D0016417

PRIVATE

PRIVATE

BRADLEY MANNING,
WIKILEAKS,
AND THE BIGGEST EXPOSURE OF
OFFICIAL SECRETS IN AMERICAN HISTORY

DENVER NICKS

CHICAGO
REVIEW
PRESS

Copyright © 2012 by Denver Nicks
All rights reserved
First edition
Published by Chicago Review Press, Incorporated
814 North Franklin Street
Chicago, Illinois 60610
ISBN 978-1-61374-068-2

Interior design: PerfecType, Nashville, TN

Library of Congress Cataloging-in-Publication Data
Nicks, Denver.
Private : Bradley Manning, Wikileaks, and the biggest exposure of
official secrets in American history / Denver Nicks. — 1st ed.
    p. cm.
Includes bibliographical references.
ISBN 978-1-61374-068-2 (HBK.)
1. Manning, Bradley, 1987– 2. WikiLeaks (Organization) 3. Official
secrets—United States. 4. Leaks (Disclosure of information)—United
States. 5. Computer crimes—United States—History. 6. Soldiers—
United States—Biography 7. United States. Army—Biography.
I. Title. II. Title: Bradley Manning, Wikileaks, and the biggest expo-
sure of official secrets in American history.

JF1525.S4N53 2012
355.1'334—dc23

                        2012003753

Printed in the United States of America
5 4 3 2 1

For Sam Wood

CONTENTS

AUTHOR'S NOTE ON SOURCES

mportant parts of this book are based on records of conversations that took place over the Internet. In most cases (excepting the chats between Adrian Lamo and Bradley Manning), those records were obtained with the assurance from the source that such chat logs, text messages, and e-mails were unaltered records of actual conversations. I used those records based upon that assurance, combined with independent corroboration and my own sense of what seemed reasonable and genuine. The logs of chats between Manning and Julian Assange were copied by hand while being presented as evidence during Manning's Article 32 hearing—one hopes that a fuller and more accurate record of those conversations surfaces someday. Much journalism depends on balancing trust in sources, documentary evidence, corroboration, and the journalist's internal compass. I believe using electronic records of conversations, rather than relying simply on memories and observations, adds an additional layer of authority to the work.

Some question the authenticity of the logs of chats between Lamo and Manning. The logs' initial publication in heavily redacted form, combined with concerns about the reliability of the source, made such questions appropriate and necessary. After long consideration I determined that the logs satisfied my sense of what is reasonable, that the tone and content of them matched what one might expect from the people involved, and that the possibility that the logs were fabricated and multiple lies were told to cover up the fact was highly unlikely. I use logs of the chats between Adrian Lamo and Bradley Manning as accurate and legitimate records.

Using chat logs and text messages as source material at book length presents singular challenges to the writer. Though text documents, they emerge from conversations that take place with a cadence and a style unique to the digital age. I generally treated such exchanges as I would verbal conversations in the physical world and, as is customary, edited selectively to fit quotes culled from chat logs into the style of traditional English prose, careful not to alter the meaning or feeling of that which I quoted. Being a nearly native speaker of chat lingo, I relied where necessary on personal experience and time stamps to deduce the rhythm and intention behind exchanges as presented in logs. In some cases while quoting from a website, blog, e-mail, chat, or the like, where I felt typographical errors were revelatory and indicative of the tone of the writer, I chose to leave errors in; I did not identify them with [*sic*].

As of this writing (February 2012) Bradley Manning has not confirmed for the public that he was the source of the leaks attributed to him in this book. Based on compounding evidence, described herein, it seems very likely that he was. Inserting the journalist's rote "allegedly" throughout the text would, I believe, fail in its purpose to keep the question open in the mind of the reader.

Following is a non-exhaustive list of sources consulted:

Steven Aftergood   Jordan Davis
Zach Antolak   Tom Dyer
Margrit Betke   Jason Edwards
Jacob Butts   Steve Fishman
Dennis Carnelli   Mike Gogulski
Danny Clark   David House
Bill Cooper   Vickey Howard
Tom Copeland   Jeremy Johnson
Dannielle Curtis   Nadim Kobeissi
Rhonda Curtis   Adrian Lamo

Kevin Lees	Keith Rose
Debbie Manning	Eric Schmiedl
Rick McCombs	Richard Stallman
Diane Musil	Berin Szoka
Jeff Patterson	Johnny Thompson
Kevin Poulsen	Shenee Watson

All opinions set forth in this book are my own, and my sources have not reviewed or endorsed this book.

Sapere aude

Sapere aude

INTRODUCTION

David Coombs strode forward toward the podium at the center of the room. He looked conspicuous in his dark suit and leather shoes, surrounded by dusty-green camouflage and sand-colored boots. Most of those watching in silence from the gallery wore civilian clothes, but the people on the other side of the bar—the four attorneys representing the government; the investigating officer; Coombs's two cocounsel; and his client, the accused—wore the army combat uniform.

"Lieutenant Colonel Almanza," Coombs said, somberly. He locked eyes with the officer at the judge's bench who was presiding over the hearing, whose job it would be to determine on what charges to court-martial the defendant. "You're in a unique position here to provide the United States government with something that it needs. And that is a reality check."

Coombs's client, a twenty-four-year-old private named Bradley Manning, was facing charges of serious crimes against the state. If convicted of all but one of the charges against him, Manning could be sentenced to 150 years in prison. But the most serious charge, aiding the enemy, alone carried a maximum penalty of life without parole or death.

"The government has overcharged in this case, and it appears they have done so in order to strong-arm a plea from my client," Coombs said, in a barely shrouded reference to Julian Assange.

Manning was accused of leaking state secrets to the antisecrecy group WikiLeaks, which had been founded by Assange years earlier.

Having spent the preceding two years publishing a leak the size of which the Pentagon had never seen, Assange, an Australian national then living in the United Kingdom, was an enticing target for the American political establishment. As Coombs spoke, there was an ongoing Department of Justice investigation into WikiLeaks exploring the possibility of prosecuting Assange in an American court. Coombs asserted that the Pentagon overreacted and charged his client with undeservedly serious offenses in order to force him into testifying against Assange. He requested that Almanza significantly decrease the charges so Manning would face a maximum of three decades in prison.

Almanza was not a naturally sympathetic audience. He'd spent much of his career as a military officer and a prosecutor with the Department of Justice immediately before presiding over Manning's Article 32 hearing, the military's pretrial investigation which is similar to a civilian grand jury. The Article 32 was a major step in the prosecution of the man responsible for the country's biggest spillage of state secrets, and the US government was keenly interested in the case. There had even been a script prepared, as if for a play, with lines for Almanza and the prosecuting attorneys. Spaces for the defense's lines were left blank.

Over the previous six days of the hearing Coombs and Almanza had frequently butted heads as the lead defense attorney pushed back against the strictures of the choreographed proceeding. When Coombs launched into a soaring, poignant oratory in his closing remarks it was clear that Almanza was not the only person he was addressing.

Journalists furiously took notes by hand while sitting in the row of seats behind the prosecution that had been reserved for media. Manning supporters filled an entire half of the gallery behind the defense table. A short drive from the courtroom dozens more journalists in Fort Meade's Media Operations Center watched through a live audio-video feed. Outside the gates of Fort Meade a rotating cast of Manning supporters held signs in protest, and people around the world followed the case through news reports and Twitter updates.

For a case that had attracted so much attention there was remarkably little agreement on who, precisely, was on trial. Coombs's final sermon in Manning's defense described a sensitive, embattled young man struggling to survive in a dysfunctional military bureaucracy. As he came to the end of his comments he shifted to describing Manning as young and idealistic. "In your early twenties, you believe when the president of the United States says 'Yes we can.'" He quoted Dr. Martin Luther King Jr. extolling the virtues of civil disobedience, and Justice Louis Brandeis praising transparency. "Sunlight," he said in closing, "is the best disinfectant."

When the lead attorney for the prosecution, Captain Ashden Fein, walked to the podium and presented his case it was as if he spoke of someone else. Manning was a shrewd and devious traitor, a skilled intelligence analyst with specialized training who had been entrusted with vital national security secrets. "He used that training to defy our trust, to indiscriminately and systematically harm us," he said. Fein went on to show a video of Adam Gadahn, the American-born al-Qaeda spokesman known by his assumed name *Azzam al-Amriki* (Azzam the American). Wearing a turban and a long, dark beard, Gadahn denounced the "Zionists" and "crusaders" in his clear American accent. Over the course of the tirade he mentioned the documents Manning leaked. The video was a dramatic, if vague, illustration of the damage Manning had done.

Outside Fort Meade the disagreement was even more pronounced, the name "Bradley Manning" appended like a slogan to wholesale denunciations and exultations alike. To some, Manning was a whistle-blowing hero, a brave soul who took a stand alone against an imperial military colossus, a Tiananmen Square Tank Man for the twenty-first century. To others, he was the worst kind of traitor, an embittered snake who had betrayed his country and the army he'd grown to hate. With the basic facts of his case in little dispute other questions loomed larger in the public debate. What was the meaning of what he had done? Why had he done it? And finally, the question underlying all others and about which so much was in dispute:

Who is Bradley Manning?

■ ■ ■

The arc of Bradley Manning's life in the 2000s was quintessentially American and post-millennial. He grew up in the relative serenity of the boom years of the 1990s before his family came apart at the end of the decade. Shortly thereafter, jetliners crashed into the World Trade Center and the Pentagon, thrusting the United States into a period of upheaval. As Manning watched that event unfold on television he knew with precocious insight that effects of the attack would ripple through American society and around the globe. He did not know then just how closely his own life would be touched by the cascading consequences of 9/11.

Manning was a computer expert in the era when words like "Google" and "Facebook" became verbs, when the Internet became the primary, and essential, network of information exchange around the world. He was a geek at a time of economic and social disturbance when geeks were becoming the new barons of industry. He anticipated the age of Zuckerberg by creating his own (far less successful) social networking site before Facebook was Facebook. He was gay in the decade when gay rights went mainstream and he nurtured a personal stake in the fight for marriage equality. As the first decade of the century wore on he confronted severe financial difficulties and became, for a time, destitute; the collapse of the global financial system followed close behind. He was driven by circumstance into the military, ill prepared for the life that awaited him there, yet he became a central actor in the endgame of America's troubled liberation of Iraq.

A deep-seated tension underlay the first decade of the new millennium. The anxiety took different forms but it rattled anywhere secrets were kept and it emanated from an old question made suddenly pressing in the Internet age: Can you keep a secret? The ascendance of the Internet meant whole lives were lived largely online. On vast social networks private lives were lived publicly, or in a new frontier realm between private and public produced by the unique circumstances of the Internet. Personal relationships were documented in unprecedented detail through chat logs and social-media profile histories. For Manning, this network was a lifeline, connecting him to friends as he struggled with loneliness and managed layers of personal secrets. But it would also be his undoing.

While Manning navigated his teen years, this same tension, between what is private and what is, or ought to be, public, was boiling to the forefront of public affairs. September 11, 2001, inspired a fearful United States to radically restructure its security apparatus and recoil into secrecy. Days after the attacks, Vice President Dick Cheney appeared on *Meet the Press* with Tim Russert, where he put the world on notice that America was not the country it had been on September 10.

"I'm going to be careful here, Tim, because I—clearly it would be inappropriate for me to talk about operational matters, specific options, or the kinds of activities we might undertake going forward. We do, indeed, though, have, obviously, the world's finest military. They've got a broad range of capabilities. And they may well be given missions in connection with this overall task and strategy.

"We also have to work, though, sort of the dark side, if you will," Cheney said. "We've got to spend time in the shadows in the intelligence world. A lot of what needs to be done here will have to be done quietly, without any discussion, using sources and methods that are available to our intelligence agencies, if we're going to be successful."

This phrase—"the dark side"—came to epitomize the seismic changes that altered the national security landscape of American society over the decade.

After the attacks, the Pentagon was caught unready for war in south Asia. The Central Intelligence Agency instead led the country into a ground war in Afghanistan—as well as covert, undeclared, and unacknowledged wars elsewhere around the world. The "sources and methods" used in prosecuting this new intensely and inherently secret sort of war trickled down to local law enforcement, into uses for which they were never intended. Overclassification in the federal government had been a growing problem since the Second World War, but after the jolt of 9/11 the juggernaut of institutional secrecy continued barreling forward under the force of its own momentum.

Further in the background during the inaugural decade of the millennium was the rise of the hacker. The term had so many overlapping and contradictory meanings as to be rendered almost meaningless, but that didn't stop the public from developing a fascination built on both wonder and fear of the superheroes of the information age. For most people the inner workings of a computer system were as unfamiliar as those of microscopic cell life but only slightly less integral to their lives. The hacker's abilities, for good or ill, to manipulate so much in human society with computers seemed almost mystical. The geeks who'd pioneered the use of computers decades earlier were increasingly empowered in the digitized, interconnected world.

With the rise of the hacker came the rise of hacker culture. Founded upon a libertarian ethos, the culture prized unimpeded exchange of information and freedom from governmental meddling with equal zeal. The world was becoming more interconnected, the information in it more digitized. Meanwhile, the US government embarked on a program of official secrecy just as the people who believed information should be free were becoming more powerful with every new Internet user. The culture that nursed the Internet in infancy gave voice to the great anxiety of the era of interconnectedness, calling for privacy in individual lives and transparency in institutions.

These discordant trends were on display at Bradley Manning's Article 32 investigation at Fort Meade in mid-December 2011. Manning had sent three-quarters of a million documents to the antisecrecy website WikiLeaks. It was the largest leak of state secrets ever seen, exposing classified records from the American military and diplomatic corps to public scrutiny. The leak was the world's first injection of an Internet-sized dose of digital transparency. Interest in Manning's case ran high.

In preparation for the hearing the military had set up an intricate system to accommodate media access. Twin flat-screen televisions were suspended from the ceiling behind the attorneys so the public and the media could see the evidence being presented. A series of voice-activated cameras were installed around the courtroom, which fed a live stream of the proceedings to a wall-sized screen in the media center, where dozens of reporters from around the world watched from tables in a room equipped with wireless Internet and landline telephones. The military provided public affairs representatives to answer media queries and assist with everything from understanding the complexities of the Uniform Code of Military Justice to ordering lunch.

But amid the high-tech efforts at transparency, the military's rules and traditions imposed a layer of secrecy over the hearing. All electronic devices were strictly prohibited from the courtroom, and reporters took notes by hand. Recording devices were also forbidden in the media center and a special sensor at the back of the room occasionally warned of the intrusion of a cell phone. During breaks journalists compared notes to ensure they had accurate records; no complete verbatim court transcript would be released to the public. The army flacks tried to institute a rule that no stories be filed until the end of each day. They turned off Internet access while court was in session, turning it back on during recesses. But the rule was circumvented by new forms of reportage. Though some old-media journalists complied, many reporters updated live blogs and posted to Twitter during the intervals when Internet access returned, further confounding efforts to manage coverage of the event. After resisting at first, the flacks relented to the intrusion of Web 2.0 into an otherwise controlled reporting environment.

Manning's life in the aughts straddled the decade's divide between private and public as his personal secrets rather suddenly became a public story. The wildly different identities ascribed to him were symptomatic of the uneven media coverage he received. Manning was a young man at the time of his arrest, and what little life he'd lived had gone mostly unnoticed. He was shy, had few friends or family, and wasn't rooted deeply in any community. For reporters covering his story there was little secondhand information about his life available. On the other hand, like many of his generation, Manning lived large segments of his life online, producing a remarkable record of conversations between confidants and off-the-cuff reflections tagged to times and dates. The world was introduced to Manning with excerpts from one such conversation between him and the man who turned him in to the authorities. The first major, long-form profile of Bradley Manning (written by this author) was built in large part around the history of his Facebook posts. Additional chat logs turned up in later pieces, including logs being published for the first time in this book.

A tremendous amount of unfiltered information about the young private was thus available to reporters, but there were few people who knew him well enough to put it into context. The result was something remarkably similar to Manning's leaks: an unvarnished, extraordinarily candid, and crucially incomplete image of an enigma. *Private* intends to fill out the story of Bradley Manning's life and the outsized effect it has had on the world. That his name was ever in a headline came as a shock to the few people Bradley Manning knew. They could not have known, when he was an inconspicuous little boy riding his bike down dirt roads in rural Oklahoma, that he would one day change the world or that in the person of Bradley Manning the great countervailing forces of the twenty-first century toward secrecy and openness would collide.

1
Crescent

Crescent, Oklahoma, appeared out of the wilderness in the fevered summer of 1899, after the lands left unassigned to Indian tribes in Oklahoma Territory were opened to white settlement. Would-be homesteaders had clamored for years for the opening up of this rare remaining tract of unsettled federal land in the fertile plains, and when, at noon on April 22, a gunshot announced the beginning of Oklahoma's first land run, a disorderly horde of people on horseback, foot, and the occasional bicycle raced to claim plots of their own. It was the last yawn of the American frontier, the triumph of Manifest Destiny, and, for those who struck out to this untrammeled Eden, a moment of profound optimism almost unimaginable in modern America. In the cross-timbers north of the Cimarron River, settlers staked out a trading post cradled in the nook of a clump of trees that formed the shape of a waxing moon. They named their new town Crescent.

Amid the fanatical confidence of the land run, Crescent's population boomed. The land was tilled into orchards of peaches, pears, apples, and grapes and fields of wheat, corn, and cotton, and the settlement grew into a one-square-mile rectangular grid, bisected by Highway 74, with a railroad stop next to the grain elevator that pumped life into the local economy. Banks, a hardware store, and restaurants grew up along Grand Avenue through the center of town. For most of the twentieth century, Crescent escaped the fate of slow decline that emptied out so many small towns in Middle America. Into this close-knit farming community of 2,800 souls in the heart of America's Bible Belt, Brian Manning moved with his Welsh wife and six-year-old daughter in the summer of 1983.

Brian Manning had grown up in Chicago but left home at seventeen. He used those first couple of years away from home to party—hard. In 1974, after a booze-soaked weekend like many before it, he made his way to a navy recruiting office, determined to get his life on track. He enlisted. He was nineteen years old. The navy trained Brian as an intelligence analyst, gave him a security clearance, and shipped him overseas.

Brian Manning met Sue Fox in Haverfordwest, where she was raised. This small but bustling market town of fewer than 15,000 straddled a tidal river in rugged southwest Wales. The young sailor was stationed at an air force base there, where he worked maintaining the military's then–cutting edge computer systems. In 1976, on the day after Brian turned twenty-one, the couple married; later that year, on December 17, their daughter, Casey, was born.

Brian got out of the navy in 1979 and completed an associate degree in computer science at a community college in Orange County, California. He planned to continue at UC Irvine, but in the summer before the start of the school year a position became available setting up and managing industrial-scale computers systems at Hertz Rent-a-Car in Oklahoma City. It was a well-paying job with the chance for advancement and substantial travel. Unlike in Southern California, in Oklahoma Brian could afford to buy a comfortable house in the exurbs for his wife and six-year-old daughter and prepare a space in the family for the next child he and his wife hoped soon to have.

The Manning family moved into a humble, two-story, white farmhouse several miles north of Crescent, on five acres of land off a remote road where the gravel thins just before conceding to the red dirt underneath. Here, on the outskirts of a rural Oklahoma town, the computer engineer and the young Welsh woman who married him assembled the idyllic home into which Bradley was born on his sister's eleventh birthday, December 17, 1987.

Brian and Sue had tried for years to have another child, and the boy was welcomed into a loving family. Casey adored her little brother. Brian could be stern and distant and spent long stretches away on business trips to Europe, but even when Bradley was a baby his dad invited him into his world of computers, letting the boy sit with him and peck away at the keyboard.

Sue loved little children. She liked to get out her Russian nesting dolls and Jacob's ladder, toys that are, notably, more for adults who are playing with little kids than for little kids playing among themselves. She was a doting mother, with little in life but her household. A small-town girl herself, she didn't work and didn't drive, instead spending her days caring for her young and keeping a neat home. She spent time in her abundant organic garden, pulling weeds; planting corn, tomatoes, asparagus, peppers, and sundry other vegetables; and picking fresh blackberries. On some mornings, she squeezed fresh juice from oranges and called to her son, who came bounding downstairs to the kitchen for breakfast with Mum. When Bradley was a few months old, the family moved to Phoenix, but they returned to Crescent before his second birthday.

Bradley had acres of countryside to explore, an aboveground swimming pool, a dog, a cat, and horses that his sister rode bareback. Neighbors were a quarter mile or more away, and he rode his bike with friends down the gravel and dirt roads, past trees and overgrown brush, cattle at pasture, fields of hay, and oil derricks. He rooted around in the dirt with toy cars and trucks. Indoors, he played video games at home on a Nintendo 64 or rode his bike to a friend's house, dropped it at the doorstep, and ran inside to play video games there. Sometimes, he spent hours glued to the computer screen playing the game SimCity.

Like his parents, Bradley was very small in stature, but he was also notoriously hyperactive. Rhonda Curtis, who was a close friend to Sue and lived around the corner from the Manning house, thought of Bradley as "a little cocker spaniel." Bradley's aunt Debbie, his father's older sister, would later describe him as a hummingbird, starting one activity and then resting briefly before bouncing frenetically to the next. The energetic little boy grew up in an exurban-bucolic wonderland, living the full range of seasons on the lower Great Plains: muggy summer with june bugs and fireflies; the long, stormy spring; mild winter with generous snow; and the cool glow of autumn.

In the fall of 1993, Bradley started kindergarten at Crescent Elementary School with around forty-five other students. He was tiny, restless but obedient, and an active participant in class. Sue got good reports from teachers when she visited the school for conferences; her boy made excellent grades and never got into any real trouble.

By the third grade, when social hierarchies and self-aware identities begin to set in for children, Bradley could tell he was different from the other kids. He wasn't tall, strong, a great athlete, or especially popular. And though in the close-knit microcosm of Crescent schools it never reached the intensity it might have in the cold anonymity of a suburban megaschool, like many small boys Bradley was bullied. But little Bradley had one asset with which he could satisfy the need common to all children to feel empowered. He was smarter than the other kids. And he knew it.

On the hour-long bus ride home with the other children who lived in the countryside around Crescent, Bradley generally spent his time finishing homework while the others fired paper wads back and forth at one another across the center aisle and over the seats. But he wasn't always quiet. "There was this one kid on the school bus showing off that he knew how to spell *Mississippi*," recalled Johnny Thompson, who was a grade under Bradley in school and, like Bradley, had one of the last stops on the school bus route. "Bradley come along and was like, well I can spell *television*. And that just kinda blew our minds." When Johnny first talked to Bradley, he thought they were in the same grade, because Bradley was so short. "I looked at his math homework, and it was algebra, and I had no idea what that was."

Whereas in a bigger, more impersonal school, a kid like Bradley might not have found a niche, in Crescent he got involved in a range of school activities. He won the science fair three years in a row—so many that there were jokes among parents about changing the rules so that one student couldn't win year after year. He was a promising saxophonist in the band and became personally close to the band teacher. For a time, he played on a youth basketball league. He became a star on the middle school quiz bowl team and took trips with other high-achieving students to competitions around the state. On such trips, he and a small group of friends would sit together on the bus and discuss questions of philosophy and morality—"stuff, for that age, that was pretty deep," recalled Shanée Watson, one of his teammates.

As an outstanding student, Bradley went on end-of-year field trips with others who made good grades. On one such trip, to Frontier City, an amusement park, he was walking around with a group of guys and a chaperone. The group stopped, with the Silver Bullet looming overhead; the rollercoaster lauds itself as the tallest in the state, and a dare to ride it is not an insignificant challenge among Oklahoma boys. The chaperone invited the boys to take a whirl on the towering coaster, but none would ride—except Bradley, who rode the Silver Bullet alone.

While other kids lived in the myopia of childhood, focused on themselves, their friends, and their possessions, Bradley's curiosity about the world was drawing his young mind outside the city limits. He developed a rich fantasy life. With his best friend, Jordan Davis— another bright kid low on the social totem pole—he created imaginary companies, hiring and firing, buying and selling, and amassing make-believe wealth. For months, he and Jordan fixated on international intrigue of Bradley's own creation, an imaginary crisis involving oil and American intervention in the Middle East, inspired, apparently, by the first Gulf War, though Bradley was far too young at the time of the actual conflict to remember it.

Consistent with his experience as a little businessman, Bradley was a politically conscious adolescent and always "very pro-business, pro-capitalism," Jordan Davis reported years later. He was never socially conservative, Davis said. He believed "that society needed to be kind of ordered and that kind of thing, but otherwise he didn't care much for that aspect of conservatism." He was also notably interventionist in his outlook on the world—a budding neoconservative. For

Bradley, like many young boys, the military held a romantic allure; unlike many young boys, Bradley thought about the wider implications of his boyhood war games. He was, according to his best friend, an advocate of what he would someday learn to call *realpolitik*. "If you have to support a dictator to keep communism out, then yeah, do that," Jordan said.

Bradley was a precocious boy of strong opinions, and in the cloistered community of Crescent he developed a certain intellectual confidence. In class discussions he was assertive, at times argumentative, and unafraid to challenge authority figures when he felt they had it wrong. To many of his classmates and teachers, it seemed Bradley Manning was too smart for his own good.

When Casey had left home for college at Oklahoma State, her room on the upper level of the house had been bequeathed to Bradley. He quickly made it his own, strewing Lego creations across the floor and setting up the computer system that would become increasingly important to him.

By the time Bradley turned eight, Brian Manning had introduced him to the C++ programming language. Brian was not a naturally affectionate dad, and that combined with the amount of time he spent away from home produced a tenuous relationship between father and son. But, as when Bradley was a baby and Brian let him sit with him pecking away at the keyboard, at the PC the two found common ground. It was the mid-1990s, and the computer was rapidly becoming an ever more interesting toy as the Internet began going mainstream; Bradley took a quick and abiding interest.

■ ■ ■

Crescent had bucked the trend of small-town decay for decades, but while the rest of the country was celebrating the economic boom of the 1990s, Crescent got left out of the party. A Kerr-McGee plutonium plant south of town near the Cimarron River had provided good local jobs until union activist Karen Silkwood's death in 1974. The dubious circumstances of Silkwood's passing—she was driving south on Highway 74, carrying, some say, documents for a *New York Times* reporter that would have revealed shoddy safety practices at the nuclear fuel plant—inspired an Oscar-nominated Hollywood movie and gave the town its first taste of the national spotlight. In 1975, a year after Silkwood's body was found in a crumpled car by the side of the road, the plant closed.

Heavy flooding in the 1980s damaged the railroad, and after one major flood it was never repaired. The train stopped coming through town, and rail cars that could accommodate three thousand bushels at the grain elevator were replaced by truck trailers with only a third of that capacity. What once fit on a one-hundred-car train required three hundred separate trucks, and the increase in the price of moving grain to market reverberated through the town's economy. Weeds grew up over the abandoned rails, businesses shut down along Grand Avenue, and Crescent continued its slow decline.

What kept the town alive were the exurbanites, families with breadwinners who commuted to work in Oklahoma City but made their homes in and around Crescent—families like the Mannings, who might have stayed had the tumult not began at home.

In the isolation of her life in the Oklahoma countryside, Sue became a heavy drinker. A little woman with perpetually rosy cheeks, she'd put vodka in her morning tea and pour vodka and Coke over ice cubes for her afternoon cocktails, taking care to be discreet about the booze around visiting friends. Late in the evenings after the family had gone to bed, she'd be flush with a day's liquor and call a friend, and they'd stay up late chatting for hours about their kids and the gossip around town. To friends, Sue seemed content with her life in Crescent, with a home and a bountiful garden to tend and a small group of women to lean on. But something was nagging at her beneath the placid exterior.

One evening on the phone her friend Diane asked Sue if she ever looked to God for help when facing life's hardships.

"God's busy," Sue told her. "He has a lot of other people's problems to deal with. He doesn't have time for mine."

To those who knew him in Crescent, Brian Manning was a peculiar man. He was standoffish—not rude, but not friendly either—and, being short like the rest of the family, accused by some of having a little man's complex. Though he lived out in the country and exuded a certain swagger, he wasn't the type to get his hands dirty, preferring to rely on others for his manual labor needs; a friend of Bradley's would later describe him as a suburban John Wayne. He went on business trips up to a month and a half long in Europe and boasted to his neighbor Bill Cooper about the women who, he said, threw themselves at him while he was away, though he insisted he never went further than buying them drinks. He ate in the English style, with the knife in his right hand and fork in the left, prongs pointed downward, claiming it was more efficient than the American method.

Sue was permissive—overly so—with Bradley, but Brian was strict, and liberal with the belt. On at least one occasion, according to his sister, when Bradley was in around the second grade, he received a spanking so severe he told a teacher at school the next day that he couldn't sit down. Bradley told his friend Jordan about once hiding in a tree to escape his father's punishing hand.

To outside observers, Sue, who was small and meek to begin with, seemed to recoil in the presence of her husband. In front of friends, neighbors, and even his kids, Brian insulted her, calling her worthless, stupid, and worse, according to numerous people who knew the family. The littlest thing would seem to set him off; sometimes it was nothing at all. The marriage came under increasing stress.

Bradley gradually learned to survive with little parental involvement. Sue started skipping parent-teacher conferences, but her son's straight A's continued. Neighbors and friends' parents gave Bradley rides to school in the evenings to, for example, set up his science fair exhibits. On school trips they'd send their own children with a little extra money to make sure Bradley had enough. When he was in the sixth grade, Bradley won a statewide academic meet—the first student from Crescent ever to do so—but when he walked onto the stage to receive his trophy, neither of his parents was in the audience.

As a child, Bradley was prone to spontaneous rage. According to Ellen Nakashima, writing in the *Washington Post*, an aunt recalled

him hurling an iron across a room at a cousin during a family vacation. When something set him off at school, Bradley would sit smoldering, his face glowing ember red before he'd slam a book down on his desk. At home he lashed out at his mother, screaming in anger at her and slinging insults like his dad.

As Bradley grew older, he retreated into video games and computers. He learned to write several languages of programming code and would access the back end of programs to edit the appearance of characters in a computer game. It was the late 1990s, and the Internet was just then becoming a truly ubiquitous, global phenomenon. For the boy sitting in his bedroom on the second story of a rural home in the central Oklahoma countryside, the Internet meant more than broadened horizons. It was an escape. His mother's drinking, his father's verbal abuse, and his growing interest in the world beyond Crescent all conspired to exhort him to explore the world online.

In the summer of 1999, Brian Manning asked his daughter, Casey, to move back home, which she did. Things were not well with the family. Mere months later, Brian came home one day and told Sue he was leaving. "I want to have my cake and eat it too," Brian said, according to what Sue later told a friend. He'd started seeing another woman, also named Susan, and he was moving to Oklahoma City.

That night Sue swallowed a handful of pills. Minutes later she woke up her daughter and told her she'd tried to kill herself. It was a classic plea for help from a woman whose life was falling apart. The hospital was many miles away, and an ambulance might take too long to reach their country home. So Casey woke her dad, but he was too drunk to drive. They woke Bradley and piled in the car. Brian went for the front seat, but Casey stopped him—sit in the back to make sure Mom is all right, she told him. Bradley could keep an eye on her, Brian said. They drove to the hospital with the eleven-year-old in the back making sure his mom didn't stop breathing.

Sue had her stomach pumped, survived, and spent about a week in the hospital under psychiatric evaluation. Brian moved out of the house promptly. He returned later with his new girlfriend to collect some belongings he'd left behind. Bill Cooper, the neighbor, was driving by and stopped to say hello. "Hi, Brian, how you been?" Bill said. They talked for a moment while the new Susan sat in silence in Brian's little red pickup. Bill invited Brian to come up to his place for a visit sometime, have a beer, and go fishing at his pond. Brian said he would, but Bill knew better. Brian then introduced his new girlfriend to Bill.

"Ah, you got yourself another Susan, so in the heat of passion you don't call out the wrong name!" Bill said, grinning.

Brian scowled, silent, and walked to the house. He grabbed the things he'd come for and left. Bill never saw him again.

The split was devastating to Sue. She had to take babysitting jobs to meet expenses, and her drinking worsened. Already a tiny woman, her weight plummeted, as the stress of losing her family—all, indeed, she had built her life around—wrought devastation on her small frame.

Without a husband and unable to drive, Sue was even more isolated, and she became more dependent than ever on the help of friends and neighbors to buy groceries and pay bills (she never learned to write a check). Ignorant as to whether or not Brian had a retirement plan, or even the specifics of his salary, Sue had to rely on attorneys to obtain the information she needed to receive alimony (Brian had taken his financial records with him when he left). Rhonda, Diane, and others would buy and deliver groceries for her, always sure to bring a supply of Sunkist orange soda for Bradley and a gallon of vodka for Sue. The women didn't realize, at first, that the others were also buying gallon-bottles of vodka for Sue, which she was finishing at a rate of at least two a week.

Friends say Bradley seemed relieved by his father moving out. He started dressing differently, for instance, wearing more stylish blue jeans that his dad had prohibited. But deep down, the eleven-year-old was experiencing significant stress while his family was in upheaval. In the months following the split, his grades dropped for the first time ever. And as with any kid that age, he was dealing with an unfamiliar cocktail of hormones pumping through his veins. With his family disintegrating, Bradley was in the midst of adolescent sexual awakening, though his sexual development was working out differently than that of his friends.

One evening, in the summer of his thirteenth year, Bradley and another friend, Zach Said, were spending the night at Jordan's house, a cottage on a large man-made pond outside of Crescent. Bradley was reclining on a couch while the three talked about video games. Jordan stood and walked out of the room for a moment and then heard Zach cackling from inside. He came back to find Zach doubled over, laughing, but Bradley seemed unfazed. Jordan sat down, and Brad spoke up.

"I have to tell you something."

Jordan was listening now. What was so funny?

"I have a crush on a boy. I'm gay."

The boy, Jordan presumed, was him—they were best friends, after all. He thought a moment. "Well . . . whatever floats your boat, man."

Bradley's coming out—at that time he had not, so far as his friends knew, told anyone else—was slightly awkward for Jordan, but the moment possessed a noteworthy lightness. This was not a cataclysmic event. Bradley was not brought before Crescent's preachers to be purified. He'd felt compelled, while living in a close-knit, rural, conservative community, to confide in his friends that he was gay, presumably just to live honestly in his own skin—a display of improbable courage and sense of self for such a young man. Then the moment passed, and the boys picked back up their conversation about video games.

Around this time, while sitting at the dining room table, Bradley also told his mother, rather matter-of-factly, that he was gay. It was fine with her, she told him. "But try not to tell other people—especially your dad."

Things were not good between Bradley and his father, who had remarried and taken on a stepson. After the separation, Bradley had remained living with his mother in Crescent—the two relocated to a smaller rental house in the middle of town, closer to school, the grocery store, the bank—but Brian did have visitation rights. One afternoon in 2001, when Bradley was thirteen, he came home early from a visit with his dad. He was fuming. His new stepbrother, Dustin, had changed his last name to Manning, and Bradley felt replaced. In a fit of frustrated rage, Bradley started charging the wall, running several vertical steps with the force of his momentum until jumping back down. Sue called her friend, Mary Egelston, for help.

Mary corralled Bradley into his bedroom, but he was no less despondent. "Nobody understands!" he shouted. It seemed his own identity had come utterly asunder, his place in the family finally supplanted, annihilated, lost. "I'm nobody now, Mum."

Something else happened that year, far from Crescent, that would dramatically affect Bradley's future.

On a clear Tuesday morning in the fall of Bradley's eighth-grade year, just weeks after students returned from summer vacation, he and Jordan were in a frenzy when they saw each other at school. An airplane had crashed into the World Trade Center in New York. When a second plane hit, the implications of the event began to sink in for the boys. Initially, Bradley hypothesized that, due to the height of the explosions, nuclear weapons might have been involved. They were, in Jordan's words, "just freaking out."

"We understood the impact and the consequence," Jordan would later recall, "the heaviness of what had happened."

The loss of life in New York was terrible, but what had them most worried were the inevitable consequences of the attack. The boys were concerned about the pandemic fear that might paralyze the American economy after September 11. And they knew American military and civil establishments would have to change in response to the attacks, perhaps dramatically.

Two months later, in November, Bradley met up with Jordan and Shanée at Jordan's grandparents' house across the street from school, where they often hung out after classes were over. The three were in the backyard, standing around under a tree, when Bradley said he had an announcement. He told the two of them he was gay, not letting on to Shanée that Jordan already knew. He followed up with the real bombshell: he was leaving Crescent, possibly forever.

Moving across the ocean to the United Kingdom was not an insignificant event. In the era before Facebook or Skype, the distance severely limited communications; for all Bradley knew this could be the last time he ever saw two of his best friends. Over the next several years he and Jordan tried to maintain contact, but for a time they lost touch. He never saw Shanée again.

Bradley, now the man of the house, booked plane tickets online for himself and his mother. They flew to Potomac, Maryland, where they stayed with Bradley's aunt Debbie for a few days. On Thanksgiving Day, Bradley and Sue boarded an airplane in Washington and bid America good-bye. Sue was going back to her home, but Bradley was leaving his.

■ ■ ■

The family moved into a three-bedroom apartment near Sue's family, in Haverfordwest. Bradley enrolled at Tasker Milward, a school about the size of the town he'd just left.

In this provincial Welsh town, the new American student was a hit. The students at Tasker Milward gave him a nickname: Bradders. He was small but assertive, spoke in an American accent, and clearly knew a lot about the world outside of their small town in the hinterlands of Wales. Bradley joined a computer club at school and, already able to write code in languages like HTML and PHP, became known in short order for his exceptional tech skills, which were a mark of pride for the new kid in school.

Bradley never lost the entrepreneurial spirit he had as a boy back in Crescent running make-believe corporations with his friend Jordan. He built websites for businesses other kids in the high school started, and he helped friends in bands put down recordings of their music. Bradley developed an online message board for the Haverfordwest community, called Angel Dyne, on which a person could create a user profile and sign in to correspond with others in town. By the end of the decade, Angel Dyne would seem dated, but in those early years the idea was original and inspired, a sort of proto-Facebook. He would later build a web interface to allow musicians to upload songs online, automatically convert them to mp3 files, and give them away or sell them at whatever rate the artist chose. The idea never took off, but it bears resemblance to tools like the iTunes Store and MySpace Music that came later. In his early teen years, Bradley honed his computer skills, displaying creativity, independence of thought, and an unambiguous ambition to do something important with his ideas.

Bradley was a student in Wales when the United States invaded Iraq in 2003. According to those who knew him in Haverfordwest, he was very openly against the war. He insisted that weapons of mass destruction were merely a pretense, masking the true reasons George W. Bush and Tony Blair conspired to overthrow Saddam Hussein: oil and revenge for the attempted assassination of Bush's father. He wouldn't hold the same position throughout the war, but his stance as an adolescent indicates a precocious, analytical mind. In expressing that opinion, he wasn't just being critical of the war—he was being critical of the vague but sophisticated-for-his-age realpolitik he'd expressed back in Crescent.

Being short, foreign, and four-eyed, he was the natural target of teasing. The British style of playful insults—taking, as it were, "the piss" out of one's friends—didn't sit well with Bradley, who preferred not to take the piss out of anyone. On one occasion, Bradley was on a camping trip with friends, but when he woke up all the tents around him were gone. The others had left while he was asleep.

Bradley was quick with a witty comeback but didn't stop there. As in his fits of frustration earlier in life, he'd lose a sense of decorum and begin yelling and kicking. The entire spectacle merely egged on his tormentors.

Despite being a target, he was known to stand up for others who were the victims of bullies' attentions. Just as he was outspoken in class and willing to stand up to teachers when he thought they were wrong, Bradley seemed unable to abide injustice in the hallways. He was willing, it seemed, to attack what he perceived as wrongheadedness wherever he saw it, at times with the ferocity (and forethought) of a Pomeranian.

Bradley's inability to get into the back-and-forth teasing of his Welsh classmates is illustrative of the cultural dissonance that was becoming a pattern in his life. In Crescent, once he developed self-awareness, the provinciality of the place and dissolution of his family worked in tandem to make him feel like an outsider. In Wales, with his strange accent, outspokenness, and precocious nature, he was every bit the alien. At Tasker Milward, Bradley got on well enough—friends remember him as generally well-liked, if a bit prickly, and prone to outbursts when teased—but he was never Welsh. He was never *one of them*.

Bradley spent much of his time at home up in his bedroom on the computer. He missed his sister, who was living out her mid-twenties back in the States, and he was worried for his mother's health. Though back among her family and the familiar sights of home, Sue's alcoholism continued. Bradley confessed to relatives that he was afraid she'd drink herself to death. The boy was taking care of his mother and living remarkably independently for a high school kid.

In 2005, Brad—he started going by the short version of his name as he grew older—decided to return the United States. He'd finished high school but not stayed for his A Levels, the optional upper-level courses taken at the end of secondary school in the United Kingdom considered prerequisites for students intending to go to university. His mother had suffered two mild strokes and was becoming helpless. Brad, an only child living with an ailing single parent, was feeling desperate and had to get out. He called his dad and begged him to help him return home. The two had barely spoken during Bradley's four years in the United Kingdom. Brian had moved on, with a new home, a wife, and a stepson, and the call took him by surprise. Nonetheless, he agreed to help Brad get settled back in Oklahoma. "He's my son," he later explained.

In early July, Brad traveled to London to have his passport renewed at the American Embassy. He spent a Wednesday night at a hostel in King's Cross. The next morning he awoke and headed toward the Tube, London's underground public transit system. He walked down into the station at the moment of the explosion. He later described the scene: "There was a horrific boom, screaming, sirens, and thick black smoke. . . . It was July 7, 2005." London had just become the victim of its first major Islamist terrorist attack.

■ ■ ■

Brad left Sue in the care of relatives living nearby and traveled back to the United States. He moved into his dad's house in Oklahoma City with his new stepmother and stepbrother.

He started a job at Zoto, a software start-up with a techie culture that would seem to appeal to the seventeen-year-old. The office was dotted with Macintosh computers, whiteboards, and meandering robots. Zoto was a great opportunity for Brad to put his intellect and computer skills to work in the real world, but the company's CEO, Kord Campbell, to whom Brad became close for a time, found him a troubled kid. Brad confided in Campbell. He told him that living with his mother back in Wales had been like living with a child. "I felt like a parent with her," he said. He also told him, "My stepmom hates me."

Campbell noticed Brad becoming increasingly detached from the world around him. On one occasion, Campbell was teaching Brad to drive when he failed to brake as the car neared a stop sign. Campbell alerted him to stop, and Brad hit the brakes but then froze. "I had to put on the emergency brakes, get out, walk around the car, open the door, and touch him before he finally snapped out of it," Campbell would later recall. As time went on, Brad seemed to have increasing trouble focusing on work. Finally, Campbell told him that, though he was sorry it had come to this, he had to let Brad go. He had, he said, a business to run.

Tensions at home mounted. Brad butted heads with his stepbrother and fought constantly with his stepmom. Ever since Brad moved home from the United Kingdom, Brian and Susan had been helping him with car insurance, a AAA membership, and spending money, and Susan was sick of it. Her own father died from emphysema and she hated cigarettes, but Brad had picked up the habit and tested the limits of her hospitality by sneaking off to the garage to smoke. Despite a strict rule against eating and drinking outside of the kitchen, Dr. Pepper cans littered the space under his bed. Brad was by now openly gay, causing friction with his dad and stepmother. And he kept overdrawing his banking account, expecting Brian and Susan to bail him out. Topping it all off, he'd been laid off from Zoto, and Susan complained that he needed a job.

In March 2006, the smoldering conflict erupted. According to Susan, she had been telling Brad to get himself employed, when the argument escalated and Brad pulled out a knife. Brian Manning, recovering from cancer and dependent upon a walker, lunged between the two to protect his wife and fell to the ground. Susan called 911.

"Oklahoma City 911."

"Yes!" Her voice shook with hysteric vibrato. "I need an officer here at my house please, and I need him here immediately. My husband's eighteen-year-old son is out of control. He just threatened me with a knife, and his father just had surgery and he is down on the floor. You get away from him!" she screamed. "Get away from him!"

"Ma'am," the dispatcher said. "Is the kid white, black, Indian, or Mexican?"

"Pardon?"

"Is he white, black, Indian, or Mexican?"

"White."

"What kind of shirt or jacket is he wearing?"

"Black."

The dispatcher asked if Brian needed an ambulance. Susan said no.

"What's he upset about?" the dispatcher said.

"Because I have been telling him he needs to get a job and he won't get a job. He thinks he should just be able to take money from us."

In the background, Brad spoke up in a voice incongruously gentle for the middle of a family brawl. "Are you OK, Dad?"

Exasperated, Susan appealed to Brian. "He ain't staying here. I ain't staying here with him. You better find somewhere for him to go because he ain't staying here."

■ ■ ■

Many years later, after Brad Manning's arrest in connection with the WikiLeaks releases, this episode would be the subject of tremendous attention in the international media. The PBS program *Frontline* uncovered a recording of the 911 call and released it online in its entirety. To some, airing it presented a distorted image of a young man's personality by highlighting one voyeur-ready, highly dramatic snippet of his life. *Frontline*'s defenders argued the call was a rare window into a key moment in Brad Manning's troubled youth.

While conducting interviews for the *Frontline* documentary, chief correspondent Martin Smith butted heads with Julian Assange on the decision to air the call, which *Frontline* had released earlier to build publicity for its forthcoming program. Smith had arrived at the English country estate in which Assange was then living, prepared to start asking questions. Instead, after the cameras and lights were set up, he found himself the subject of an interrogation, as WikiLeaks turned its own camera on him and Assange began his inquisition.

"Events in the home, these are—"

Smith cut Assange off. "Do you think I should *not* report on a 911 call?"

"Yes, I think you should not report on it," Assange said.

"Well, I would disagree with that."

"Because, in the broad sweep of someone's life, that is *one* event, of someone age eighteen, et cetera," said Assange.

Smith appealed to WikiLeaks' own principles. "So, I would have censored that."

"Yes," Assange said, hesitating. "Because it would be distortive. It would have a distortive effect on the broad sweep of someone's life, because it is so emotive."

"I think you're not giving the audience enough credit, Julian," Smith said, arguing that the circumstances of the dispute—an eighteen-year-old living at home with a stepmother—was context enough for the viewer to understand what the call did, and did not, reveal.

The debate over *Frontline*'s decision to release the recording of the 911 call was emblematic of the controversies that would arise over the media's coverage of Manning. Were these intimate details of Manning's early life relevant to the story? And if so, was it proper to release them with the implicit suggestion that the leaks were inspired more by the leaker's troubled past than by higher motives—before the accused was able to speak for himself?

Furthermore, Manning remained innocent until proven guilty. Yet the media storm that erupted after his arrest, and subsequent investigations into his short life (investigations that this writer took part in), served, slowly over time, to convict him in the court of public opinion, despite an astonishing-in-retrospect lack of publicly available evidence that he was guilty. In the months after Manning's arrest, the single piece of evidence available to the public linking him to the leak was a series of excerpts from easily edited logs of chats he allegedly had online over a several-day period with a stranger, Adrian Lamo. But Manning had suddenly become a public figure, his name now associated to a massive leak of state secrets, and the people wanted answers. Just as significant was journalists' own hunger for information about the story, which had special relevance to their profession. In discussions about Manning, "alleged" became a stock phrase, appended to sentences by supporters and journalists alike with such imprudent, almost comical frequency that it began to lose all meaning. The media at large effectively skipped over the natural first question, "Did he do it?" and added to it the more interesting preamble: "Why?"

■ ■ ■

When the police arrived at Brian Manning's house in Oklahoma City, they escorted Brad outside and drove him to an overnight shelter. Brian called Casey, who was living nearby with her husband, and told her what had happened. Casey called her husband, who picked Brad up from the shelter and took him back to their house, where he stayed for a few days.

Unable to go back to his dad's and unwilling to be a burden on his sister, Brad packed his few belongings into the little faded red pickup truck his dad had given him and called up his old friend Jordan Davis to tell him he was moving to Tulsa. Jordan, now living in Tulsa with his parents, asked where he was going to stay. Brad said he didn't know. It seemed like an odd move to Jordan, abandoning home with what little he had and moving to a new city.

Brad told Jordan he'd gotten into a fight with his stepmom and been kicked out of the house. He didn't have a lot of options. Considering the circumstances, Jordan thought he sounded improbably cheerful. "You gotta do what you gotta do," Jordan said.

Brad drove onto the Turner Turnpike, barreling eastbound out of Oklahoma City toward an uncertain future in Tulsa. For the first time in his life he'd struck out on his own. He knew he was smart and capable—made, if he was bold enough to try, to accomplish great things. But ahead lay a mix of uncertainty and opportunity. He'd been fired from his first real job, and he needed an education but didn't have a clear route to one. He'd just returned to the States after spending several of his formative years abroad, and he didn't have a network of high school buddies to lean on. He was eighteen years old, effectively homeless and nearly alone. But he was free. For the first time in his life he was free.

It was the grand finale to a childhood thrown into chaos. Brad hadn't felt at home in his hometown, and now, he didn't have a home in his own family. For Brad Manning, much of the next four years would be a continual and variously disguised search for home.

2
Hack the World

"It was a philosophy of sharing, openness, decentralization, and getting your hands on machines at any cost to improve the machines and to improve the world."

—From *Hackers: Heroes of the Computer Revolution* by Steven Levy (1984)

I n a small, terraced house across the street from the University of Melbourne, a thirty-four-year-old undergraduate in mathematics and physics was working vigorously on a plan to transform the world.

"He was always telling me about ideas," recalled the girlfriend he was living with at the time. The computer programmer was a self-styled activist-philosopher. He'd grown up among nonconformists, mistrusting the establishment, and devoted much of his time to thinking about the nature of authority. He intended nothing less than to change the basic functioning of government on earth.

By late 2005, he'd settled on an idea. His girlfriend remembers coming home one day to find him in his room, next to a massive whiteboard appended to the wall. He described a website on which "anyone in the world can post documents, anonymously," she later said. Written on the whiteboard was one made-up word, which stood for both the name of an organization and a concept; neither was revolutionary in the literal sense, but both would transform the world.

WikiLeaks.

■ ■ ■

Julian Assange was born in 1971, in Townsville, on Australia's northeast coast, but much of his youth was spent seven miles offshore in the rustic resort community of Magnetic Island. In the 1970s, the island was a haven for artists, nonconformists, and back-to-the-land types. Assange's mother, Christine Hawkins, suspended fruit from the ceiling to protect it from wildlife, found taipans in her son's bed, and hacked a path to her front door with a machete. She lived, she later recalled, "in a bikini, 'going native' with my baby and other mums on the island." Assange described much of his youth as like that of Tom Sawyer—riding horses, fishing, building rafts, and exploring the wilderness.

The family's three stints on Magnetic Island were placid interludes in Assange's otherwise unsettled childhood. His mother lived as an itinerant artist, carting Assange and later his half-brother on her odyssey through the lefty bohemia of 1970s Australia. The family moved often: Sydney, Brisbane, the Adelaide Hills, Perth, and a string of towns along Australia's western coast. Later in his childhood, from age eleven to sixteen, Assange was led to believe the family was being pursued by his half-brother's father who had joined a powerful and dangerous cult known as the Family (a custody battle over Assange's half-brother led Christine to take to the road). Assange had changed residence more than a dozen times by the time he was fourteen (he has claimed a number as high as thirty-seven). Traipsing around Australia with his mother and a changing cast of father figures, at times in paranoid flight from a supposed stalker in a shadowy cult, made for a disjointed and unconventional childhood.

Assange's mother burned her schoolbooks when she left home on a motorcycle at age seventeen; she showed no more esteem for formal education in the rearing of her son Julian. The family's frequent changes of residence made consistent education impossible, and Assange had difficulties in school, which Christine explained were due to his "high level of genius." For eighteen months he was taken out of school entirely, purportedly due to an illness. During this time he was homeschooled.

Despite the absence in his life of academic rigor, Assange was driven by an innate curiosity. He read widely and voraciously, developing an interest in science and philosophy. Relatives of the young Assange described him as sensitive and geeky, but he could also be pedantic and self-important. Other kids called him "the Prof" due to his penchant for trying to teach them about what he learned. Assange told Raffi Khatchadourian, writing for the *New Yorker*, "We were bright, sensitive kids who didn't fit into the dominant subculture and fiercely castigated those who did as boneheads."

When Assange was eleven years old, the wandering family lived across the street from an electronics store, into which the boy would venture to tool around on a computer in the shop. He was drawn to the computer, unraveling and manipulating the code in well-known programs. So taken was the boy with the machine that his mother moved the family to a cheaper rental house, where she could save money to buy one for him. Eventually, she did.

Released in 1982, the Commodore 64 was to the personal computer what the iPod was to the digital music player. Compared to the personal computers that came before, it was sleek, fast, and cheap, selling seventeen million units over twelve years. The bestselling personal computer of all time, it set off a revolution in home computing, bringing the high-powered computer to the middle-class home. And in its mass-produced interface, Assange found a world that satisfied both his intellect and his disposition. "The austerity of one's interaction with a computer is something that appealed to me," Assange has said. "It is like chess—chess is very austere, in that you don't have many rules, there is no randomness, and the problem is very hard."

In 1987, Assange got his first modem. He was living with his mother in Emerald, a slow-paced exurb of Melbourne that the precocious sixteen-year-old found mind-numbingly boring.

In those days, there was no such thing as a website—there was still no World Wide Web—and no publicly accessible connection from Australia to the then-nascent Internet in the United States. But there were smaller local computer networks. On these, Assange made his first forays out of his stultifying exurban existence and into the interconnected digital world.

He communicated with other computer users, often bright teenagers like himself, via online bulletin board systems (BBS). For teens whose offline social lives barely existed, the conversations were like digital parties. Talk revolved around the technical questions early-adopter computer techies were interested in, like hardware, software, and programming languages. Users explored the possibilities and limitations of computer networks and what it took to push beyond those limitations, sharing with one another what they learned along the way. The same curiosity that compelled these young men—they were almost all males—to learn for themselves the inner workings of still fairly uncommon computing machines attracted them to further explorations of digital networks. Assange, under the moniker "Mendax," formed common cause with two other teenagers who were keen on embarking on these sorts of expeditions. Displaying an early proclivity for the theatrical, Assange and his teenage friends proclaimed themselves "the International Subversives."

Piggybacking on the superior computing power of the mainframe at the Royal Melbourne Institute of Technology, the young techies accessed the computer system at the Australian National University, through which they accessed the Lonsdale Telephone Exchange, a doorway into computer networks worldwide. Over a period of several years, through skilled guesswork, programming, and "social engineering"—a term for operating in the real world to deceive people into divulging confidential information—they got into such sensitive systems as those of the United States Air Force and Navy, the defense contractor Lockheed Martin, NASA, Motorola, Unisys, Xerox, the

US Department of Defense's unclassified MILNET, and the nuclear research laboratory at Los Alamos.

When Assange was seventeen, he moved out of his mother's house and in with his girlfriend, Teresa. They relocated into Melbourne proper, Australia's buzzing cultural and intellectual capital. As the central node of the country's particularly irreverent brand of countercultural politics, Melbourne became a sort of real-world BBS chat room for the Australian hacker underground.

Assange and Teresa married in an unofficial ceremony and the next year had a son, Daniel, but in 1991 the couple had a bitter split. In the confrontation that ensued, Teresa tore through the house, throwing open drawers as she grabbed her belongings and left. She took their son with her. Assange was devastated and descended into depression.

With Teresa and Daniel gone, the house was half-empty and in disarray, tousled clothes littering the floor. Assange nearly stopped eating. He sank into unsettled lethargy, tortured by melancholy on restless nights. And he became careless.

On the evening of October 29, 1991, Assange was reclining on a couch at home, reading *Soledad Brother*, the collected letters of a black man wrongfully imprisoned by the state of California. He had a speaker system connected to his computer modem, which was connected to the phone line, and the slow staccato of a busy signal droned through the house, an electric mantra for his sense of futility and his resignation to it. The incriminating disks he usually kept hidden in his beehive were strewn around the computer.

At 11:30 PM, a loud knocking sounded from his front door. Standing outside were nearly a dozen officers of the Australian Federal Police.

The so-called International Subversives were bound by an ethical code. They forbade themselves from doing any harm during their online expeditions or taking any malicious action based on what they found. It was a kind of perversion of the Boy Scout principle to leave no trace. They changed as little as possible on their ventures into the digital wilderness, only adding or removing code so as to leave a secret door ajar for their next foray or in order to cover their tracks. They were, and considered themselves to be, "hackers," but their illicit explorations of closed networks bore greater resemblance to teenagers breaking into a high school for kicks on a Friday night than to the sort of illegal activity the media would come to label with the grossly misunderstood term *hacking*.

Indeed, the first hackers hadn't been criminals at all, nor had they been primarily interested in computers. They had been college kids with a railroad hobby.

■ ■ ■

At the Massachusetts Institute of Technology in the late 1950s, two sometimes hostile factions comprised the Tech Model Railroad Club (TMRC). There was the nostalgic faction, who painstakingly constructed train replicas, tinkering and painting in fine detail. They subscribed to railroad magazines and took trips on aging lines, reveling in railroad lore. And there was the S&P faction, with members concentrated in the Signals & Power Subcommittee. What held their interest was not sentimentality for the railroad or the meticulous reconstruction of model trains but the interconnected system of switches and rail lines on which trains traveled. A tweak in one part of the network rippled throughout, in vibrant, alluring complexity. The interlinked system seemed to move and breathe in dynamic unison, a living puzzle begging to be dissected, understood, and optimized.

Fueled by the Coca-Colas they seemed always to have at hand, the S&P crew spent late nights tinkering with the system. "Using dials appropriated from telephones," Steven Levy wrote in his seminal tome on the subject, *Hackers: Heroes of the Computer Revolution*, "the TMRC 'engineers' could specify which block of track they wanted control of, and run a train from there." The hours their classmates spent studying, they devoted to experimenting with and improving the system. Levy writes, "A project undertaken or a product built not solely to fulfill some constructive goal, but with some wild pleasure taken in mere involvement, was called a 'hack.'" The most inventive and productive members of the S&P Subcommittee proudly donned their moniker: *hackers*.

From the beginning, the term was colored with a shade of mischief. The intricate pranks for which MIT students are still renowned, like disguising the campus's Great Dome as the *Star Wars* character R2-D2 or placing a full-size replica of a campus police car atop it, had long been called *hacks*. An association with the unbridled creativity of these perennial high jinks was not likely lost on the TMRC hackers.

In the bowels of one building at MIT was the Electronic Accounting Machinery Room, a climate-controlled citadel that housed one of MIT's most expensive pieces of equipment: the IBM 704. The massive proto-computer filled an entire room and was jealously guarded by those who ran the machine, who were known commonly as "the Priesthood." Mere laymen were not allowed direct access to the IBM 704 but could submit requests to the priests, who would feed the machine the punch-hole cards it used to make computations. Hours and sometimes days later, if the instructions laid out on the cards were without error and the machine did not break down, it would spit out the results of its processes.

The IBM 704 was not merely a shortcut for calculations. It was a system unto itself, into which a set of instructions could be plugged, the results analyzed, the instructions tweaked, improved, improvised, and, for the creative, unruly few tempted to think beyond the rules and regulations—the very purpose of the machine—*hacked*.

In 1959, MIT offered its first course in computer science (it was ridiculed, initially, as a hairbrained notion for a discipline). The class was taught by John McCarthy, the mathematician who coined the term *artificial intelligence*, and, mystifyingly to his critics, pioneered the use of a programming language to "teach" a computer to play chess. Under McCarthy's tutelage, the world's first computer hackers pushed the boundaries of the possible and began creating the digital world as we know it today.

As computers steadily improved, the complexity and possibilities of programming expanded. Early hackers turned computers into numerical translators, converting Arabic numerals into their Roman counterparts. They tweaked their computers to play music, rendering Bach fugues and Gilbert and Sullivan operettas in humming electric tones. Then they turned the machines into musical instruments. Much to the annoyance of his befuddled professor, one MIT hacker wrote a program that allowed him to make computations for the homework from his numerical analysis class; in irreverent homage to the still multimillion-dollar machines, he called his program the "Expensive Desk Calculator." Hackers built one of the first video-game controllers and even the first video-game. (It was called Spacewar and, as it was endlessly being hacked and thus improved, was a significantly more interesting game than Pong, born years later.)

In tandem with the computing power of their machines, an unwritten set of guidelines evolved for the nascent hacker subculture. Levy identifies five principles that composed, and still compose, the essence of the Hacker Ethic.

"Computers can change your life for the better." The computer is the ultimate tool, and the world can be made better by using it in innovative and useful ways.

"Art and beauty can be created on a computer." Music and graphics are impressive, but the true beauty in a computer resides in the code. Elegant in its logic, beautiful in its dynamic unity, the perfect program could be every bit as magnificent as the most complex life form.

"Hackers should be judged on their hacking, not credentials, age, race or position." Hacking is a meritocracy. Logic and utility reign, and arbitrary status symbols, which corrupt meritocracy, are worse than meaningless—they are contemptible.

"Mistrust authority, and promote decentralization." Ever since the early days, when hackers were kept at a distance from the IBM 704 by the Priesthood, authority figures and their bureaucratic rules had only hindered exploration and innovation.

"All information should be free." Hacking depends on information about systems moving freely among people. In the ultimate free marketplace, the best programs are quickly shared and improved and the improvements shared, and thus, through laissez-faire exchange, creativity is at a premium, and the meritocracy of hackers and hacks prevails. How can a system be dissected and improved if its internal workings are kept secret?

The Jargon File, a regularly updated repository of hacker slang and culture, offers several concise definitions for *hacker*. First on the list is, "A person who enjoys exploring the details of programmable systems and how to stretch their capabilities, as opposed to most users, who prefer to learn only the minimum necessary." And another, "One who enjoys the intellectual challenge of creatively overcoming or circumventing limitations."

"Hackers," Steven Levy writes, "believe that essential lessons can be learned about systems—about the world—from taking things apart, seeing how they work, and using this knowledge to create new and even more interesting things. They resent any person, physical barrier, or law that tries to keep them from doing this."

The Internet Engineering Task Force is the closest thing the Internet has to a governing body. Its "Internet Users Glossary" offers as good a definition of *hacker* as any, with an added nod to the substantial confusion that has come to surround the term. A hacker, according to the glossary, is "a person who delights in having an intimate understanding of the internal workings of a system, computers and computer networks in particular. The term is often misused in a pejorative context, where 'cracker' would be the correct term."

This usage of the term *cracker*, according to *The Jargon File*, was coined in 1985 by hackers who sought to distance themselves from those among their ranks who used their skills to penetrate secure networks. It hasn't stuck. To the extent that the English language is socially constructed—which is to say to a large extent—among the meanings of *hacker* is still a tech-savvy computer user who breaks into closed computer systems.

The fact is, there are two basic and often overlapping categories of hackers unified by a shared sense of playful, subversive whimsy and, ostensibly, the principles laid out above. There are the builders, heirs to their Tech Model Railroad Club forbearers, who take things apart to put them back together, to innovate and optimize. And there are the raiders, who employ many of the same talents to circumvent network security and penetrate closed systems. Julian Assange and the International Subversives were of the latter sort. But even within this category there are key distinctions, which the hackish culture has looked to Hollywood to help describe.

In the classic formulation of the old Western film, there is a villain, wearing a black hat, in conflict with a hero, wearing a white hat. A "black hat" is thus a hacker who uses his computer skills with malicious intent, such as writing a virus program or breaking into the secure network of an online merchant to steal credit card information. A "white hat" is a hacker who uses his powers for good, chiefly to test and shore up network security to defend against black hats. Along this gradient is the "gray hat," a hacker who may break the law in the course of penetrating a secure system but who does so without malicious intent. In this sense, the gray hat comes closest to the purest essence of the hacking ethos—he doesn't do it for the money or because he's told to; he does it, ultimately, for the thrill of the hack.

When the Australian Federal Police raided Julian Assange's house in 1991, one of the world's great, budding gray hats was temporarily taken offline.

■ ■ ■

The police ripped through Assange's house with enthusiasm exceeding his wife's rampage in leaving it. They took his computer, tore up the carpet, and took every book and scrap of paper. They even confiscated Assange's collection of old *Scientific American* magazines. They tried to interrogate Assange, but he said little, and after consulting an attorney on a legal-aid hotline, he said nothing at all.

The months after the police raid were among the lowest of Assange's life. He didn't touch a computer for six months. The state waited years to formally press charges, and amid the uncertainty Assange descended further into the aimless depression his wife's abrupt departure had wrought. His mental condition became so unstable that he checked himself into a psychiatric ward, but after a brief stay he began to feel the institution was doing more harm than good. He moved in with his mother, but that living arrangement proved untenable, and he left after only a few days. He wandered the countryside surrounding Melbourne, sleeping in city parks, grassy meadows, riverbanks, and the eucalyptus forests of eight-thousand-acre Dadenong National Park, in Melbourne's outer suburbs.

By the time Assange received his charges in the mail, in July 1994, he was in better spirits. He was making money as a programmer and consultant and, with his mother, had launched a personal campaign to recover custody of his son, Daniel. He formed an organization that fought "corruption and lack of accountability" in the government of the Australian state of Victoria. According to *Underground*, a book about the Australian hacker scene by Suelette Dreyfus, for whom Assange worked as a researcher, he "acted as a conduit for leaked documents" that were used in court cases against the state government.

When he finally went to court to face his hacking charges in late 1996, Assange was given a relatively a minor sentence. Total damage claims from the hackers' activities, incurred not from repairing vandalism but from diverting resources to fight the intrusions, totaled more than $160,000 (AUD). In the end, Assange was ordered to pay $2,100 in reparations to the Australian National University and given a three-year good-behavior bond of $5,000. The judge cited Assange's unorthodox upbringing as a mitigating factor in sentencing but added, "highly intelligent individuals ought not to behave like this, and I suspect it is only highly intelligent individuals who can do what you did."

Despite the leniency of his sentence, Assange's first-person confrontation with the legal establishment profoundly shaped his political thinking. He alluded to the experience years later, in mid-2006, when he wrote, with characteristic hyperbole:

> If there is a book whose feeling captures me it is First Circle by Solzhenitsyn. To feel that home is the comraderie of persecuted, and infact, prosecuted, polymaths in a Stalinist slave labor camp! How close the parallels to my own adventures! . . . Such prosecution in youth is a defining peak experience. To know the state for

what it really is! To see through that veneer the educated swear to disbelieve in but still slavishly follow with their hearts! . . . True belief begins only with a jackboot at the door. True belief forms when lead into the dock and referred to in the third person. True belief is when a distant voice booms *'the prisoner shall now rise'* and no one else in the room stands.

While he was waiting to be charged as a cybercriminal in the early 1990s, Assange became involved with the Cypherpunks, a movement interested in the use of technology to protect individual privacy from government intrusion. The core group formed in the San Francisco Bay Area in 1992 out of the young Silicon Valley computer programmers who were striking it rich and retiring early. Australian academic Robert Manne writes, "It must have been more than a little gratifying for a self-educated antipodean computer hacker, who had not even completed high school, to converse on equal terms with professors of mathematics, whiz-kid businessmen and some of the leading computer code-writers in the world."

For nearly a decade, Assange was active on the Cypherpunks mailing list, a lively thread of impassioned back-and-forth on issues related to privacy, encryption, and freedom in the digital age. The Cypherpunks were, in large part, libertarians of the Ayn Rand variety: purist anarchists fervently opposed to Big Brother–style government surveillance and elitists in favor of a strict and cold-hearted meritocracy. Assange too cast his lot squarely with autonomous individuals and against the surveillance state, but when others on the mailing list delivered laissez-faire diatribes, he criticized their political bent with equal zeal. In one post, he refers to labor unions as "those devious entities that first-world companies and governments have had a hand in suppressing all over the third world by curtailing freedom of association, speech and other basic political rights we take for granted." The group had a profound influence on his political development, but records of the correspondence also reveal Assange tacking away over time from the rightist anarchism of Cypherpunk custom.

"At the core of the cypherpunk philosophy," Manne writes, "was the belief that the great question of politics in the age of the internet was whether the state would strangle individual freedom and privacy through its capacity for electronic surveillance or whether autonomous individuals would eventually undermine and even destroy the state through their deployment of electronic weapons newly at hand."

This point is essential. A first cousin to the hacker ethic, with its creation story of overthrowing the IBM 704 Priesthood at MIT, the Cypherpunk worldview was fundamentally about empowering individuals and disempowering the state. To this end, the Cypherpunks advocated a dual-pronged program: autonomy and privacy for individuals and transparency with oversight for institutions, namely the state. Put more simply, they called for individual privacy but institutional transparency.

In 1995 a New York City–based architect and former 1960s radical named John Young joined the Cypherpunks mailing list. The following year, Young came across a federal report released only in hard copy that dealt with regulatory issues and encryption products. Inspired by the impassioned exchanges he was following on the Cypherpunks thread, Young scanned the report and posted it online. And so began Cryptome.

Young created the website Cryptome.org to host documents related to "freedom of expression, privacy, cryptology, dual-use technologies, national security, intelligence, and secret governance," including "open, secret and classified documents." By 2000, Cryptome had amassed an online archive of more than four thousand documents. Young's Cryptome.org was ruffling feathers at the FBI, NSA, and CIA and as far afield as Japan's Public Security Investigation Agency and Britain's MI5. Julian Assange remained active on the Cypherpunks mailing list as the Cryptome project took off. All the while he was paying attention.

Assange corresponded with the Cypherpunks using two primary e-mail addresses: proff@suburbia.net and proff@gnu.ai.mit.edu. Suburbia.net was an Australian public Internet-access system in the early 1990s, which, according to the site's About page, had "members from all walks of life. From magistrates and politicians to convicted computer hackers!" who shared "a common interest in the free flow of information and ideas." Assange was, as he put it, "the chief technical brains" for the Suburbia Public Access Network, which he called "a low-cost, power-to-the-people enabling technology."

The gnu.ai.mit.edu domain was a similarly publicly available Internet access system, maintained at MIT, by the philosopher-king of the GNU project, Richard M. Stallman. Both the GNU and Suburbia accounts were available for free, but, as Stallman would say, they were also "free as in freedom." As an icon and guru in MIT's hacker culture, Stallman's ideas would have an important influence on both Assange and Brad Manning.

■ ■ ■

By the 1970s, the hacking culture midwifed in Cambridge, Massachusetts, had spread. The growing popularity of academic computer centers and a torrent of Defense Department funds—long the lifeblood of the computer research central to the growth of hackerism—led to the development of hacker hives across the country, most notably at Stanford, planting the seed of what would become Silicon Valley. Though the once-tiny hacking subculture at MIT had established colonies as far away as northern California, MIT's hacker core remained. On the ninth floor of a building at MIT's Tech Square, in the Artificial Intelligence (AI) lab, the hacker ethos was safe and strong—for a while. And that is precisely what drew Richard Stallman to the computers across town.

Stallman had grown up in New York City in a politically conscious household during the tempestuous 1960s. He enrolled at Harvard in 1970 to study mathematics and science, and quickly developed an interest in computers. But Harvard's computer labs were stodgy and laden with regulations, bureaucracy, and graduate student gatekeepers, like the Priesthood who guarded the IBM 704 at MIT back in the 1950s. Time at Harvard's computer terminals was allotted based on academic rank, forcing undergraduate peons like Stallman to wait patiently until their elders were finished before they could use the machines.

In 1971, as the end of his freshman year approached, Stallman heard about a computer lab near the eastern end of Cambridge where the programmers had overthrown their Priesthood, where the computer terminals were first-come, first-serve, open to any and all, and where social standing was strictly meritocratic, unlike the dull, academic hierarchy at Harvard. Stallman made the two-mile trek to the Artificial Intelligence lab at MIT, and by the time he left that day he had a job writing code. A hacker was born.

"That's the way it was back then," Stallman later said, as recounted in Sam Williams's *Free as in Freedom: Richard Stallman's Campaign for Free Software*. "That's the way it still is now. I'll hire somebody when I meet him if I see he's good. Why wait? Stuffy people who insist on putting bureaucracy into everything really miss the point. If a person is good, he shouldn't have to go through a long, detailed hiring process; he should be sitting at a computer writing code."

The fresh-faced, timid Harvard geek was subsumed into hacker culture. When not doing work for his classes at Harvard, he was at the MIT AI lab, writing code, chowing down on Chinese food during all-night marathon hacking sessions, and, as had become tradition among MIT hackers, busting through whatever stood in the way of his access to AI lab computers. MIT professors who, out of forgetfulness or spite, left AI lab computer terminals behind locked office doors at the end of the day had their offices routinely broken into either through surreptitious means or with something as inelegant as a battering ram. While other computer labs around the country were installing password-protected security systems, MIT's hackers stood steadfastly against such measures. Hacking, after all, depended on openness, collaboration, and the free exchange of information. Passwords and the like were, the hackers felt, antithetical to their ethos.

The hacker scene awakened Stallman's social being. Once a wallflower, it wasn't long before he was actually seeking out social interaction and speaking out politically. The Watergate scandal, which grew to a boil during Stallman's college years, affected him deeply. Williams writes: "To the hackers, Watergate was merely a Shakespearean rendition of the daily power struggles that made life such a hassle for those without privilege. It was an outsized parable for what happened when people traded liberty and openness for security and convenience."

The proud atheist Stallman took to wearing an "Impeach God" button—a hack on the then-ubiquitous "Impeach Nixon" buttons and the doomed president's infamous "secret plan" to end the Vietnam War. When people questioned him about the button he would answer: "I have a special plan to save the universe, but because of heavenly security reasons I can't tell you what that plan is. You're just going to have to put your faith in me, because I see the picture and you don't. You know I'm good because I told you so. If you don't believe me, I'll throw you on my enemies list and throw you in a pit where [the] Infernal Revenue Service will audit your taxes for eternity."

The late 1970s and early 1980s were, many argue, the end of a golden age of hacking. The spirit of radical openness and collaboration was suppressed by what the hackers felt were exigent bureaucrats, protecting the interests of the powerful at the expense of innovation and all that hacking could offer. MIT professors who demanded passwords to protect sensitive research data eventually got them. More and more hackers were pulled away from the Eden of the AI lab and into the growing private sector around computers, amid dwindling Pentagon funds for computer science research in the post-Vietnam era. For Stallman, a watershed was reached in 1982, when the AI lab upgraded its computers and in so doing switched to a new, proprietary operating system with inbuilt security measures and source code the hackers were strictly barred from altering. The battle lines had been drawn.

Stallman had already developed a reputation for his aversion to secrecy. After the use of passwords was instituted on AI lab computers, it was widely known by hackers around the country that all one needed to log on to the MIT network—and through it to ARPAnet, the precursor to the Internet—was to get access to an MIT machine and supply the initials RMS in the log-in field and RMS again for the password.

Thus, when a message went out to the net.unix-wizards newsgroup declaring the intention to undermine in absolute terms the new system, it came as little surprise to those who knew him well that Richard Stallman was the author. The message began:

Free Unix!

Starting this Thanksgiving I am going to write a complete Unix-compatible software system called GNU (for Gnu's Not Unix), and give it away free to everyone who can use it.

Stallman asserted, "The golden rule requires that if I like a program I must share it with other people who like it. I cannot in good conscience sign a nondisclosure agreement or a software license agreement." He continued, "So that I can continue to use computers without violating my principles, I have decided to put together a sufficient body of free software so that I will be able to get along without any software that is not free." Stallman ended his message thus: "If I get donations of money, I may be able to hire a few people full or part time. The salary won't be high, but I'm looking for people for whom knowing they are helping humanity is as important as money."

GNU is a computer operating system similar to the widely used Unix system, which, in the computer world, is a behemoth (Macintosh's OS X system, for example, is Unix-based). The GNU project set off a revolution in computer programming, leading to a flurry of mass, democratic, global collaboration. Through the spirit of openness, free access to information, and cooperation, programmers gave the world open-sourced operating systems, including GNU/Linux, which, in various iterations, is in use all over the world. A partial list of major GNU/Linux users includes Dreamworks Animation, Amazon.com, CERN, the Chicago Mercantile Exchange, the New York Stock Exchange, IBM, and the United States Army.

In 1985, Stallman founded the Free Software Foundation, through which he refined and continued to spread the gospel of "free software" over the following decades. Stallman's ideas gave birth to both the free software and open source movements, between which there is a slender but deep ideological chasm. Stallman writes, in an essay titled "Why Open Source Misses the Point": "The two terms describe almost the same category of software, but they stand for views based on fundamentally different values. Open source is a development methodology; free software is a social movement."

"This is a matter of freedom, not price, so think of 'free speech,' not 'free beer,'" Stallman writes. The freedom to share, cooperate, and collaborate with unfettered access to software source code is essential, says Stallman, for the health of society in general. But equally important is the freedom to protect the ability of people—"users" in Stallman's hacker parlance—to use computers as they wish. Software can, for example, censor the websites you're able to visit; limit the way you manipulate audio, video, or pictures; restrict your ability to dispose of data; or track your activity online. Software that is "closed" keeps a programmer from being able to, for instance, tweak a program so that it stops tracking your online activity. Free software preserves the ability of a programmer to optimize software to suit the needs of users or to eliminate restrictions it might place on a user. To understand the concept, it can be helpful to think in terms of the predigital era. The technology to write a letter is free in the Stallman sense: if you can hold a pen, then you are free to write a letter however you want—invent a new language; write backward; draw a picture; fold, tear, scratch, hide, burn, or give away a copy of your note. "In a world of digital sounds, images, and words," Stallman writes, "free software becomes increasingly essential for freedom in general."

In the early 1990s, MIT forced Stallman to stop the practice of allowing just anyone to access MIT machines through his account with the RMS log-in name and password combination. But the GNU project had machines of its own, on which, in the freewheeling, collaborative spirit of hackerism, free guest accounts were allowed under the gnu.ai.mit.edu domain. Open to anyone who wanted to access the Internet or open an e-mail account in the era before ubiquitous use of Gmail, Hotmail, and other such services, Stallman's GNU machine was a sort of free Internet service provider. "[The accounts] were easy to get, and that's because we believed in hospitality," Stallman says. During the 1990s, Julian Assange devoted many hours to developing free and open software. He kept multiple e-mail addresses, but one of them, out of solidarity or convenience, or both, was held through one of Stallman's free accounts. Assange had become a devoted free-software partisan.

■ ■ ■

The late 1990s and early 2000s were happier times for Assange. With his legal troubles and his gray-hat hacking days behind him, he was making a decent living as a computer consultant. He traveled widely through Asia, Europe, and the United States. He donated his technical expertise to NGOs and activist groups. Back home, Assange reveled in the politically charged atmosphere of Melbourne, a hotbed for the leftist anti-globalization movement.

By age thirty-two, Assange had enough financial and personal stability to seek a university degree. He enrolled full-time at the University of Melbourne, where he studied mathematics and physics, with mediocre academic success. He lived in a communal squat and slept, roommates said, with his bedroom bathed in the glow of red light bulbs, which he claimed helped him sleep; early humans waking in the middle of the night, he explained, would have seen only the glow of a campfire.

Assange did wake often in the middle of the night, his mind racing with ideas. He'd become deeply preoccupied and was so focused, spending hours working on his computer, that he'd fail to eat for days. He would scrawl his midnight brainstorms onto loose paper or, when no scraps could be found, the walls and doors. The computer code covering available writing surfaces might have looked like arcane hieroglyphs to the illiterate, but to the lanky Australian with electric-white hair, whose specter would come to haunt governments around world, the code was the language of insurrection.

Julian Assange saw the world through the eyes of a hacker of the old school. There were principles he held to be sacrosanct. In a piece of writing from mid-2006 regarding an open-source project he'd spent years working on, we hear echoes of Stallman in Assange's refusal to sign a nondisclosure agreement: "I felt it was the antithesis of what motivated me to be involved with the foundation (building something out of the love of creation and intellectual competition)."

He was deeply suspicious of authority. By his thirties, Assange's primary philosophical preoccupation was the relationship of the individual to the state. For Assange, the abstraction "the state" applied to either end of the traditional political spectrum and carried very definite undertones of totalitarian persecution, conformity, and cruel, crushing power. He was, Manne writes in an analysis of Assange's correspondence from the period, "a profound anticommunist. But he regards power in Western society as belonging to political and economic elites offering ordinary people nothing more nourishing than a counterfeit conception of democracy and a soul-destroying consumption culture."

Perhaps most importantly, Assange saw problems as puzzles. In the hackish tradition stretching back to the Tech Model Railroad Club at MIT, complex systems begged to be dissected, analyzed, and optimized; a part of the system that didn't work properly was just a glitch waiting to be fixed. A barrier to information access, like an unjust authoritarian government, was no more than a web of puzzles, and the natural response to a web of puzzles was to untangle and solve them. And busy untangling puzzles he was.

On October 3, 2006, Julian Assange sent an e-mail to John Young, founder of Cryptome.org.

> Dear John,
>   You knew me under another name from cypherpunk days. I am involved in a project that you may have feeling for. I will not mention its name yet incase you feel yu are not able to be involved.
>   The project is a mass document leaking project that requires someone with backbone to hold the .org domain registration.

He went on to explain that the domain registrant should know as little about the project as possible but still be willing to publicly stand behind the domain name. "Will you be that person?" he asked. The next day, the domain name WikiLeaks.org was registered in the United States, under the names John Shipton—Assange's biological father—and John Young.

Assange's chosen name for the WikiLeaks project is instructive. In 1999, he registered leaks.org and did nothing with the site. But by 2005, when he apparently first settled on the name WikiLeaks and wrote it on his whiteboard in Melbourne, he'd been profoundly impressed by the success of Wikipedia. Steeped as he was in the ethos of the free software movement, Assange sincerely hoped WikiLeaks would become a node for mass, open, journalistic collaboration. Leaked documents would be posted online, and visitors to the site from around the world would analyze and comment on the documents. In this "wiki"—originally a Hawaiian word meaning "quick," now generally understood as a website that allows collaborative editing—users would create useful, collaborative, and trustworthy works of journalism through radical openness.

Over the following months an e-mail list developed between members of the international crew Assange was assembling to form the WikiLeaks organization. Among them, according to records of the e-mail exchange, were cryptographers, academics, an ex-hacker, a businessman, and others. Assange reached out to Daniel Ellsberg, famous leaker of the Pentagon Papers, but, in what would prove to be something of an irony, Ellsberg missed the e-mail.

By the winter of 2006, Assange had put his ideas to paper. In a document titled "Conspiracy as Governance," he laid the foundation for his argument. The piece is written in Assange's typical style, obtuse to simulate academic rigor, but simplified to its basic parts his logic has a certain elegance. It goes something like the following.

A nexus of authoritarian governments and multinational corporations (they are one and the same in Assange's view) dominates the world. It operates as what Assange dubs a conspiracy, and its survival depends on both secrecy and on communication among its members. One way to destroy a conspiracy is to sever the links of secret communication among the conspirators. This can be accomplished by dramatically lowering the cost of leaking information, so leaks become easier, secrets become harder to keep, and communication inside conspiracies, which depend on secrecy, becomes increasingly difficult to maintain.

A "leaky" world, in Assange's estimation, works like herbicide on a weed-infested lawn. Herbicide is sprayed over the entire lawn, but by design only the weeds are vulnerable to its poison. The weeds are destroyed, and the desirable plants in the lawn are left, ostensibly, as healthy as ever.

Similarly, a world in which leaking information is safe and easy affects all the world's governments. But only unjust governments, which wholly depend on secret communications, are harmed by widespread and uncontained leaking. "The more secretive or unjust an organization is, the more leaks induce fear and paranoia in its leadership and planning coterie," Assange wrote in a later blog post. "Hence in a world where leaking is easy, secretive or unjust systems are nonlinearly hit relative to open, just systems."

The key difference between Assange's vision and the classic information leak is in the crosshairs. Traditionally, a whistleblower leaks information for personal gain, to undermine an adversary, or to reveal an injustice. In the case of WikiLeaks, the target is not any specific adversary or policy or even any particular injustice that might be revealed. The target is secrecy itself.

3

General Manning

B rad had been sleeping in his truck. After the screaming match at his dad's house in Oklahoma City, he'd driven to Tulsa in his old red pickup. But when he got there he was confronted with the facts: he had little money, few friends, and limited education. Fighting with his dad and stepmother, who had been providing for him, and opting to take to the road rather than staying in the area and begging forgiveness was, to understate things, a bold move. He was effectively starting over, and with very little going for him.

Considering the circumstances, he was in surprisingly good spirits. It was Brad's first real taste of freedom, and if he was wanting for money, credentials, and a network, he was not for faith in his own abilities. What he needed was a little help to get started, which an old friend from Crescent could provide.

Jordan was in his senior year at Memorial High School, living in his parents' home in South Tulsa, where the family had relocated a few years earlier. He didn't like knowing his friend was sleeping in a pickup truck and invited him to move into his house. He knew his dad didn't like people staying the night but figured Brad's presence could be hidden long enough for him to get settled in Tulsa. Brad took a little convincing but eventually agreed.

He slept on a pallet on the floor in Jordan's closet, spoke in a hushed voice, and hid on the rare occasions that Jordan's dad ventured upstairs. He parked his truck down the block from the house to avoid raising suspicions. For the two best friends, reunited after years apart, the whole cloak-and-dagger operation had a dash of adventure.

Brad lived covertly at Jordan's house for a couple weeks before he got his own place at the Copper Mills apartment complex nearby with help on a down payment from his dad. The furnishings were sparse, but Brad was fastidious. He kept a neat home, with a bed, a PC, and a stack of books, among them volumes by Tom Clancy and Immanuel Kant's intricate opus, *Critique of Pure Reason*.

In mid-April 2005, Brad and Jordan got jobs at Incredible Pizza, a massive family-friendly pizza parlor and arcade, with a facade like a neon castle, looming over a South Tulsa strip mall. Wielding a clipboard and wearing a smile and a cheesy yellow bowling shirt, Brad greeted customers and directed them onto the game-room floor or to one of the many parties happening that day. With the constant din of gleeful children and the bells and dings and whirs of a massive arcade, Incredible Pizza gets loud fast. Guiding the endless flow of stressed parents and excited children through the chaos—it's especially busy during the weekend shifts Brad and Jordan always worked—can be taxing. Playing host at a pizza place contrasted starkly, in both pay and prestige, with his previous job at Zoto, and the search for a new job started soon after his stint at Incredible Pizza began.

Brad came to work one day and told his manager he needed the day off—he had an interview for a job at a bank. He'd neglected to make arrangements to have a coworker cover his shift or even to call in sick, but he wasn't going to let bad planning stand in the way of a position better suited to his abilities. The manager told Brad if he left not to come back. He went anyway.

He didn't get the job. Again unemployed, Brad got a job at F.Y.E., a retail entertainment chain, peddling DVDs and CDs at Tulsa's Woodland Hills Mall. But he wanted more than eastern Oklahoma could offer. His time in Tulsa was over.

Again Brad struck out on his own, this time with even less familial support than before. He drove north to Chicago, where he got a job at Guitar Center and spent nights in his truck.

In late June, not long after his move to Chicago, Brad's Aunt Debbie, a financial-industry power attorney and adjunct law professor living with her family in the Maryland suburbs of Washington, DC, got a phone call from her Welsh sister-in-law, Sue. Brad had called Mum, and Mum had called her daughter Casey, who suggested she call Aunt Debbie for help.

"He was exhausted, mentally and physically," Debbie later recalled. He'd run out of money and, with nowhere else to turn, called his mum in Wales to ask for help.

Brad and Debbie were by no means close. He'd stayed at her house a few times over the years for brief visits, but she hardly knew him. Nonetheless, by 2006, with an alcoholic mother an ocean away and a father he didn't get along with, his aunt Debbie was Brad's last best chance at a stable life.

Her nephew was nearly a stranger to her, but family was family, and Debbie sprang into action. She wired Brad two hundred dollars and called his cell phone with an invitation to stay in her home while he rested and built a more steady foundation for young adulthood. Brad left immediately, completing the thirteen-hour drive in little more than a day. He showed up at the doorstep of his aunt's quaint, two story, red-brick house, with a mowed lawn and curbside mailbox, in Potomac, Maryland, on a warm, overcast Sunday—July 2, 2006.

Ever since his family had begun to fracture back in Crescent, Brad's life had been unstable, and coming home from the United Kingdom had only precipitated more upheaval. "He moved to America, and it was just like chaos after chaos after chaos," recalled Jordan. As he carried his belongings from his truck into the room he would share with a cousin who was home from college for the summer, Brad was beginning what would be one of the most tranquil periods of his life. He'd not yet had the chance to contemplate his future with anything like the comfort and stability Debbie was offering.

Though he was penniless and living in a shared bedroom at his aunt's house in the suburbs, in one short Metro ride, Brad could ascend into a gleaming city, throbbing with youthful energy. Never before in his nineteen years was opportunity so near at hand. He was fiercely interested in current events, the currency of everyday conversation in DC. The Bush years were waning, and the gay rights movement—energized even as he arrived by a failed effort in the House of Representatives to pass a constitutional amendment banning same-sex marriage—was gearing up for the 2008 election cycle. The nation's capital, like nowhere else in the country, was pulsating with his kind of energy. Brad Manning had been on a personal crusade, living in bold pursuit of the life he believed befitted his abilities, and he had reached the Holy Land.

Almost.

■ ■ ■

The suburbs of Washington, DC, look much like other suburbs throughout the eastern United States. Meandering roads wind through patches of thick brush that host thriving deer populations, past strip malls and mowed grassy easements with groomed young trees, into placid neighborhoods with cul-de-sacs and large, postwar homes. They differ from other suburbs in their demographic makeup. The Washington, DC, metropolitan area is the best-educated major metro area in the United States, with more university degrees per capita than any other. Residents of the inner suburbs, including Montgomery County, where Brad's aunt Debbie lived, are better educated than those of both the district and its outer suburbs. And even among the inner suburbs, Montgomery County is near the top of the list. DC suburbanites commute to jobs in the upper echelons of the federal bureaucracy and the nation's leading think tanks and interest groups. They are a uniquely concentrated population of highly educated, upper-middle-class news junkies personally invested in national and international affairs. These are the people to whom Brad spent his days serving coffee.

Brad got a job at a Starbucks in a strip mall near his aunt's house, working essentially full-time. It was another low-end job, but this wasn't like working at Guitar Center in Chicago while living out of a truck or peddling DVDs or greeting noisy kids at a pizza joint in a

South Tulsa strip mall. Compared to other service super-chains, Starbucks has a reputation for treating its employees well. Brad enjoyed the work, and the customers surrounding him each day were intelligent, educated suburbanites with whom he shared an abiding interest in current affairs. One such contact, with whom he claimed to have had a brief sexual relationship, worked at the Defense Intelligence Agency. Army recruiters were also among his frequent customers.

Brad wrecked his truck just after he arrived in Potomac, smashing one side of the front end and badly damaging a headlight, so he didn't drive much at night. When he wasn't at work, he was often at home. He spent hours in the bedroom he shared with his cousin, until the cousin returned to college at the end of the summer and Brad had the room to himself. Eventually he moved into a carpeted room of his own, with a window near the ceiling, in the basement and connected to the laundry.

He created an account on a personals website for single smokers, describing himself as a "flirt, shy at first, but warm up quickly," and a "geek, intellectual, liberal, preppy." He kept his room tidy and had few possessions—mostly books, a computer, and a Korg Electrible MX synthesizer, on which he wrote his own electronic music and remixed that of other artists. "He was used to living and coping with life on his own and never asked anything from us," Debbie later recalled. She tried her best to feed him a proper diet, but Brad was resistant. He lived, she said, on a staple meal from his favorite restaurant, McDonald's: Big Mac with cheese, large fries, and a Coke.

Much of the time Brad spent in his room he was playing EVE Online, a massive online multiplayer role-playing game. It's a seductive sci-fi universe, with a story extending back thousands of years and hundreds of thousands of players piloting spaceships, each with a destiny of his own making. In this alternate reality, you are free to be a trader, miner, pirate, or mercenary, to build or spy or fight intergalactic battles, all in real time. As an EVE player you create your own character, customizing a new human from scratch. You choose its gender and appearance, from wrinkles and facial scarring to eye color, freckles, facial hair, and clothes. The game is up-front with its appeal: "You are about to become what all men should fear. You will roam the heavens commanding the most powerful machines ever built," a disembodied voice declares in the game's opening sequence. "Dare to be bold, pilot. Forge your own path to greatness." After assuming a new persona of your own design, you enter the EVE universe, and the first thing you hear is a woman's soft voice: "Welcome to your new life."

One can imagine the appeal of spending long nights in the EVE universe for five-foot-two Brad Manning, who had little in the world but an unshakable faith in his own abilities if he could just get the chance to use them.

Brad eventually got a second job at Abercrombie & Fitch (his wardrobe rapidly came to reflect his new employee discount), and enrolled part-time at Montgomery College, the local community college. He took first-year, introductory classes in history and English while continuing to work full-time.

Brad failed a test and dropped out after one semester. He later told a friend, "Community college sucks," and described the semester he spent "covering old topics" while balancing school with work: "It didn't pay off," he said. But his aunt Debbie had a different take. "He was used to everything coming easily and seemed shocked that he didn't know everything," she said.

Brad Manning was not a star athlete growing up. He wasn't a charmer, a comedian, a rich kid, or a Casanova. He was, however, fiercely intelligent. Brad derived a sense of empowerment from his intelligence, which was unique in the small towns he grew up in. He'd grown into a cocky, if quiet, young man, and to challenge Brad's intelligence—to fail him on an exam, for instance—was to challenge that which validated his existence. Brad did what many of us have done at times in such instances. He dodged the issue.

■ ■ ■

By the fall of 2007, Brad was again directionless. He'd finally achieved the stability he sought at Debbie's house, but his truck had broken down completely, he'd dropped out of community college, and his jobs were leading him nowhere. He liked working at Starbucks and Abercrombie & Fitch, but again as before he knew he was capable of greater things. "As fun as those jobs were they weren't really getting me anywhere," he later told a friend online. "I wanted to go to college."

Brad called his aunt Debbie one afternoon and asked if the two of them could go out for dinner: he had something he wanted to tell her. They went to Broadway Diner, a kitschy, faux–old fashioned eatery, like a set piece from *American Graffiti*. As he sat across the table from Debbie—a woman he hardly knew only a year before but who'd become the closest thing he had to a stable, involved parent—Brad calmly explained that he'd decided to join the army.

His reasons for joining were few. He told her he was focused on going to college to study physics and that the army would pay for it. He chose the army over the other services because "the army said they would use his intellect," Debbie recalled. "He didn't want to end up doing something useless."

He didn't tell Debbie that his father had spent weeks prodding him to talk to a recruiter. "Bradley, you're really not going anywhere," Brian had told his son, remembering his own boozy teenage years and how only the navy had rescued him from aimlessness. "You haven't got transportation. You're working in a coffee shop and maybe going to go to community college." In the military, he said, "you're going to have three square meals a day. You're going to have a place to sleep and a roof over your head. And as long as you follow the path, you know, it's all you have to do."

Debbie was stunned. She protested, but Brad stopped her. It was, he said, a fait accompli—he'd already signed his papers. It was another bold venture for the young man from Crescent, but Brad was no stranger to risk. In a few days he was scheduled to report for duty at a Baltimore recruiting station. As of October 7, 2007, Bradley Manning was in the United States Army.

■ ■ ■

The US Army Manning joined was, to paraphrase the Oldsmobile ad campaign, not your father's army. The military was more diverse than ever before and by some measures more equitable than the civilian world. In 1973, when the US military became an all-volunteer force, just 1.6 percent of active-duty personnel were women; by 2005, females made up 15 percent of the active-duty armed forces (figures for the army in particular were roughly equivalent). Discrepancies in pay between men and women, and people of different races, were much smaller in the military than in the civilian world. Salary and benefits for entry-level military jobs exceeded those on offer for comparable starting positions outside the military. The Post-9/11 GI Bill increased educational assistance above the already-existing program through which millions of veterans had gone to college.

Homosexuals had been serving in the army for as long as there had been a country to serve and had come under increasing pressure under Don't Ask, Don't Tell, as discharges of gays spiked after 1994. But even active-duty gays were in better shape than before, after discharges under DADT peaked in 2001 and then dropped steadily in the waning years of the policy.

Brad had clearly and openly "demonstrate[d] a propensity or intent to engage in homosexual acts," as the language of the legislation read, and it was technically illegal under federal law for him to enlist in 2007. More than ten thousand gay and lesbian service members had been discharged under DADT, including soldiers with specialized training like that which Brad was to receive as an intelligence analyst. But the very real threat of getting fired didn't stop an estimated 65,000 gays and lesbians who served under DADT at any given time or an estimated one million gay and lesbian veterans from serving in years past. Brad was taking a risk in enlisting, but there was nothing particularly drastic about it. By 2007, a gay man enlisting in the army was, for all intents and purposes, rather ordinary.

The early years of the new millennium in the United States were a carnival of patriotic swagger. The stream of volunteers that flowed through recruiting stations to serve after the 9/11 attacks and the inauguration of the War on Terror continued through the invasions of Afghanistan and Iraq. Support for the Iraq War remained high through 2004, and the president who took the country to war won reelection that year on a campaign largely fueled by the fire of patriotic sentiment he'd stoked throughout his first term (e.g. the "Mission Accomplished" speech on the USS *Abraham Lincoln* and the Republican National Convention that year held in New York City near the site of the World Trade Center attacks). But by 2005, all was not well for Uncle Sam's fighting forces.

A February 2005 Pew Research poll revealed, for the first time, that half of Americans felt going to war in Iraq was a bad decision. In June that year, a *Washington Post*/ABC News poll reported that nearly six in ten Americans said the war was not worth fighting and two-thirds felt the military was "bogged down" in Iraq. The relatively low casualty rate in 2003 had given way to sustained high body counts over the following years; 2007 was the deadliest year for American soldiers in Iraq.

As casualties rose and ever more stories of mangled bodies, PTSD, and traumatic brain injuries crept into the American mainstream, the popularity of the war tumbled, and the quality of volunteers followed the trend.

Because the actual number of troops in the armed forces is set by Congress, and the military almost always meets its recruitment goals by lowering standards as necessary, the best way to judge the country's enthusiasm for enlistment is to look at the quality of new recruits. In response to the dwindling supply of qualified volunteers, in 2004 the army lowered its enlistment standards, increasing the number of waivers for applicants with criminal backgrounds, for example, by 65 percent from 2004 to 2007. Between 2004 and 2009, the armed forces failed to meet its goals on the number of recruits with high school diplomas. Over that same five-year period, the military let in more low scorers and fewer high scorers on its aptitude tests than it planned to. The strain of two wars and troop commitments around the world was clearly weighing on the army, and the caliber of its enlistees suffered.

Though the army was diminished from years past, Brad Manning was not one of those let in under lowered standards. As an intelligence analyst, he was among the top scorers on the army's aptitude test, and he had no criminal background or history of drug abuse. He was at a ripe age for recruitment, healthy, and just above the five-foot minimum-height requirement. The army's standards had dropped to the lowest levels in decades, and he entered along with some recruits of lowered quality, but even in a banner year, Brad Manning could have seemed to a recruiter like the cream of the crop.

Within months of his enlistment, many of those training with him would come to a different conclusion: in the words of his bunkmate at basic training, Brad Manning "was not army material."

The moment Brad signed his papers his identity fractured in two; henceforth he would have a civilian life and an army life. Though he barely concealed his homosexuality, he was still prohibited from serving as an openly gay man. In the army, he was no longer Brad the DJ, the gamer, the gay and single twenty-something in the suburbs of Washington, DC. In the army, he was Manning, just another new recruit in need of a dose of army discipline.

■ ■ ■

Brad Manning reported for duty in Baltimore and shipped off for basic training at Fort Leonard Wood, Missouri, in early October 2007. He went first to the reception battalion, where he was treated to a haircut and a new set of clothes, administered a barrage of medical exams, and taught how to properly make a bed. His personal items were confiscated, and he was issued a new military identification card. He was then transferred downrange to the training battalion, where boot camp truly begins.

The first part of the US Army's basic training program, known by its initials, BCT, for Basic Combat Training, is a highly ritualized, physically and mentally rigorous ten-week program. New recruits are trained in army core values and combat fundamentals, like tactical maneuvering and rifle upkeep. They're subjected to physical trials to build fitness and to instill tenacity and discipline. A day at BCT begins long before sunrise with the snare of a flashlight pounding on the door. Formation and physical training starts several minutes later, leaving just enough time to quickly shave, brush their teeth, and throw on workout clothes before running out the door.

The program is an intentionally strenuous introduction to army life designed to shock the system. From a legal standpoint alone, the change from civilian to soldier is significant, and the break with the civilian world is severe for good reason. The moment they enter the army, new recruits join a special class of citizens under the command of military officers, their lives governed by a unique legal code. To disobey orders is to violate the law. To quit and walk away is to be a deserter, the penalty for which can range from nothing to death.[1] Boot camp is intended to upset a new soldier's sense of equilibrium, forcing him or her to adapt to an unfamiliar and challenging environment.

The reality of enforcing Don't Ask, Don't Tell, particularly during a troop shortage, created special peculiarities for gays in the military. As the name of the policy plainly says, so long as one didn't tell, no one was allowed to ask. Even if a soldier was perceived to be gay, official action could be unlikely, and in some cases active-duty service members who came out were not discharged immediately. After the September 11 attacks, for instance, the Marine Corps declined to discharge some troops who came out of the closet while on deployment, waiting instead until they returned home. Considering the reduced flow of volunteers and general manpower shortage, evidence suggests that the army, as an institution, *wanted* qualified gays to serve, so long as they were serving in the closet.

---

1. Since the Civil War, the American military has executed only one soldier for desertion (in 1945), but desertion rates in the army skyrocketed in the years following the 2003 invasion of Iraq—nine of every one thousand army soldiers deserted in 2007.

In basic training, Manning had a pink cell phone; other soldiers teased him for having a picture of his sister hanging in his locker; he had a slight build; and his attitude in boot camp was described as effeminate and "kinda gayish." Anyone might have a pink phone, a picture of a sister, or an attitude perceived as "gayish" in a macho environment. But Manning *was* gay, and out, determined to skirt as close to the DADT line as possible. His closet door was effectively transparent.

"Basically, when a drill sergeant does not want you in the army, they'll just treat you like crap until you quit," said Steve Rodriguez,[2] who was in the same company as Manning during basic training. "Typical things that a lot of people would not get yelled at for, he would get picked on a lot for." Talking in line, cleaning too fast, running too slow—Manning, it seemed, could do nothing right. And though he was singled out for particularly harsh scrutiny, he also brought trouble upon himself—he was chronically late for morning formation. "He got a lot of 'drop and give me twenty' type corrective actioning," Rodriguez said. "Every time I looked, Manning was doing push-ups. He was always doing push-ups. Just getting yelled at a lot for the smallest little thing . . . most of the time he just sat there and took it."

Then he snapped.

Reflecting on Manning's personality, Rodriguez described him as a "quiet, nice pit bull." The boy from Oklahoma by way of Wales was no stranger to bullying, and, resentful of the special attention he was getting, Manning started fighting back. Drill sergeants yelling at him to "Shut up!" while he stood in line in the cafeteria elicited outbursts. "I'm not talking!" he'd scream, slamming his food tray on the table. In groups of three, drill sergeants would berate him while he stood toe-to-toe with them (and, one would imagine, nose to chest), staring back and shouting in return. He became so audacious that the drill sergeants, demonstrating that they weren't entirely humorless, took to calling him General Manning—"What the fuck is wrong with you, General Manning!?"—and the term caught on among the rank and file.

---

2. At the request of the source, this name has been changed.

By the end of October, Manning was reassigned. While the army processed his papers, they let him cool his heels in the RHU, the Rehab and Holding Unit, commonly known as the discharge unit. They were sending him home.

Ostensibly, he'd sustained a nerve injury in his left side causing his arm to go limp. "Also, I'm suffering from dropfoot," he wrote in a November 5 post to his Facebook account, "meaning my left foot is numb and unable to walk correctly without a limp." This was his official story, and the one he repeated to nearly everyone in his civilian life. But it wasn't the full story.

■ ■ ■

The discharge unit is an island of castaways segregated from the rest of the population while they wait for weeks or sometimes months on end to recover from injuries or be processed out of the military.[3] People land in RHU for sundry reasons, but they all share one thing in common: none of them wants to be there. Deemed unfit for military service, they are the boot camp failures, the fat, slow, or injured. They are the quitters who wanted out and convinced the army to discharge them or the thieves and sadists who couldn't suppress their criminal instinct long enough to make it through basic training. A sizable contingent is made up of women who decided the army wasn't for them. And some are "Chapter 15," army jargon for gay. The unit's denizens are known commonly as washouts or cripples in army slang. While Manning was there, they liked to call themselves the Crips.

The rabble is lorded over by drill sergeants who no more want be in RHU than do the washouts and cripples themselves. They've been assigned to babysit the discharge unit as punishment for failures and infractions of their own or because they're near the end of drill sergeant duty and waiting to get back to the real job they specialized in.

---

3. In an official response, Fort Leonard Wood public affairs wrote that an average stay in RHU was about three weeks. The reporting process revealed stories of significantly longer stays.

"It's traumatic walking into the discharge unit," said Dane Thompson,[4] who was in the RHU at Fort Leonard Wood when Manning arrived. "It's like walking into Oz. You're scared shitless."

When the army learned that Steve Rodriguez didn't reveal a serious medical complication prior to enlisting, they sent him to RHU to be discharged. Soon after Rodriguez walked into his RHU bay, he was introduced to Dane Thompson, a former cop and an old man among the washouts, most of whom were in their early twenties or younger.

Thompson was a Chapter 15. He reported that one of the drill sergeants looked like a man who molested him when he was ten years old, and he was so attracted to the man, he said, that he couldn't focus on training. It was a lie. "I wanted to get the fuck out," he said later. "I joined the military because I wanted discipline and I wanted camaraderie." Instead, Thompson, with his perennially under-siege outlook on life, felt surrounded by incompetence and brutality.

Thompson showed Rodriguez around the bay, a long room with cream-colored walls and fluorescent lights where the men slept. Lockers flanked rows of bunks with forest green blankets folded neatly over foam mattresses. Rodriguez's first task was to find a good bunk—it would be his home base during the long, idle days in the RHU.

"You're in the suburbs," Thompson said.

"What?"

"Over there in that corner?" said Thompson. "That's the Ghetto, that's Harlem. And over there? That's Chinatown." The place was as segregated as a prison yard. There was the Barrio, the Trailer Park, and West Hollywood for the gays. "And over here? This is where we take care of each other. We're quiet. We relax. We're clean. This is the Suburbs."

Rodriguez spotted an open top-level bunk in the corner and claimed it. Thompson introduced him to the small white guy on a lower bunk nearby.

"Hey!" He recognized Manning from the training company. "You're in here?"

---

4. At the request of the source, this name has been changed.

Manning explained that he'd hurt his arm.

Probably a good thing you did, Rodriguez thought.

Malaise hung over the discharge unit. Long presentations on army values ended with the Crips sitting aimlessly for hours on end in a classroom, prohibited from returning to their bays. Drill sergeants directed them to clean and reclean the same places, ad infinitum, or suit up and walk outside for formation only to be directed back indoors. The guys spent long stretches of time in the bays playing board games, watching movies, or scheming out operations to sneak in contraband, like cigarettes and the ingredients to make prison hooch. ("All they ended up doing was getting this rancid slop that smelled like feet and mold," said Thompson.) One of the most popular hang-out spots was the latrine. Guys would sneak porn into the bathroom to jerk off as often as possible. "Copious amounts of masturbation," recalled John Christopher,[5] who spent more than half a year in RHU and was the bay leader for part of the time Manning was there. "It was a steady decline in respect and humanity each day you spent there," Christopher said.

Though he was generally miserable and wracked with anxiety, Manning got along well enough with the guys in the Suburbs. Thompson sometimes lent Manning his mp3 player, which, Thompson said, Manning would return with almost teary-eyed gratitude. With little else to do, Suburbanites goofed off a lot, teasing one another. Rodriguez has fond memories of sneaking out of bed in the middle of the night and hiding Manning's shoes in different parts of the bay. In the morning, Manning woke up, searched frantically around his bunk, and ran outside after him yelling, "My shoes! You bastard!"

One night, Thompson heard Manning lying in bed, quietly whimpering to himself.

"Manning, go to sleep." Thompson said.

"Shut up, Thompson," Manning said.

"Oh, you need help going to sleep?"

---

5. At the request of the source, this name has been changed.

As if on cue, Thompson, Rodriguez, and others jumped out of bed, pillows swinging. Manning grabbed his own weapon, and a massive pillow fight ensued. Laughter echoed in the quiet of the darkened bay.

From the beginning of his time in the army, Manning appears to have been of two minds about the experience. Despite his difficulties at boot camp, he was publicly adamant during his stint in the discharge unit that he wanted to continue his training. A November 5 Facebook announcement ended thusly: "Anyway, I'm hanging in here, and as far as I know I'm not yet going to be discharged from the army, and may be recycled for training by January! Peace out everyone." While in RHU he spoke on the phone to his father and his uncle, and they both encouraged him to be firm in asking for another chance. According to some who were with him in RHU, he insisted that he had no business being in the discharge unit and fought vigorously to be allowed to continue basic training.

But those closest to him in RHU say he was ambivalent at times about finishing and that he complained often about the endless and seemingly arbitrary persecution he received at the hands of drill sergeants.

Over time, Manning and Rodriguez came to be close buddies. They spent many nights together on Fire Guard, an anachronism from the days of wooden barracks and wood-burning stoves, in which at least two people from the unit must be awake at all times to guard against a fire. They'd do their one-hour shifts together, sitting in the dark with the beams of their flashlights dancing on the wall on front of them. In the midnight quiet, they spoke in hushed voices about their lives and their hopes of getting the hell out of discharge.

"I'm just sick and tired of how they're treating me," Rodriguez recalls Manning saying. "I can't wait to get the fuck out of here. I want to go back. I've got so much music to write."

"He basically just concentrated on getting the hell out of there, leaving the army. It was a bad decision. [Manning would say,] 'Why are they taking so long to get me out of here, what's the holdup?'" Rodriguez said. Manning complained about getting picked on by everyone from drill sergeants to other basic trainees.

"That's because you're very pickable," Rodriguez told him. "You're small. And you're General Manning; you should be able to take it."

Rodriguez opened up to Manning too. He and Manning spent a lot of time talking about computers, and eventually Rodriguez let him in on a secret from his past.

In the early 1990s, Rodriguez was a hacker—a black hat—who went by the online handle the Fang.

"I think he really liked the part of how I had my own BBS system," Rodriguez said. The Fang's "Electric RoXXy" BBS was a distribution site for the underground hacking magazine *PHRACK*. "I was in full control of hosting docs for anyone in the world.

"I guess you could say my system was a WikiLeaks-type system before there was a WikiLeaks," Rodriguez said. He hosted "thousands of documents that related to hacking, cracking, phreaking, government secrets . . . many leaked documents. Lots of anarchy, bomb-making stuff. Credit card hacking, how to get into concerts for free, call in and get free airline tickets. This was the '90s, can't do that now. Patriot Act would nail you to the wall.

"Back then there weren't many computer geeks, so many of us got hired to fix computers, install networks, servers. There was zero security, so hackers could copy whatever documents they wanted. Plus, many networks had no passwords or security. Wild West days."

Manning seemed impressed, Rodriguez said.

Everyone in RHU wanted to be somewhere else, and the frustration often boiled over. Under the command of drill sergeants who tormented underlings for sport, the discharge unit became a trickle-down economy of cruelty. Fights were common, and the sizable contingent of sadists got their jollies by making the rounds and fucking with the smaller and weaker residents or anyone they found without a posse. They especially liked to fuck with the queers. "They're bored, and they're bullies," said Thompson. "They don't have any sense of empowerment at all, so what do they do? Pick on somebody else."

In one instance, a notorious nineteen-year-old redhead named Butts was ridiculing Manning. "Manning turned around and barked at him," Thompson said. "'Quit picking on me!' like a little Chihuahua.

And as soon as he did that it was like gas on a fire." Two of Butts's comrades came running, and the three pushed Manning back into a corner.

"Take a shot, pussy!" they goaded him. "Come on, faggot!"

"Leave me alone! Fuck you! Leave me alone!" Manning screamed.

Rodriguez ran over to break it up, followed by Thompson and others. By the time Manning was separated from the group, a dark circle had spread through the crotch of his gray sweatpants. Like a puppy getting kicked around an alley, he'd peed himself.

It wasn't the first time. "Manning had severe anxiety," and would urinate on himself from time to time, said Christopher. "He tried very hard to hide it.

"Manning was very shy," Christopher continued, "very withdrawn. He liked his stuff a certain way and would get so upset to the point of tears if you messed with anything of his. His pink phone got him a lot of grief from the guys. He would get so angry it would cause his nose to bleed."

The battle buddy system in basic training mandates that no one be allowed to go anywhere alone—one must always be with a buddy. On two occasions, Thompson accompanied Manning to medical exams. "When we went over to the hospital, we weren't going up to fucking neurology," Thompson said. "*Twice* I took him over to the psych ward."

Whatever was troubling Brad Manning during the beginning of his army career, it wasn't limited to a nerve injury. After just a few weeks in basic training Manning was to be discharged, and, in the nerve-racking world of the RHU, he expressed to at least some confidants that he wanted to be let go. But in late December, just before Christmas, the army changed course, and in his more reflective moments it seems Brad was excited about getting another shot at a career in the army.

Considering the deluge of convicted criminals and high school dropouts the army had been reduced to accepting for the three years prior to Manning's enlistment, it isn't difficult to see why the leadership would work hard to allow, or encourage, him to stay. He was smart, in good health, and the right age. Surely the officers had all seen boys made into men in the crucible of basic training—Manning was just a hard nut to crack. They decided to let him have another chance. Manning was ecstatic. He would have to start basic training over again in January, but after finishing he'd finally be off to Fort Huachuca to do intelligence training with troops with whom he hoped to have more in common. The army was Brad's best chance at fulfilling his dream of going to college, and his brush with failure was temporarily averted. He went home for the holidays a relieved and optimistic young man.

Brad returned to Debbie's house for Christmas. He told his family how excited he was to get another chance to finish basic training. His nerve injury had healed, he explained, and he was looking forward to January when he could get back to Fort Leonard Wood and give basic training another shot.

Brad didn't hang around Debbie's house in Potomac long. Shortly after he got in, he went to the Metro station and headed south, to hang out in the big city and go clubbing downtown. That night, at Apex, one of DC's most popular gay clubs at the time, he met Toby Quaranta. And through Toby, Brad nearly found home.

4
Dixie Charm

"Home is a place not only of strong affections,
but of entire unreserve; it is life's undress rehearsal,
its backroom, its dressing room."

—Harriet Beecher Stowe

A child growing up in Oklahoma in the 1990s was at once bliss-
fully oblivious to the world beyond the state line and acutely
aware in peculiar ways that he lived in what many considered
flyover country. Nationally televised events, like the Super Bowl, were
announced in Eastern Standard Time, subtly implying that somewhere to the east the people were a little more important. The Okie's
place in the world came into clearer focus in 1995, after the bombing
of the Murrah building less than an hour's drive south from Crescent
thrust Oklahoma into the spotlight. Headlines screamed intriguing
messages like "Myth of Midwest Safety Shattered," informing a child,
perhaps for the first time, that Oklahoma is in a place called the "Midwest" and there was once a myth about how safe it was.

As Brad Manning grew into an adolescent, the wider world came
into view. He moved to Wales, where he was a novelty in a novel

world. He visited Japan with his Welsh schoolmates, expanding his known universe to a place most Americans will never see. By the time he returned to live with his father not fifty miles from where his life began, he was a world traveler; it's easy to imagine him pining for something more exotic than a life in Oklahoma City.

For some kids in the great expanse of Middle America, Babylon is New York City. For some it is Los Angeles, Paris, or London. But for those who are seduced by the intricacies of affairs of state, it is, to paraphrase Jack Kennedy, a city of Yankee charm and Dixie efficiency: Washington, DC.

Brad Manning landed in the suburbs of DC by happenstance—the disintegration of his family set in motion events that led him to destitution in Chicago and thus to live with his aunt in Maryland—but it was a fortuitous move. Washington, DC, was exactly what he'd been looking for: a place to call home. By the winter of 2007, the outlines of that home had begun taking shape.

■ ■ ■

Swirling lights and thumping beats, cheap drinks and shirtless guys dancing carefree in a club electric with sexual energy—an evening at Apex could be exhilarating. After Velvet Nation closed, the under-21 nights at Apex on Thursday and Friday were the best thing on offer for an underage gay kid in DC. One cold evening in December, Brad made the hour-long trip from his aunt's house to Dupont Circle to hit the club with a group of friends. He'd just returned to the civilian world after months in discharge-unit limbo. He'd also just celebrated his twentieth birthday. In a few days it would be Christmas Eve.

Toby Quaranta spotted Brad first, standing apart from his group—he seemed like a bit of a wallflower. Toby walked up and introduced himself. Brad was slow to open up, but the two eventually hit it off.

Toby was the yang to Brad's yin. Whereas one was small and quiet, the other was tall and outgoing. Brad didn't make friends easily, and Toby was the kind of person people described as a "force of nature," the guy who knows everyone. He'd come from a difficult upbringing in stolid, suburban Virginia, and he and Brad related to each other's experiences coming out of the closet in conservative America. Toby worked at Human Rights Campaign, America's leading LGBT advocacy group, and Brad was a struggling kid fresh off the boat, as it were, from the gay-unfriendly Bible Belt, and a soldier living under Don't Ask, Don't Tell. Their personalities and interests fit like puzzle pieces.

Brad spent most of the next two weeks at Toby's apartment in downtown DC, and they grew close fast. They spent the cheery, work-free days of late December lounging at home, watching movies, cooking, and listening to music. They walked around the city for hours while Toby showed Brad around DC and introduced him to his seemingly endless group of gay friends, many of them influential leaders in their respective fields. As a professional politico a few years older, Toby played the sage, introducing Brad to a world of big-city professionals and to the life of a bright, gay twenty-something that Brad might have led had circumstances been different. It was the closest thing Brad had yet experienced to a real romance, a brief snapshot of domestic bliss in his otherwise nerve-racking life as a soldier-to-be. Those weeks provided a more refined image than ever before of the life he might one day have.

Brad and Toby said good-bye after the new year but decided to keep in touch; Toby promised he'd be there when Brad graduated from basic training in April.

On January 3, Brad returned to Fort Leonard Wood to start basic training over. He and Toby talked on the phone once a week when Brad was allowed, and they wrote letters back and forth every few days. Though Brad's second stint in basic started out well, within weeks he was miserable once again. But this time he stuck it out, played by the rules, put his head down, and, as they say in the army, "soldiered on." On April 3, six months after enlisting, he graduated from boot camp. Keeping the promise made months before, Toby flew to St. Louis, rented a car, and drove to Fort Leonard Wood for the ceremony.

Brad was deeply relieved to finally get out of boot camp, but he wasn't altogether at ease that graduation weekend. In addition to his aunt Debbie and Toby, his dad was there, and distinct parts of his life met—Brad's unsettled, chaotic past collided with his hopeful future.

Though he worked at Hertz Rent-a-Car, Brian didn't rent a car for the weekend. Toby had to pick him up from the hotel where he was staying and chauffeur him around, and he resented it. He'd heard plenty from Brad about his childhood in Crescent and the strained relationship he had with his father. The tension was palpable as Brian regaled Toby and Brad with stories of his own time in the service while they toured around the army post. Brian was proud of Brad and told him so, but there wasn't much warmth between father and son. Brad seemed anxious around his dad and anxious too around the other soldiers graduating from basic training; he didn't share the sense of camaraderie the other soldiers expressed, embracing one another and introducing their families to their new army buddies. He seemed, in the summation, to be eager to put the whole episode behind him and get on to intelligence training.

Toby had to catch a flight before the graduation ceremony, but before he left he took a photograph for the family in the lobby of their hotel. Wearing his green dress uniform and a black beret, with his dad on one side and his aunt on the other, Brad stood between the two familial pillars in his life and grinned widely. Toby snapped a picture. Two years later, the picture would be cropped on both sides and spread around the globe at cyberspeed. Emblazoned on T-shirts, patches, and protest signs, it would become the iconic image around the world of the traitor, or the hero, of his generation.

■ ■ ■

As Brad had hoped, life got better outside Fort Leonard Wood. He went to train as an intelligence analyst at Fort Huachuca, an ochre-tinged army post in the Arizona high desert, not far from Tombstone and a day's hike from the Mexico border. Manning stayed busy, spending ten hours or more a day in classes, and he got along well enough with the other soldiers.

Three weeks into his training, Brad posted three video messages to his family and friends on his YouTube account. Sitting in his two-man dorm room in the trainee barracks, with the camera pointed at himself, he relayed simple messages about how his day was going, and in the process he talked about the inside of a SCIF (pronounced "skif"), short for a Sensitive Compartmented Information Facility. These secure rooms are dedicated to the handling of classified material, and information about the room itself is considered sensitive. About twenty-five of his fellow classmates brought the videos to the attention of Manning's platoon sergeant. Manning was ordered to remove the videos from the Internet, write a brief statement detailing the regulations, and create a PowerPoint presentation about the importance of securing classified information to be shown in front of the other trainees at Friday formation.

The videos represented a minor lapse in judgment, but the authorities determined no classified information had been revealed. "In a training environment, where we're dealing with young people who aren't used to the army, we deal with a wide variety of folks doing inappropriate things," an army spokesperson later commented. "They have issues, and it's dealt with, and they go on to do great things for the army and the country."

The incident reflected the pride Manning was beginning to take in his job. Though his friends say he was always coy and careful not to reveal classified information, he clearly felt empowered by what he was learning and was eager to talk about his new career. He felt valued by the army and, perhaps for the first time in his life, felt he was doing truly valuable work. Peering behind the curtain of government secrecy, Manning, the avid news consumer, was seeing and being trusted with the behind-the-scenes story of global affairs. He was being inducted into an intelligence community that had quietly metastasized into a behemoth of a size theretofore unseen in American history.

■ ■ ■

Little more than a year after the 9/11 attacks, on September 26, 2002, Cofer Black was in a conference room at the Hart Senate Building, seated at a table with a microphone extending toward him like a silver proboscis. The career intelligence officer wore a dark suit, and he was balding and chubby with droopy eyes that gave him a somber but determined air. Facing him on a raised platform were members of the House and Senate Select Committees on Intelligence, as well as cameras recording the proceedings for the benefit of journalists and the public. The joint committee had called Black to testify in its inquiry into the intelligence community's failure to prevent the September 11 attacks and to ask what had been done in the meantime to remedy the problems.

Black began by thanking the committee for its offer of a screen to protect his identity during his testimony. "Good security is always a very good idea, and if this were normal circumstances I would accept your offer," Black said, smiling out of one side of his mouth and stretching his shoulders back. "The work of this committee and this hearing is just too important." He held a pause and continued in a flat and ominous tone. "I don't want to be just a voice behind a screen. When I speak I think the American people need to look into my face, and I want to look the American people in the eye. My name is Cofer Black. I'm a case officer of the director of operations of the Central Intelligence Agency."

From July 1999 until May 2002, Black had been the head of the CIA's Counterterrorism Center, and he spoke defensively about the agency's efforts leading up to 9/11. "We provided strategic warning. Our intense efforts were unable to provide tactical warning on 9/11," he said. "We all share a profound and horrible sense of loss." Black himself, he noted, had been a target of al-Qaeda. "In this long fight, my CIA colleagues operating with me in Khartoum, Sudan, in 1995, preempted preparations of Osama bin Laden's thugs to kill me. Six years later Osama bin Laden and his al-Qaeda are the killers of 9/11."

To understand how 9/11 happened, and what had changed in its wake, Black said, "you need to fully appreciate choices in three areas. These were choices made for us." First, personnel at the agency had been cut in the late 1990s, he said, leaving officers such as himself responsible for managing a growing threat with declining manpower. Second, he said, his budget was too small, giving him about enough money each year to purchase two modern jet fighter aircraft. (Verifying the statements is impossible as the budget and size of the CIA remain classified.)

"My third point—operational flexibility." He spoke slowly and deliberately. "This is a very highly classified area. But I have to say that all you need to know is: there was a before 9/11"—he gestured to one side—"and there was an after 9/11. After 9/11, the gloves come off."

Black's phrase—"After 9/11, the gloves come off"—drew substantial attention from journalists. A year after the attacks little was known about how the United States was waging this new conflict the president had been calling the "War on Terror." Dana Priest, who'd spent years reporting on the military for the *Washington Post*, was intrigued by Black's statement. Since 9/11 she'd heard anecdotes about controversial methods of interrogation and been oddly stymied in her efforts to get confirmation from officials. But the part of Black's testimony that drew her ear closer was lost on most of the public: "all you need to know."

"Why was it up to this civil servant, no matter how well respected he was among his colleagues, to decide what anyone else, even the elected representatives he was addressing, did and did not need to know about the deadliest enemy facing the United States?" Priest wrote. She and a colleague, William Arkin, began an intensive and unprecedented investigation into the national security bureaucracy. The groundbreaking study, released in July 2010 under the title *Top Secret America*, revealed an intelligence world profoundly changed from that which had existed prior to September 11, 2001. Cofer Black had complained that the intelligence community's resources had diminished in the 1990s, and in the panic that followed the attacks, the United States severely overcorrected.

As the country recoiled and prepared to respond in the hours after the September 11 attacks, a new kind of war was in the making. A band of stateless terrorists had struck a confounding blow to the American homeland, and suddenly terrorism, which had been treated largely as an issue for law enforcement, became a defense department priority. But the Pentagon was organized to fight a traditional conflict against an opposing military, not a shadowy international network of criminals headquartered in the backwater of Afghanistan, and it was the Central Intelligence Agency that was poised to take charge of the fight. "Where everybody else was looking for their maps on Afghanistan, [the CIA was] ready to rock, ready to roll," Cofer Black said. "I mean, we were waiting for the bureaucracy to catch up."

With Black at the forefront, the CIA drew up a plan codenamed Greystone and presented it to President Bush within days of the attacks. On September 17, Bush issued a presidential finding, which is required to authorize covert CIA action, and the war was on. "I had never seen a presidential authorization as far-reaching and as aggressive in scope. It was simply extraordinary," said John Rizzo, CIA general counsel from 2001 to 2009. With an initial down payment of a billion dollars, plus tens of billions to follow in congressionally authorized funds, and instructions to the Pentagon to assist however it could, President Bush directed "the CIA to undertake the most sweeping and lethal covert action since the agency was founded in 1947," wrote Priest.

The decision to place the CIA at the helm of the new global War on Terror would have far-reaching impacts on American society. Covert action, legally distinct from clandestine action, is designed to be so secretive that the United States maintains plausible deniability. With the CIA leading a war in which the primary mode of operation was covert, the culture of secrecy took hold stronger than ever before. Top Secret America expanded into a corpulent bureaucracy, deformed and encumbered by its sudden growth spurt, amid a massive influx of cash, with no one in government making a real effort to identify waste and duplication.

Priest's investigation—the first of its kind in or out of government—found at least thirty-three new building complexes built since 9/11 which hosted top-secret intelligence work. In the decade after September 11, 2001, the intelligence budget had grown by 250 percent. Due to the secrecy and sheer size of the new intelligence world, its total budget was literally incalculable, but a safe, albeit rough, estimate, Priest said, was well over $100 billion. Priest found 1,271 government organizations "related to counterterrorism, homeland security, and intelligence located in about 10,000 locations across the United States," but that figure drastically undersells the situation. The War on Terror had brought on the mass privatization of the national security bureaucracy, and Priest found 1,931 private companies engaged in the same work as government agencies, but at a much higher cost to the American taxpayer. Among the most prominent of these companies was the private security firm Blackwater, of which Cofer Black became vice chairman after he left government in 2005. Indeed, amid a severe global recession there was a bonanza happening in Top Secret America. For someone with the right experience, the private sector promised incomparable earnings and job security. With his top secret clearance there was a sea of opportunity awaiting Brad Manning once he got out of the army.

Priest found Top Secret America to be woefully dysfunctional. A breakdown in oversight made it a natural habitat for waste and overlap. The congressional committees tasked with monitoring the intelligence world were understaffed to handle the sudden expansion, and worse, essential staffers and even elected representatives were deliberately left in the dark about key elements of the secret activities they were supposed to scrutinize. The Information Security Oversight Office (ISOO) is responsible for overseeing the security of classified documents, but in the decade after 9/11 its staff grew hardly at all. Meanwhile, the amount of newly classified documents tripled to more than 23 million, protected at a cost of $10 billion a year.

"Today's classification system is in crisis," the ISOO head told Priest. One of the most dangerous aspects of Top Secret America, Priest found, was that it had grown so large that no one even knew how big it was, and its culture of secrecy was infecting deeper layers of American life. The CIA had mutated into a military force, blurring the line between covert actions and clandestine military operations and infecting the military with its brand of reflexive secrecy. Terrorism became a national security imperative, and the Patriot Act removed the separation between intelligence work and law enforcement. The culture of secrecy thus leached into the justice system, with the FBI running sting operations to catch "pre-terrorists," people guilty of having the intent to commit or help facilitate terrorism (a misdeed Orwell might have called thoughtcrime). Terror suspects were tried while pertinent information remained classified by the government, unavailable to the defense counsel and sometimes even the prosecution and presiding judge.

The culture of secrecy spread beyond terrorism investigations. Between October 2006 and October 2009, federal courts issued 2,332 "sneak and peek" warrants—the secret search warrants authorized by the Patriot Act—but only 1 percent of them were for terrorism-related investigations; 69 percent were drug related. New "fusion centers" were created to expand the ballooning intelligence community into local law enforcement agencies around the country, turning city cops into frontline warriors in the War on Terror. More often, however, fusion centers simply injected the tactics of the War on Terror into everyday local law enforcement activity.

In all, Priest found that 854,000 people held a top-secret security clearance from the American government; the number astounded the public after the report was published, but it turned out to be a significant undercount. A belated government review of the number of people holding security clearances found that in 2010 more than 1.4 million government employees and private contractors held a top secret clearance. In all, the government study found, more than 4.2 million people had access to classified information. The revelation blew all other estimates out of the water and shocked observers in and out of government. Indeed, until Priest's report on Top Secret America, nothing resembling a comprehensive assessment of the growth in the national security industrial complex post-9/11 had ever been undertaken.

In the early 2000s, while a culture of secrecy was malignant in the expanding military-industrial complex, a countervailing trend was emerging in Washington. Inquiries into the 9/11 attacks found that the attacks might have been prevented had information been more readily shared between territorial government agencies, and policymakers thus moved to encourage information sharing throughout the intelligence world. Pursuant to these recommendations, in 2006 the State Department launched the Net-Centric Diplomacy program through which classified reports filed from American diplomatic outposts around the world would be available to properly cleared individuals. The Department of Defense, which paid to implement Net-Centric Diplomacy, had access to State Department cables through the Secret Internet Protocol Router Network, known as SIPRnet (pronounced *sip-er-net*), the Pentagon's equivalent of the Internet for secret communications. Diplomats designated cables for inclusion on SIPRnet by simply tagging them with the phrase "SIPDIS" (for "SIPRnet distribution"), an action that eventually became routine.

The immense growth in Top Secret America created waste and duplication, a shadow economy, and a dangerous culture of secrecy that spread through American society, but it also made America more vulnerable. The expanding bureaucracy combined with rampant overclassification and new protocols for sharing secret information—more people with more access to more secrets—made for a tenuous situation. As Priest wrote in *Top Secret America*, "Secrets cannot be totally secured by locks or code names or encrypted e-mail or even vaults underground, and acting as if they can be is dangerous, even to national security. The security of secrets ultimately depends on human beings."

■ ■ ■

Fort Drum is the approximate geographical opposite of Fort Huachuca. The post, more than 100,000 sprawling acres in upstate New York, is green and partly wooded during the mild summer months and blanketed in snow for most of the long winter. The shoreline of

Lake Ontario is a mere half hour away by car, and Watertown, the nearby city of 30,000, is even closer. After he completed intelligence training, Brad Manning was stationed at Fort Drum as an intelligence analyst with the 10th Mountain Division, 2nd Brigade.

Toby had started a new relationship. (He and his boyfriend would later marry.) His friendship with Brad had changed, but they remained close. They talked on the phone regularly, often about the gay rights issues Toby was steeped in as an organizer for Human Rights Campaign.

Through Toby, Brad could get the inside scoop on politics within the gay rights movement, such as the intramovement rivalries influencing events in California and the backstory on the long campaign to achieve marriage equality for gays in America.

Brad had long been interested in politics, but living under Don't Ask, Don't Tell inspired a new level of passion in him. In November, he made the hour-and-a-half drive from Fort Drum to the Syracuse city hall for a rally against Proposition 8, the California ballot initiative that overturned a state supreme court decision allowing same-sex marriage. At the protest, Brad was interviewed anonymously by a student reporter. "I was kicked out of my home, and I once lost my job," he told her. "The world is not moving fast enough for us at home, work, or the battlefield." He went on, "I've been living a double life. . . . I can't make a statement. I can't be caught in an act. I hope the public support changes. I hope to do that before ETS [Expiration of Term of Service, when an enlisted soldier finishes his commitment in the army]."

Over the rest of the year, Brad settled into military life. He spent his days preparing intelligence reports for superior officers, studying maps and charts, and working with the army's Linux-based computer system. His unit was preparing to deploy to Iraq in the fall of 2009, and as an "all source" intelligence analyst it would be his job once in that country to make sense of the information coming in from an array of sources, such as monitored enemy communications, detainee interrogations, or even the hidden patterns of enemy movement. Brad was being trained to use the multiple databases available to him, most importantly CIDNE, short for Combined Information Data Network Exchange, on which various reports could be found, many from soldiers in the field. He became familiar with the ubiquitous Significant Activities Reports, called SIGACTs for short, the daily ground-level reports of IED attacks, sniper fire, and other such instances of engagement with the enemy. At Fort Drum, through classroom lessons, hands-on experience, and solo exploration inspired by his inborn, insatiable curiosity, Brad was learning about a world shrouded in arcane acronyms: the vast, tangled bureaucracy of the national security state. It was both fascinating and empowering for the young man. Only a year before, he'd been a transient with few friends, no credentials, and a string of low-end jobs: a veritable nobody. In the army, it seemed he was finally becoming somebody.

Brad's first summer and fall at Fort Drum was a period of uncharacteristic tranquility. He got to know other gay soldiers and was introduced into the small gay community in Watertown. He was making a good living and playing the stock market with some of his earnings. Later in the year he started dating Tyler Watkins, an effusive polymath from Ithaca studying neuroscience and psychology at Brandeis University in Boston. Tyler was a classical musician—oboist, cellist, and organist—of exceptional quality; a theatrical conversationalist and an occasional drag queen; a devout Catholic; a witty, energetic extrovert; and a man about town. He was many of the things that Private Manning, the semi-closeted intelligence analyst at Fort Drum, was not, and Brad fell into the innocent, consuming, and volatile love we all recognize as our first.

He was happy and optimistic, making more money than he'd ever made and forming the kinds of emotional bonds that had been largely absent from his life. In the words of a close friend, "Bradley was living the normal gay life. He was making friends. He was feeling good about himself. . . . He was, you know, living life for the first time." It was in this spirit that he traveled from upstate New York back to DC for the holidays in December 2008.

■ ■ ■

A good origin story is a valuable asset in nearly all spheres of American life, but particularly in politics, and especially in gay politics. We love our Horatio Alger tales of hardscrabble youth, of success through pluck and tenacity, of coming from hardship in places with names like Hope, Arkansas, and Stonewall, Texas, and making it to the bright lights and promise of the Big City. The compelling version in the gay world is a tale of enduring homophobia in Middle America, coming out of the closet, struggling through the abandonment of family and friends, and finally arriving into the embrace of a gay-friendly community. With a few tweaks to the narrative—like simplifying the reasons he got kicked out of his dad's house down to his being gay—Brad Manning had such a story, and, better still, it was mostly true. When Brad traveled from Chicago to his aunt's house, the DC area was merely the best of very few options—nonetheless, he'd come to the right place.

At the heart of the United States' capital city is a bustling gay village. By percentage, DC is one of the gayest cities in America, and gays make up a greater proportion of the District's population than any state in the country. DC residents marry later in life than residents of any other state, and the effect for gay men is only more pronounced. Gays have children less, socialize more, and even when coupled off are more likely than heterosexuals to have non-monogamous—or, in the parlance of Dan Savage, *monogamish*—relationships. Blondes be damned, the facts are in: gays have more fun.

The resulting community is a vibrant web of DC professionals who tend, as a group, to have more social capital, as it were, than others. As in other immigrant communities—and it remains true that elite DC, both straight and gay, is primarily an immigrant community—there is an ethos among gays to help out newcomers. (The old joke of the "gay mafia" might have a little more truth in it than you thought.) In Toby Quaranta, Brad Manning had the best guide to DC that a person could ask for.

Brad wore his origin story like a badge of honor. "Pay to play politics, but open bars. I'm all for it," Brad once said in a conversation online with a close friend. "I donate $50 to a cause (Stonewall Dems,

SLDN, HRC), sit at the bar, grab a drink, and talk to people about my life. Then they empathize and tell me I should meet someone. So I get introduced to so and so, and we talk, exchange business cards, and boom, I hit up Facebook, track down their contact info and we persist in the conversation."

And thus in 2008, over the course of occasional visits back to DC, Brad gained a foothold in the center of American power. In downtown Washington, through Toby, he was introduced into a social circle like he had never before known. He met lobbyists and activists. He could call White House aides friends. And he was no longer a failed college student or a forgettable barista, retail clerk, or pizza parlor host. He was Private First Class Bradley E. Manning, a well-connected intelligence analyst in the United States Army. Such a change can be exhilarating, in the words of Berin Szoka, the founder and president of a DC-based libertarian think tank, "for somebody who is just out of the provinces to come to the imperial city and meet people who have things like 1930s parties."

The director of the Center for Internet Freedom at the now-closed Progress and Freedom Foundation and an ardent libertarian in Washington's primarily left-leaning gay community, Berin Szoka threw parties known for their good food and booze. His second-story apartment played host to myriad social events for gay DC professionals, and in tongue-in-cheek homage to the approaching inauguration of an apparently leftist president at the outset of a serious economic crisis, Berin threw a 2008 New Year's party themed "New Year's Eve, 1932." Vodka martinis were the drink of the evening and Michael, Berin's boyfriend, kept the drink glasses full all night. Nearly everyone drank his way to well past tipsy.

That chilly January evening, Brad traveled into DC from Debbie's house and met up with Toby and his boyfriend. The three headed to Berin's townhouse apartment in Shaw, on the gentrifying edge of downtown Washington.

Berin's guests were, as they tended to be, well-educated, successful gays in their late twenties and early thirties, and all were encouraged to come dressed as someone famous from the Depression era.

Berin was Charles Lindbergh. Jason Edwards, a teacher of Greek and Latin at a DC-area private school, came as the man who famously abdicated the English throne for love, Edward VIII, or, as Jason introduced himself, "His Royal Highness, the Prince of Wales."

Jason was standing near the door when Brad climbed the steps to Berin's apartment and walked inside. Brad hadn't come dressed as anyone. "He was kind of short and a little small and pretty," Jason said later. "And he had that bright, bright blond hair. I immediately said, 'Well, we've got to come up with a character for you!' And the first thing that comes to mind was Jean Harlow." Brad didn't recognize the name of his new persona, the blonde bombshell whose dazzling ascent to Hollywood stardom ended with her untimely death in 1937, at the age of twenty-six.

Though he was a lot younger than most at the party and not, by nature, a social animal, Brad was in his element. He excelled that evening, having lively conversations lubricated by alcohol in a room full of gay nerds. He carried on discussions with people much older and more credentialed than he was, and he was always sure to trade business cards with a reminder to keep in touch.

He spent much of the night talking to Jason Edwards. As a high school teacher Jason was, perhaps, more comfortable than most talking to a much younger man. And he had a certain caretaker quality—the type, one of his friends commented, to mend broken wings.

As midnight approached, the party moved upstairs to the roof-deck. Hanging Chinese lanterns encircled the deck, glowing in the darkness, and beyond them the flickering lights of the district, with the yellow-lit Capitol building and the blinking red tip of the Washington Monument in the distance. On all sides, fireworks exploded, lighting up the night in flashes. Drunk and happy, loose and alive, the party toasted the new year.

This was Brad's hour. He was newly in love, with a good job and a growing network of influential politicos to look to in a few years when he got out of the army. "Sometimes there are these central and poignant events," said a close friend, "where someone goes from always being the outcast, always having one gay bar in town, if there is one, always being the one gay person in their group of friends, to realizing, 'I can live a life that is normal *and* gay.' And I think that was that night for Brad . . . and I am really sorry that he didn't get to live that."

■ ■ ■

Brad visited Tyler in Boston briefly and then returned to the snowy expanse of Fort Drum. As always, he went to Facebook after Berin's New Year's party and sent friend requests to the people he met. "I hold on VERY close to my contacts," he once said to a friend online. One of these was Jason Edwards, who, Brad discovered, used AOL Instant Messenger like he did. He sent Jason a message, and the two started chatting regularly.

Jason had the erudite manner one would expect in a scholar of Greek and Latin, paired with the earnest sensitivity and patience one hopes for in a schoolteacher. He taught classics at the Heights School, a Catholic all-boys school in Potomac, Maryland, established by Opus Dei, and known for the same stalwart conservatism as the religious society that founded it.

Jason, who was in his early thirties, lived and worked near Brad's aunt's house. (The two of them joked that Brad might have made Jason coffee a few times at Starbucks.) When Brad visited DC, they'd meet to take a walk together, go browsing at a bookstore, or pick up a movie and watch it in a classroom at the Heights School.

The two became good friends, despite Jason's Catholic faith and Brad's dogmatic atheism. Jason recalled one incident early on in their friendship, in which they were driving in DC, near Dupont Circle, and they passed St. Matthew's Cathedral on Rhode Island Avenue. "It's impressive from the outside, but it is absolutely beautiful inside," Jason said.

Brad glanced out the car window at the century-old red brick church. "One day," he said, "we'll turn all the churches into lecture halls." They dropped religion from their stable of conversation topics.

Jason found that, beneath an exterior demeanor that swung between standoffish and cocky, Brad experienced emotions deeply and at times uncontrollably. He recalled watching movies with Brad—*The Last King of Scotland*, a 2006 film about the cruelty of Idi Amin's reign in Uganda, and *Dancer in the Dark*, a Danish film about a young Czech mother's struggles as an immigrant to the United States. "Both of those movies bought him to tears," he said, "and it took him a while to recover. For the rest of the evening he was just kind of crying. Crying for a long while, and then when he would think of it again he would start crying again. He just had such very, very sensitive emotions. Something could really enter his psyche and just kind of stick there, and he would hold onto that and just react to it over and over and over.

"He had that quality of youth which is not just years, but it's just that kind of vulnerability," Jason said. "Not so many years of cynicism and jade over his heart.

Brad and Jason had a comfortable, platonic friendship. "I'm a schoolteacher, and I tend to have this really approachable, nonthreatening quality," said Jason. "He knew that I didn't place any expectations on him, as far as either having him impress me or, you know, any sexual expectations.

"It got to the point where my role with him became less that of an equal and a peer and more that of a—I don't even want to say counselor, because I don't know how much he actually listened to me—but it was more that he just needed someone to kind of vent to." And vent he did.

Brad felt isolated. Life on base was dreary, especially in the depths of winter, when cold air moving across Lake Ontario piled snow in heaps on the communities near the downwind shore in what is known as the "lake effect." Though the army had given him money, pride, and prestige at levels he'd never before experienced, he was increasingly conflicted about being a soldier. He'd endured six months of basic training, much of it in the purgatory of the discharge unit, and was finding active duty life to be a mixed bag. He took immense pride in his work and in his job title but lacked an intellectual or creative outlet in the community he lived in. Brad did not react constructively to the army's machismo culture—he felt paranoid, as though his every move was being scrutinized. "He was always very insecure about his masculinity," said Jason. "He had two ways of responding to it. There was either the flippant disregard and rejection of it, [or] he could be—I'm not even sure you could even call it effeminate so much as childlike." Feeling stifled, he pushed back against army culture rather than adapt to it. "He would complain about being surrounded by people he just considered stupid," said Jason. "His intellectual inferiors."

Tyler was Brad's first long-term romance, and he invested in him wholly and recklessly. He made regular trips to Boston to see him, and Tyler made trips to Watertown to visit Brad. Sometimes they met up in Tyler's hometown of Ithaca. For the itinerant boy from a broken family, the stability of his first long-term relationship became the foundation upon which to build that for which he had been searching for many years: a home.

"There's always that sense with him," said a close friend to both Brad and Tyler, "that he really wanted roots. Because his family moved around and all those things, he never was really in one place long enough to really put down strong roots, which I think is one of the reasons that his relationship with Tyler was so intense for him, because he felt like it was something he could really hold on to."

For Valentine's Day, Tyler bought Brad a dozen roses, and Brad bought the two of them matching equality bracelets. Brad—and just about everyone else at Fort Drum, it seems—routinely flouted the rule forbidding soldiers from traveling beyond a certain distance from the base while on leave without prior authorization. The men saw each other as often as possible. Tyler went public with his disdain for Don't Ask, Don't Tell, identifying himself on his personal blog as a "queer army wife."

"It wasn't until I join[ed] the ranks of all the other gay military spouses that I really ever understood how unjust our country's policies towards the queer community in the military [are]," he wrote. "Not only am I fed up with DADT but I'm sick and tired of the Obama administration's failure to serve and uphold the rights of ALL citizens of the US."

They kept their relationship "open," easing the stress of living hundreds of miles from each other, and Brad nurtured that effect which distance has upon the heart, committing himself ever more to Tyler. He put Tyler on the list of people to be alerted should he be hurt or injured at work and made him the beneficiary of his life insurance policy.

A devout, churchgoing Catholic convert, Tyler was in some ways an unlikely pick for Brad, the zealous atheist fond of doing verbal combat over religion for kicks. In one instance, recounted by Brad to a friend, he and Tyler took a quiz together and came to the question: Who is most important in your life? "I answered with his name," Brad said. "His response was God."

Those who watched the relationship develop from the outside saw a clear dissonance of affections. Brad was new to the negotiations, compromises, and disappointments of romance, and he loved Tyler with a naivete and totality that Tyler couldn't reciprocate. Brad seemed to take for granted that their relationship would hopefully lead to marriage; for Tyler that possibility was distant and ultimately irrelevant to the lush, fun life he was leading in his early twenties.

"When he actually would meet with Tyler," said Jason Edwards, "Tyler wanted to go out and meet with his friends and wanted to dress in this provocative manner, sometimes wearing makeup or kind of off-the-wall clothing. Bradley just didn't know what to do with it. He had this idea that he would go and visit Tyler and they would have this time where they would just hang out. And he said that every time he visited, Tyler wanted to go out with his friends or he wanted to have sex, and it was just too much."

As with so many youthful romances, the promise of its demise was written when the relationship began.

■ ■ ■

On a Saturday evening in late February 2009, Brad was sitting at a computer at Fort Drum, in a barracks that had been mostly deserted for the weekend. He'd been rooting around online, letting his curiosity be his guide, and found a kindred spirit. He was alone, socially isolated in upstate New York, and decided to reach out to someone with whom he hoped he might have something in common. He sent a message on AOL Instant Messenger to a young man around his age whom he had never met.

"Hi," Brad said.

"Hi," said Zach Antolak, a transgender blogger from the suburbs of Chicago.

"You don't know me, I apologize. I got this from your YouTube channel."

"No problem," said Zach, "there's a reason I put it on there :P ."

"I did a search on info theory, books, videos, etc. Bought books on it, watched some of your videos, then I saw your more personal stuff and figured you were on the same page.

"I do computations and analytical work," Brad continued, "as well as preparing weekly intel briefings for the commander. Uhhm . . . I'm politically active, even more so after enlisting—living under Don't Ask Don't Tell will certainly do that."

"Yeah," Zach said, "I can't say I'd ever enlist, for that reason in particular."

"Yes," said Brad, "but seeing as it will get me through college, and I get a bit more of a story . . . maybe its worth it =L ."

Zach and Brad chatted for three hours that night. Thus began a series of exchanges that would last the better part of the year.

Under the pseudonym Zinnia Jones, Zach blogged about a variety of issues, but he had a special preoccupation with gender identity and religion. He self-identified as a lesbian and heaped scorn upon "homophobes" and "bigots," particularly those inspired by religious beliefs. Brad and he had common interests in LGBT issues, computer programming, math, science, and evangelistic godlessness. One from Midwestern suburbia and the other from the rural Bible Belt, the two arch-atheists shared the zeal of the apostate.

Their conversation topics were wide ranging. They commiserated with each other's tribulations being "gifted in a public education system." They compared personal histories. They discussed their way from programmer shoptalk and cryptography to Camp X-Ray at

Guantánamo Bay. With a tinge of condescension, Brad tried to wow Zach with his insider's familiarity of military intelligence and computer programming prowess.

"Military is all f'd up," he said. "Contracts with closed source developers with incompatible software. Drives me NUTS."

"That is ridiculous," Zach said. "It's hard to ensure security when the source is unavailable."

"Yes. Even worse, it's often lowest bidder. Used to be the cream of the crop. Now it's outdated non-backward compatible suites of buggy software that were originally used for civilian purposes, then modified for military but not exactly thoroughly tested. Then they get contractors who don't know anything about computers to teach it. And its all OKAY, because we can't exactly complain out in the open, because the software which bugs out is often times on machines which are stamped with big red SECRET stickers."

Through many of their conversations, Brad was gloating. He fabricated a story about how army recruiters found a copy of his resume and hounded him to join the military. He complained about the bureaucratic inefficiencies and cultural vapidity he saw in the army, reserving special scorn for boot camp.

"The Army took me, a web dev[eloper], threw me into a rigid schedule, removed me from my digital self and threw me in the forests of Missouri for 10 weeks with an old M-16, Reagan-era load bearing equipment, and 50 twanging people hailing from places like Texas, Alabama, Georgia, and Mississippi . . . joy."

The chat logs reveal Brad as a young man driven by juvenile insecurities to impress a stranger, but also, it seems, himself. In the myopia of young adulthood, he saw himself, a low-ranking, enlisted intelligence analyst, as an actor in the inner orbit of the national security universe. His inflated self-importance contributed mightily to the pride he felt in his job, but it also weighed on him.

With few social distractions at Fort Drum and an inborn, ravenous curiosity, Brad spent much of his time exploring the constantly replenishing reservoir of national security information now available to him. At times, he obsessed over what he learned, pondering the big picture questions of political theory and questioning basic assumptions about foreign affairs, as if conducting the International Relations 101 college seminar he never took. All the while, he felt a sense of personal responsibility incongruous with his lowly position in the intricate interplay of foreign affairs.

■ ■ ■

March 2, 2009 . . .

Brad: Would you call Iraq and Afghanistan wars?

Zach: Not like, a WWII kind of war or anything. Depends on the criteria for war.

Brad: I was just thinking about how we refer to them as wars, commonly. Would you say that there is a "war" in Mexico, even though more casualties from drug cartel related violence are occurring there?

Zach: Hmm. I'm not sure, really. For either, you could use the more generic term conflict.

Brad: I know, it's weird. I was just thinking about that this morning. We've been watching carefully since it's in our back yard, of course. Sinaloa, Gulf, Los Zetas. 6000 killed last year, and that's not the ACTUAL total >nudge<.

■ ■ ■

March 8, 2009 . . .

Brad: >sigh< I've got foreign affairs on my mind constantly now. Mexico's spiraling violence, Pakistan's instability, North Korea's rhetorical posturing . . . blah blah blah. One of the bad parts of the job, having to think about bad stuff.

Zach: I've just been catching up on *24* [the TV spy drama]. I suppose it's like foreign affairs for complete idiots.

Brad: Hehehe . . . well, the Jason Bourne club isn't as fun as television and movies make it out to be. Just read a state department release, keep a smile on your face, and a knife behind your back. I'm going to Boston this weekend. That might put my mind at ease for at least a moment.

■ ■ ■

In late April 2009, Brad went back to DC for several weeks. He stayed at a hotel in Virginia and was busy during daylight hours doing classroom training with the army, but in the evenings he crossed the Potomac and waded back into the DC life he loved. He visited his family and old friends. He went hobnobbing with Washington politicos, attending a Stonewall Democrats fund-raiser. He had a picture taken with one of his personal heroes, Gavin Newsom, the Californian politician who, while mayor of San Francisco, began unilaterally issuing marriage licenses to same-sex couples in violation of state law. Back in DC, Brad felt like he fit right in.

He and Jason Edwards met up for dinner one night, and he excitedly showed Jason a PowerPoint presentation he was working on. "He talked about how he had been praised by a four star general about his intelligence for such a young man," Jason said. "He just had a really great sense of self."

Jason stayed the night, but before they went to bed Brad received a strange text message from a number he didn't recognize. "It said, 'Hey I'm Derek, I met you out. You're really cute and we should hook up some time,' and Brad was surprised by this," said Jason. "He didn't know anybody by the name of Derek." Brad tracked the number to another soldier there at the hotel; he wasn't gay, and he wasn't named Derek. Brad was being baited.

"[Brad] never actually said 'Hey, I'm gay.' He did everything *but*, so that way he could say, 'Well, my political causes that I support say nothing one way or the other about my sexual orientation,'" Jason said. "I don't tell, you can't ask. That was the premise he was working off, and it did not serve him well."

As the fall deployment date grew closer Brad's unsuitability for life in the army was creating manifest problems. On one early morning at Fort Drum in May 2009, Brad failed to show up for formation. Jihrleah Showman, the leader of his unit, went to his room in the barracks. When she knocked on the door he answered wearing civilian clothes and looking bleary-eyed, as if he'd just woken up. She told him to get dressed and get to formation in a hurry.

As the two walked back to formation Showman asked what had caused him to be late. Had he slept all right? Did his alarm not go off? Brad was unresponsive to her questions—oddly quiet, she felt. When they came in sight of First Sergeant Paul Adkins however, the senior noncommissioned officer in charge of the unit, Brad erupted in emotional fury. Just as Showman began to explain that she'd have to report his tardiness to Adkins, Brad began screaming unintelligibly at the top of his lungs, waving his arms wildly and salivating at the mouth, Showman later said. When Adkins walked up Brad lowered his voice and made grunting noises with clenched fists. Adkins asked what was wrong and Brad said he couldn't take messing up as he had.

After Brad calmed down Showman set up a time to have a longer conversation with him about the incident. As his superior in the unit, it was her responsibility to counsel him regarding the outburst, but Showman was also from Tulsa, a fellow Oklahoman, and she got along with Brad better than most other soldiers did. She asked Brad if he was suicidal. He said he wasn't but that he "really felt paranoid because he felt people were listening and watching his every move," Showman would later recount.

Brad was small and fragile in a macho world. He wasn't adapting well to army life and the stress was taking its toll. Showman recommended to Adkins that Brad's outburst be referred to higher-ups for counseling; Adkins said he'd reported the incident but Showman heard nothing more about it. She also suggested that, due to his mental state, his access to classified information be taken away and he not deploy with the unit in the fall. Under pressure to meet the army's manpower needs, Adkins declined to follow Showman's advice.

The isolation and pressure of Fort Drum would be nothing compared to life in Iraq.

■ ■ ■

Early in the summer of 2009, Tyler Watkins and his friend Danny Clark were preparing to carpool from Boston to Provincetown, the gay and lesbian resort community at the far tip of Cape Cod. When Danny stopped at Tyler's house to pick him up, he realized he'd forgotten to pack anything to read. He grabbed a book off Tyler's shelf—*Surely You're Joking, Mr. Feynman,* the zany memoirs of the Nobel Prize-winning physicist Richard Feynman—and asked if he could borrow it. Tyler said sure, adding that the book belonged to his boyfriend.

In mid-June, Brad went to Boston for a long weekend with Tyler and then headed back upstate to report for duty at Fort Drum on Sunday, June 21, sad as usual to be leaving his boyfriend.

Tyler mentioned to Brad that a friend of his had borrowed the Feynman memoir and enjoyed it. As Brad had done months earlier with Zach Antolak, he reached out again to a man he'd never met or spoken to but with whom he thought he might share common interests. On Friday night he called Danny, didn't get an answer, and then sent him a text message.

"Hello, it's Brad Manning," he wrote.

Danny texted back, "Hi, this is Danny Clark, you got me :) ."

"Its not hard to track you down ;) ."

"Yeah, I'm sure I'm quite Google stalkable. Once you learn [his e-mail address] you'll find all kinds of scandalous details regarding filesystems and free software ;-> ."

5
Building WikiLeaks

Within weeks of Assange posting the "Conspiracy as Governance" document online, in which he outlines his theory of radical transparency, the small coterie of WikiLeaks insiders were sending e-mails back and forth at a fevered pace. By mid-December 2006, the organization had gotten its hands on a secret memorandum from Somalia's Islamist government in Mogadishu directing the assassination of the head of the rival, Western-backed transitional authority. In a rapid-fire discussion that continued through the Christmas holiday, John Young of Cryptome, Assange, and others crafted what would be the opening volley in WikiLeaks' war on government secrecy.

Notably, this first of WikiLeaks' disclosures appears not to have been a leak at all but an act of classic espionage perpetrated by what Assange has called the "open source, democratic intelligence agency": WikiLeaks.

■ ■ ■

In 1995, the US Naval Research Laboratory created a software program to facilitate secure, anonymous communications over the Internet. The program, called Tor, remains an essential tool for diplomacy and intelligence work for governments around the world. But, as with the Internet itself, WikiLeaks turned Tor against its creator.

Tor works through classic misdirection. Normally, a computer in, say, Japan connects to a computer in Estonia via a server in order to exchange data. The Tor program allows the computer in Japan to send data on a randomized pathway through any number of the servers around the world that make up the Tor network before finally delivering the data packet to Estonia. The more people using Tor—that is, the more crowded the network—the more secure it is. An eavesdropper might note the data sailing between two Tor nodes along its randomized pathway from Japan to Estonia, but he loses the trail there. He can't read the encrypted data or follow it to its next destination, and the identities of the original Japanese sender and Estonian recipient are undetectable.

Each Tor node to which the data bounces on its random path from Japan to Estonia adds a layer of encryption. These layers are "peeled off" as the data reaches its final destination—hence the program's name, the Onion Router, or TOR for short. These days the acronym has been discarded, rendering the proper noun Tor. A free software iteration of the program, supported by the Tor Project, went live for the general public in 2004 and became an essential piece of WikiLeaks' encrypted data submission system. By the end of the decade it had become a leader among technologies used to circumvent censorship and surveillance online. In a 2011 awards ceremony, the Tor Project was given the 2010 Project for Social Benefit Award by Richard Stallman's Free Software Foundation.

One of the members of the WikiLeaks "advisory board" was the owner of a volunteer server on the Tor network, and, it has been reported, he discovered a serious vulnerability in the program. Whereas communications *through* the network were encrypted and sent on randomized pathways to throw off any possible tails, communications at the beginning and the end of the pathway—where the layers of encryption had been peeled off—were vulnerable if users did not encrypt their own data in the beginning. Though the sender in Japan could transmit information over most of the network with confidence, if he sent it unencrypted, his data could be intercepted by the owner of the server to which he first connected. Similarly, while data might safely make it to the last server in the pathway, where the Estonian could pick it up, the owner of the last server could nab a copy of unencrypted data on its way out the door. This, it appears, is how WikiLeaks got its first scoop.[1]

Around New Year's Day, before the group's home page had even gone live, WikiLeaks posted a downloadable file online that contained the secret memorandum from Somalia. The response from the media was swift and predictable, as the news of WikiLeaks' existence instantly eclipsed whatever revelations may have been in the Somali document. Assange excitedly wrote to John Young, alluding to the source of WikiLeaks' first document.

> We are going to fuck them all. Chinese mostly, but not entirely a feint. Invention abounds. Lies, twists and distorts everywhere needed for protection. Hackers monitor chinese and other intel as they burrow into their targets, when they pull, so do we. Inxhaustible supply of material. Near 100,000 documents/emails a day. We're going to crack the world open and let it flower into something new.

The Somali document episode illustrates an essential part of Assange's vision. Though presented in the popular narrative as a venue to allow whistleblowers to securely transmit data, the ideological underpinnings of WikiLeaks were more ambitious. In a world where governments protect themselves from embarrassment and democratic oversight by keeping secrets buried, Assange intended to crack the system open and set its secrets free. WikiLeaks did indeed seek to rectify injustices, but the method it used to do so was an all-out assault on government secrecy, and if the source of leaks wasn't always a whistleblower, then so be it.

Even before the WikiLeaks.org site went live, its vision of radical transparency stirred controversy among other transparency activists.

---

1. Julian Assange has flatly denied that the Somalia document was culled from the Tor network. Considering the contemporary e-mails leaked by Cryptome and the insufficiency of Assange's denial, this writer remains unconvinced.

Writing on January 3, 2007, in the Secrecy News blog of the Federation of American Scientists Project on Government Secrecy, Steven Aftergood, who had been invited to take part in the WikiLeaks project at its inception, wrote that he did "not favor automated or indiscriminate publication of confidential records." Foretelling later debates about the impact and ethics of WikiLeaks, he wrote: "In the absence of accountable editorial oversight, publication can more easily become an act of aggression or an incitement to violence, not to mention an invasion of privacy or an offense against good taste." Already, WikiLeaks' methods were striking discord even among freedom of information activists, and it is no wonder; neither the media nor WikiLeaks itself could come to final agreement on what exactly WikiLeaks was.

In the media, at times, Julian Assange has been called a whistleblower. The label is nonsensical on its face. A whistleblower, as commonly understood, is a person on the inside of an organization who reveals its incriminating secrets to the outside world. Assange has acted strictly as a conduit for information whistleblowers have provided him.

The distinction is important on two fronts, representing two sides of the same question: who's responsible? To those for whom a leak is an act of heroism, the whistleblower—that is, the responsible party with some skin in the game—is to be celebrated. Those who see a leak as traitorous condemn the whistleblower for his treachery. Journalists—who are not whistleblowers themselves but conduits of whistleblown information—have been left out of the calculus.

In law the distinction is particularly clear. Heretofore in modern American jurisprudence the US government has declined to fully prosecute a journalist for publishing a leak, while it has targeted whistleblowers with increasing enthusiasm. (In Obama's first year and a half as president, the Justice Department prosecuted more whistleblowers than under any other president in American history.) The press has mightily enjoyed its perch beyond reproach, but the WikiLeaks project muddles the distinction. Though it may make journalists squirm in their seats, there is no question that Assange bears much greater resemblance to their kind than to any whistleblower past or present.

What, then, makes WikiLeaks different?

After posting the Somalia document, WikiLeaks produced a press release that described more lucidly than before what it intended to accomplish in its campaign for global justice by way of combating secrecy.

> Public scrutiny of otherwise unaccountable and secretive institutions pressures them to act ethically. What official will chance a secret, corrupt transaction when the public is likely to find out? . . . When the risks of embarrassment through openness and honesty increase, the tables are turned against conspiracy, corruption, exploitation and oppression. Open government answers injustice rather than causing it. Open government exposes and undoes corruption. Open governance is the most cost effective method of promoting good governance.
>
> Today, with authoritarian governments in power around much of the world, increasing authoritarian tendencies in democratic governments, and increasing amounts of power vested in unaccountable corporations, the need for openness and democratization is greater than ever.
>
> WikiLeaks is a tool to satisfy that need.

As envisaged by Assange, the site would eventually become a full broadside attack on secrecy the world over. It would, by design, be nondiscriminatory in its targets, creating a leaky world in its assault on the very notion of government secrecy as it was then practiced.

But a traditional whistleblower is discriminating. Having seen incriminating information that is kept from the public view, she is compelled to release it to (in the best of the tradition) reveal a specific injustice. The conflict that arises is clear—if a whistleblower intends to reveal a specific injustice, and WikiLeaks is an indiscriminate assault on secrecy itself, aren't whistleblowers being co-opted by an organization with ambitions of its own?

For the first years of WikiLeaks' existence the answer was yes, and vice versa. A symbiosis of whistleblowers and radical transparency activists existed, each using the other for their own ends. Only after Brad Manning arrived in Iraq did the two purposes—traditional whistleblowing and radical, collaborative transparency—meld into one revolutionary whole.

■ ■ ■

On January 7, 2007, days after the Somalia document's release, Assange announced a plan to raise five million dollars by July. John Young issued a scathing response.

"Announcing a $5 million fund-raising goal by July will kill this effort. It makes WL appear to be a Wall Street scam. This amount could not be needed so soon except for suspect purposes."

But Young's concerns weren't limited to Assange's grandiose fund-raising plans. "I'd say the same about the alleged 1.1 million documents ready for leaking. Way too many to be believable without evidence. I don't believe the number. So far, one document, of highly suspect provenance."

Young advised Assange to temper his impatience, operate on a "shoe-string for a few months," and establish WikiLeaks' "bona fides by publishing a credible batch of documents." He closed with a prescient critique of Assange's bloviating style. "The biggest crooks brag overmuch of how ethical their operations are. Avoid ethical promises, period, they've been used too often to fleece victims. Demonstrate sustained ethical behavior, don't preach/peddle it." In a quick addendum e-mail, Young suggested that the US Central Intelligence Agency was the only viable—and possibly intended—source of such a large sum. He suggested, with evident sarcasm, that if it was the CIA WikiLeaks was soliciting, they should ask for something closer to $100 million. He signed off: "In solidarity to fuck em all."

"Advice noted," Assange responded. "We'll polish up our sheers for cutting fleeces golden."

By the end of the day, the founding core of the organization had disintegrated. Young e-mailed the entire WikiLeaks listserv. "Cryptome is publishing the contents of this list, and how I was induced to serve as US person for registration. WikiLeaks is a fraud."

■ ■ ■

Assange pressed on, traveling widely throughout the year spreading the gospel of WikiLeaks. Though largely forgotten in the popular narrative, many of WikiLeaks' first releases were astonishing, at the least in their origins. In August, WikiLeaks posted a leaked report exposing the expansive corruption of a former president of Kenya. In September the group posted two thousand pages of leaked documents listing equipment in use by the US Army in Iraq and Afghanistan, all in searchable format and unredacted. Articles written by WikiLeaks insiders and allies in reaction to the documents alleged they reveal corruption, war profiteering, and the use of banned chemical warfare agents by the US military in Iraq.[2] The United States rejected these claims. In November, the group posted the Standard Operating Procedures of the military jail at Guantánamo Bay, which, WikiLeaks and others have asserted, exposed systematic attempts on the part of the military to limit the access of the Red Cross to prisoners held at the detention facility.

Though it was receiving secret documents and attracting the attention of US authorities, WikiLeaks wasn't garnering the press attention it had hoped for, and the organization struggled to secure funding. To keep its operations running, it depended on volunteers. Among them was a German computer security specialist active in the open source community, Daniel Domscheit-Berg. After being trusted with menial tasks, like cleaning up front-end code on the site, Domscheit-Berg arranged a lecture for Assange at the annual congress of the Chaos Computer Club, an influential hackers organization based in Berlin. The congress would be their first meeting in real life.

WikiLeaks missed the registration deadline. When Assange arrived at the Berliner Congress Center he wasn't listed on the speakers list and had no lecture scheduled at the event. Undeterred, Assange

---

2. WikiLeaks asserted that the use of CS gas, or "tear gas," in combat operations, as revealed in the leaks, is banned under the Chemical Weapons Convention of 1997. The US government contends that the language of American law allows for the use of CS under certain circumstances.

set up camp in the pressroom, literally. As described by Domscheit-Berg in his tell-all, *Inside WikiLeaks: My Time with Julian Assange at the World's Most Dangerous Website,* Assange turned the room into his personal office and bedroom, working there on his computer throughout the day and sleeping in the room at night.

Last-minute arrangements were made, and he delivered his lecture in a basement to a group of fewer than twenty people. Domscheit-Berg describes the scene: "He wore the same clothes every day. The gleaming white shirt that had so impressed me when we first met lost some of its shine as time went on. If Julian was disappointed by the small number of listeners he attracted, he didn't let it show. He spoke for forty-five minutes, and afterward, when three people in the audience wanted to know more, he patiently answered their questions. . . . Julian was tireless in his attempts to get audiences excited about his ideas."

Though Assange had always presented the organization as a robust network of activists from around the world, in truth the number of people actively involved in WikiLeaks' operations was small. In addition to Assange and Domscheit-Berg, two technically savvy people whom Domscheit-Berg calls "the technician" and "the architect" built and maintained the site's secure submission system. Assange and, to a lesser extent, Domscheit-Berg were the public faces of WikiLeaks. They traveled almost constantly, speaking to audiences around the globe about their work, applying for grant funding, and working to beef up the security of their submission system. The cadre moved about the world with a growing paranoia that agents of the security state were one step behind them, always watching and waiting.

WikiLeaks continued to receive leaked documents: the contents of vice presidential nominee Sarah Palin's e-mail account; the membership list of the far-right British National Party; a ten-year archive of e-mails between climate scientists at the influential Climatic Research Unit; records from the Swiss bank Julius Baer's offshore operations in the Cayman Islands; closely guarded secrets of the Church of Scientology. Momentum was growing for the transparency insurgents, whose ambitions far exceeded their clout. On October 12, 2009, WikiLeaks tweeted, "Celebrating our first 10k followers! As long as that's only 1/150 of @mchammer, we still have a lot of work to do though."

The US Army was growing concerned about the group. A classified March 18, 2008, study from the Army Counterintelligence Center reveals the army's early preoccupations regarding WikiLeaks, which are both prescient and, when viewed in hindsight, comical. The report discusses articles written by "the foreign staff writer for WikiLeaks.org, Julian Assange." The army report repeatedly refers to WikiLeaks' supposedly stated policy of not verifying the authenticity of leaked documents before posting them to the web; e-mails leaked by Cryptome and stated WikiLeaks policy reveal that the organization was preoccupied from the beginning with ensuring the veracity of documents it posts (as well as its willingness to depend on the wiki—mass collaboration—to verify documents after they're posted).

The report concludes that, with the increase in Internet access around the world and the spread of attendant digital technologies, the threat to the United States from WikiLeaks is substantial and growing. "It must be presumed that Wikileaks.org has or will receive sensitive or classified DoD documents in the future," the report says. "Various open or freeware applications used in the development and management of Wikileaks.org continue to improve with time" and "will provide greater privacy and anonymity of persons who leak information to Wikileaks.org." The most effective weapon against WikiLeaks, says the report, would be to attack its greatest asset and greatest vulnerability: trust.

> Web sites such as Wikileaks.org have trust as their most important center of gravity by protecting the anonymity and identity of the insider, leaker, or whistleblower. Successful identification, prosecution, termination of employment, and exposure of persons leaking the information . . . would damage and potentially destroy this center of gravity and deter others from taking similar actions.

WikiLeaks would later publish the classified US Army counterintelligence report on its operations.

■ ■ ■

At the end of November 2009, WikiLeaks published over half a million lines of pager messages from the morning of September 11, 2001. The correspondence included messages sent to government personnel, journalists, office workers, and others and offered remarkable insight into the second-by-second development of events in the hours after terrorist attacks struck the World Trade Center and the Pentagon. The origin of the leak was remarkable in itself: it was, to someone who knew what he was looking at, obviously from a classified National Security Agency database.

For the first three years of WikiLeaks' existence the group struggled to secure financing and notoriety. Though people in the intelligence community certainly followed the organization's goings on and many of secrets the group published made headlines, in the popular narrative WikiLeaks largely receded into the background. On December 23, 2009, under severe financial strain, WikiLeaks announced it was going offline.

The radio silence would be a sort of strike. WikiLeaks would continue to accept leak submissions, but no new content would be posted and all previously published content would be taken offline (though still accessible in some cases on mirror sites). Only when enough donations came in to fully support the site's operations would the site go back online.

Assange and Domscheit-Berg were in Iceland during this time, in the early stages of creating the Icelandic Modern Media Initiative, a proposal they and others had been working on with Icelandic politicians, principally the leftist parliamentarian Birgitta Jonsdottir, to create a press freedom haven in the island nation. Iceland had been hit particularly hard by the financial crisis of 2008, but when WikiLeaks published documents that proved malfeasance at the country's largest bank, Kaupthing, a court injunction prevented a news station from reporting on the leak. Instead, the news anchor could only direct viewers to the WikiLeaks website. It was a powerfully symbolic moment representing the absurdity of blundering state censorship and of the establishment's fundamental misunderstanding of the threat cyberpowered transparency activists now posed to its position. In equal measure it was an expression of the importance and the promise of WikiLeaks' transparency insurgency.

While Assange was in Iceland, the US Embassy hosted a cocktail party at the home of the new *chargé d'affaires*, Sam Watson. As a member of parliament, Jonsdottir was invited to the embassy event, and she suggested Assange come along as her guest. "I said it would be a bit of a prank to take him and see if they knew who he was," she said. "I don't think they had any idea."

Jonsdottir arrived late to pick up Assange for the party, didn't find him, and went on a short jaunt looking for him at the places around Reykjavik she knew he liked to hang out. But Assange had gone on to the party without her. "I crashed it under the guise of Birgitta's plus-one," he wrote in his autobiography. Assange had come to the party with copies of leaked documents he'd received relating to the shady dealings of another Icelandic bank, Landsbanki. "I was feeling perky that night," he wrote. At the party Assange met the former head of Kaupthing, the bank at which WikiLeaks had exposed malfeasance. "That didn't go particularly well," Assange wrote. He also spoke with Sam Watson—though neither man knew it at the time, only a few months hence Assange would release a diplomatic cable sent by Watson that would cause a minor scandal in Iceland and presage a later wave of major scandals the world over.

Days after the announcement that WikiLeaks was going offline, Assange and Domscheit-Berg flew to Berlin for the Chaos Communications Conference, this time as keynote speakers. In their address, they explained that they'd gone offline for lack of support from the public and spoke at length about plans for the Icelandic media haven initiative.

"First one member of the audience," wrote Domscheit-Berg, "then two, then three stood up, and suddenly they were giving us a standing ovation. The noise was deafening. I felt waves of enthusiasm floating up to us like a cloud from the masses down below."

The enthusiasm of the crowd of hackers notwithstanding, in the circus of the mainstream media WikiLeaks was still a sideshow, and donor funding to support its operations was not forthcoming. Days later, Assange and Domscheit-Berg returned to Iceland to continue the work of creating a media haven, and WikiLeaks.org remained offline.

6
Carl Sagan

"My life goal is the expansion of human knowledge,
and the elimination of the earth-moon system
as the boundary of human influence."

—Bradley E. Manning

On the heels of a trip to DC and a long weekend in Boston with his boyfriend, Brad was back at Fort Drum. It was Friday night, June 26, 2009, and he was lonely again. After exchanging introductory text messages with Tyler's friend Danny Clark, Brad followed up with a phone call.

A conversation that started with their shared fondness for Richard Feynman quickly developed into a wide-ranging, half-hour-long discussion about mutual interests and personal histories. As usual, Brad regaled Danny with his origin story as a gay kid from Oklahoma who overcame obstacles to claw his way into the inner sanctum of military intelligence. Large segments of their conversation covered their greatest commonality, computers, and their respective jobs, Danny at a nonprofit and Brad in the army.

"He told me about joining the military where the actual work he seemed to like a lot and really excel at, but the entire social structure just seemed unspeakably awful," Danny said. "I got the sense that he was sort of starved for any kind of intelligent conversation, especially about topics he was interested in."

Danny was a computer expert and a Cambridge native in his early thirties. While in high school, he worked as a systems administrator for Cambridge-based Interlock Media, a film production company with a bent toward environmentalism and social justice. After graduation, he spent a year at Oberlin College, an institution known for progressive activism, but left school for a job at the software firm Lotus and then went to work for IBM after the tech giant acquired his firm. He left IBM for a stint at One Laptop per Child, a nonprofit dedicated to making computers cheap, durable, and widely available across the developing world. Next, he worked for the cause that was, perhaps, the closest to his heart: the free software movement. He worked as a systems administrator for the Free Software Foundation and developed a personal relationship with Richard Stallman, the legendary hacker who'd spearheaded the movement decades earlier.

Having spent most of his life in Cambridge, Danny, though not an MIT student, was a staple in the community around "pika." Briefly a chapter of the national Pi Kappa Alpha fraternity (known commonly as Pike), pika became coed in 1975 and by 1982 had officially severed ties with the national Pike office. The pika house is a three-story maze like a live-in Rube Goldberg machine, with space for thirty-two occupants, living and study areas, pantry, study room, kitchen, workroom, garden, and a tree house connected to the multilevel outdoor deck by a retractable drawbridge. Art covers the walls, creativity abounds, and community-relevant decisions are made by consensus. One pikan said, "It's really sort of like an autonomous collective, to use the Monty Pythonesque phrase." A commenter in an online forum said she "wouldn't call it a very social environment, and when people do socialize, it's usually doing weird things: union songs, potato guns, speed chess, hacking." Pika is the hacker's paradise.

For Danny, a longtime resident of the cloistered, progressive, and reflexively intellectual community of Cambridge, Massachusetts, Brad was a unique specimen. "I don't know how he managed to become as smart and well-read as he did, having never had the benefit of an environment with a lot of people who were into the same kind of things," Danny said later. "But he did. So you had this person who was clearly much better informed on all this political stuff, but then McDonald's was his favorite restaurant. You know? You don't meet people in Cambridge like that. He was just this sort of fascinating person I hadn't met before."

Like Brad, Danny had a quick mind, but his social anxiety sometimes made extended real-life conversations with strangers strained. They hung up their phones, and thirty minutes later continued their talk online, an environment in which they both felt comfortable.

"Do you come to Boston on work, or when on leave?" Danny asked.

"I visit Tyler there on occasion, while on pass that is, usually a 3-4 day weekend," Brad said.

Danny joked about them being eavesdropped on by ECHELON, the signals intelligence program operated by the National Security Agency that monitors communications worldwide.

"So is ECHELON recording our every word RIGHT NOW TERRORIST ATTACK ON GAYS IN OBAMA'S CLOSET?" he typed. "Just trying to get in some good name entities."

"NSA's ECHELON, as I found out, was a disaster," Brad told him. "SIGINT [signals intelligence] is a weird beast. It's only supposed to collect on foreign nationals."

"Yeah," said Danny, "but everyone is a foreigner to some country."

"If it collects on American citizens, it has to throw it out and destroy it for legal reasons," said Brad. In any case, Brad said, it would be infeasible for the NSA to monitor and store data collected on all Americans. He went on about arcane aspects of the government's encryption and surveillance methods. There was a long pause. Danny didn't have much to add on the subject.

"<3 block ciphers. Sorry, I got carried away =L ," Brad typed. "I spend way too much time on SIPRnet and JWICS." Pronounced "jaywax" the Joint Worldwide Intelligence Communications System (JWICS) is a computer network shared by the Pentagon and the State

Department to transfer material classified at Top Secret and SCI, or Secure Compartmented Information, levels.

"My point," Danny said, "was just that I had heard there may have been collusion with Australia and the UK SIGINT to get around the citizen-of-the-country limitation."

"Ah the ACGU =) ," Brad said.

"Wow, you guys have more TLAs [three-letter acronyms] than IBM! C'est que ACGU?" Danny asked.

"Aussies, Canooks, Great Brits, and Uncle Sam."

Without provocation, Brad changed topics.

"I'm way underpaid," he said.

"Do you get anything on top of the standard for your peon-rank for doing more specialized work?" Danny said.

"A pat on the back, and a wink from the odd major and colonel. Not to mention, it gets me out of DUMB work, like inventories, key control, and being the guy who moves boxes."

Brad went on to talk about a White House official who, he said, was creeping him out.

"Won't stop texting me, hitting on me," he said. "I wish I lived a normal-ass life xD" His description of the relationship revealed a measure of arrogance coupled with his characteristic desire to impress.

"I don't do too bad under DADT =L ," Brad continued. "I seem to be having a lot more fun than Dan Choi [the Iraq War veteran who came out publicly to protest DADT] and all those other vocal types."

Throughout the four-hour conversation, Brad gave his standard self-introduction. He was cocky and a braggart, but self-consciously so, simultaneously proud of his work and frustrated with being under-appreciated. He boasted about the political connections he'd made over the past year.

"I'm a DC guy," he told Danny. "I got caught up in the DC homosphere."

"Oh, just like just the mainstream gay bars/clubs there?" Danny asked, adding, "Homosphere . . . nice."

"Well, that and the cocktail parties," Brad said. "Pay to play politics, but open bars. I'm all for it."

Brad's expressions of inflated self-importance weren't limited to conversations with friends online. Back at Fort Drum, he was not getting along well in the army and was increasingly prone to fits of rage, screaming at superior officers with clenched fists and lashing out at other soldiers by tossing chairs.

Though he put on a happy face for friends on the outside, living under Don't Ask, Don't Tell was adding a singular level of stress to Brad's life. Already an emotionally fragile young man with few deep friendships and little going for him in the civilian world, the strictures of the DADT policy made Brad's home life—that is, the life he led most of the time among other soldiers at Fort Drum—anything but the comfortable, safe environment that comes to mind when one imagines home.

Brad and Danny continued chatting over the next several days. Mostly they made mundane conversation about Brad-centered topics, like electronic music, Brad's ill-fitting army-issue uniforms, his now-abandoned EVE Online account, and his changing plans for the future. "I've been so determined to go to a fancy college and kick ass. I almost don't need to go to college anymore," he said. He listed off his dream schools anyway, with MIT at the top.

There were bits of silliness. Brad wrote to Danny one day out of the blue. "Ninja," he said. "Coolest thought I had all day. Imagine a ninja. Doing the running man. In the air."

"Ninjarific," Danny replied the next day.

Brad talked about using his personal network to help his cousin, a recent college grad, find a job. "Put him in touch with my best friend Toby, staffer for senator Barbara Boxer of Cali," he said. "I have a habit of working outside the bounds of formality."

"I've heard congressional staffing is much more gay than one would think," Danny said.

"It's what got me so far so fast," said Brad. "Twinkish gay soldier, intel, science, and computer geek boy with a political agenda."

■ ■ ■

In the summer of 2009, Brad's unit, the 2nd Brigade Combat Team, 10th Mountain Division, was preparing to deploy to Iraq. Brad returned to DC for the Fourth of July, and on July 7 he departed for Fort Polk, the sprawling army post in the middle of Louisiana, where his unit spent several weeks at the Joint Readiness Training Center (JRTC). JRTC was the army's predeployment clearinghouse, at which soldiers were running realistic-as-possible simulations of life in the field in Iraq. Once back from "the swamps," as Brad called his time at JRTC, he described the experience to Danny.

"I think I've just realized the outrageousness of the situation I am in," he said.

"More so than it has been before?" Danny asked.

"I'm living under DADT, making huge progress in my intel job, but I have a micromanaging bull-dyke as my first line supervisor who absolutely loves the army, but has no intel talent whatsoever." Brad's attitude was again clashing with military culture.

"She's trying to push all this 'hooah, hooah' army, 'everyone is a soldier and needs to do this, this and this' on me, while I'm questioning the policies of the military. And because of my emotional situation I was strongly recommended to see the chaplain," Brad said. "Yet he's not at all very religious, knew exactly what secular humanism was, and we talked about my situation, and how it ties in with humanist/atheist philosophy.

"Pretty boy (me), questioning military because oppressed by bull dyke, went to see religious person who talked about the whole thing from a reason/philosophy standpoint. Is that not absolutely hiliarious xD"

"That's pretty good," Danny said. "The swamp-training was hard on you? Last time we talked you seemed to be doing pretty well emotionally."

"No, it went amazingly well for me. I accomplished much. But she's destroying everything intel-wise for some 'soldiery' crap, destroying the pre-deployment intel process." Brad seemed genuinely, if presumptuously, concerned about his unit's readiness. "Everyone is suffering," he said, "but this old-style military tradition is possibly

"I was a short (still am), very intelligent (could read at 3 and multiply / divide by 4), very effeminate, and glued to a computer screen at these young ages [MSDOS / Windows 3.1 timeframe]. I played SimCity [the original] obsessively." —Bradley Manning

Bradley as a toddler.

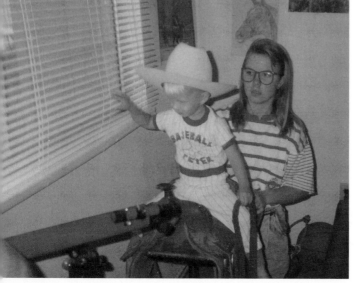

Bradley Manning and sister Casey.

Bradley Manning circa first grade.

(left) Bradley had acres of countryside to explore, an aboveground swimming pool, a dog, a cat, and horses that his sister rode bareback.

(below) Bradley at home outside Crescent, Oklahoma.

Manning family at Casey's prom. Left to right: Sue, Casey, Brian, and young Bradley.

Casey Manning and teen Bradley.

(above) Bradley on trip to Japan with Welsh schoolmates. Courtesy of the Bradley Manning Support Network

(left) Brad Manning passport photo for return from the UK to the United States. Courtesy of the Manning family

(right) Brad celebrating his birthday at Fort Drum.
Courtesy of the Bradley Manning Support Network

(left) Tyler Watkins and Brad Manning. "He never was really in one place long enough to really put down strong roots, which I think is one of the reasons that his relationship with Tyler was so intense for him, because he felt like it was something he could really hold on to." —Danny Clark
Courtesy of the Bradley Manning Support Network

The New Year's Eve party at Berin Szoka's apartment. Left to right: Jason Edwards, Toby Quaranta, Brad Manning. COURTESY OF THE BRADLEY MANNING SUPPORT NETWORK

Brad Manning and Danny Clark on an impromptu trip to Washington, DC.
COURTESY OF THE BRADLEY MANNING SUPPORT NETWORK

Brad and Danny at pika.
COURTESY OF THE BRADLEY MANNING SUPPORT NETWORK

He tended to be quiet and reserved in a group of strangers, but at pika, where smarts and quirks were celebrated in equal measure, Brad was instantly among friends. COURTESY OF THE BRADLEY MANNING SUPPORT NETWORK

Private Manning during a training exercise in Kuwait. COURTESY OF THE BRADLEY MANNING SUPPORT NETWORK

Julian Assange and Daniel Domscheit-Berg speaking at the Chaos Communication Congress in Berlin, December 2009.
© ANDREAS GAUFER "ANDYGEE1," LICENSED THROUGH CREATIVE COMMONS

Left to right: Adrian Lamo, Kevin Mitnick, Kevin Poulsen, circa 2001. Photo by Matthew Griffiths

About 400 Manning supporters rallied outside the gates at Quantico Marine Base in Virginia in March 2010. Dozens were arrested. Photo by the author

Protestors rally in support of Bradley Manning on the first day
of the Occupy Wall Street demonstrations in New York City, September 17, 2011.

Brad Manning, center in handcuffs, is escorted from his Article 32 hearing at Fort Meade. Manning
was charged with 22 counts, including aiding the enemy and violations of the Espionage Act.

killing soldiers in the future, since we're not going to be prepared when we arrive now. Instead of doing my job like I was doing this morning, the focus has shifted to doing inspections, making sure I can recite military propaganda, clean up the office, and do nothing until I'm told to do something."

While Brad expressed his frustrations with the military to Danny, he didn't reveal to him anything near the degree of his alienation. By August, his behavior had deteriorated so far that his supervisor Sergeant Adkins said he showed signs of "instability" and referred him to a mental health specialist for anger management issues. Unable to confide in his army-appointed therapist due to Don't Ask, Don't Tell, however, Brad went to only one initial counseling visit. He sought therapy on his own off base, but even that was ineffective. Instead, Brad confided in friends back home. "His emotions could turn on a dime," said Jason Edwards. "When he called from Fort Drum it was bad. When he called it was basically just this kind of screaming and crying, and there wasn't a lot that he would say that was terribly coherent."

Concerned that he could be "a risk to himself and possibly others," according an official statement issued later, Adkins considered following Showman's advice and leaving Brad behind when the unit deployed. But there was a shortage of intelligence analysts in Iraq, and Brad's temperament was showing improvement. The army weighed the risks of deploying Brad Manning with his unit, and the exigencies of a protracted war won out in the calculus.

■ ■ ■

Among the stresses in Brad's life was a growing concern about his relationship with Tyler. "He doesn't talk to me much anymore =L ," he told Danny in a chat online on August 8. "Maybe I'm just being needy, but he is the only thing I have that I care about."

But Tyler wasn't the only thing weighing on his mind. He saw himself as a deep-inside player in the intelligence world, and the heaviness of the responsibility was not sitting well.

"I have this increasingly awful feeling," he said in the same conversation. "It comes from the realization that I am a trusted government employee with the highest security clearance. I know too much."

"Have you talked to many people that have been deployed before?"

"Yes, I have. That and I've seen the public affairs responses to potential questions if media asks. But media knows that it won't look good if it starts to question the military's handling of war. God I know too much."

"Really, *the* highest?"

"Yes. TS/SCI. With a need to know for almost everything involving foreign policy," Brad said. "I'm the only damn person that's smart enough to know which resources are available to me, that research not only military, but other-government-agency reporting. I'm so far deep rooted in reality I cannot escape." Brad was exaggerating his level of access to government secrets, but not by much.

Contrary to the image promulgated in spy movies, the American federal government's system for handling state secrets is an inexact, patchwork scheme of obscure origins. Regulations for the handling of sensitive information in matters of state were inherited or implemented from the time of the American Revolution onward, but in general, issues requiring the utmost secrecy were simply handled on what later generations would call a "need-to-know basis." The basic structure of the military's modern system of classification appears to come from the First World War, when the American Expeditionary Force had to coordinate its activities with the French and British armies. Borrowing from its allies, the Americans instituted ad hoc restrictions on information controlled up to the highest level, "Secret." Further changes came over the years, including instituting the "Top Secret" designation during the Truman era.

Brad had been given a TS/SCI security clearance, short for Top Secret/Sensitive Compartmented Information, and he was correct, in one sense, to say it was the highest-level designation available. The SCI clearance level restricts information into compartments, access to which is granted on an individual, need-to-know basis. Though he was a lowly private in the chain of command, the digitization of classified communications and the government's twenty-first century information-sharing initiatives conspired to give him unprecedented access to state secrets. Through SIPRnet and JWICS, Brad and others in his position had more government secrets at their fingertips than enlisted men and women of any earlier era. There was, of course, plenty of information "involving foreign policy" for which Brad Manning did not have a need-to-know clearance, but his access to the State Department communications through JWICS was remarkable enough on its own.

"I don't know if you can imagine the pressure," Brad said. It had become a familiar yarn, Brad playing on his own vanity to tease out frustrations in his military life. It's clear he'd become intoxicated by the glamour of his ability to peer behind the curtain of state secrecy, but his misunderstanding, or misrepresentation, of his level of access had become a burden as well.

"Nope, not really. The fear is if you are captured it could be really bad?" Danny said.

"I wont be captured. But if I were to be, I'm one of the few military personnel considered a liability. I'm strategically worth more dead than tactically alive."

■ ■ ■

As the date of Brad's deployment approached, his plans for the future were very much on his mind. "I'm not sure how my life is going to pan out over the next 26 months," Brad said after initiating a chat online with Zach Antolak, on August 1, 2009, two months before he was scheduled to deploy. "Two months pre-deployment, 12 months of Iraq, and another 12 months of recovery and garrison, all assuming I don't get discharged under DADT. But the moment I leave the military, I'm planning on breaking out in all directions."

"Man, stay safe in Iraq," said Antolak.

"I'm an analyst, I shadow a brigade commander," Brad said. "Also, the Shia majority in the location we are going doesn't want to screw around with the US. They're stockpiling fresh weapons, because the moment we leave, they plan on removing Sunnis out of the region to the southeast and northeast of Baghdad." As usual Brad seemed to carry a sense of responsibility for the outcome of the war incongruous with his humble rank. "I'm trying to figure out a way to prevent a civil war the second we leave."

During his predeployment months, Brad chatted often with his new friend Danny Clark. In one conversation, Danny asked Brad what he'd like to do on a perfect leave—in a couple months he'd be en route to the Middle East, with no leave to be taken.

"I'd like my family and friends to get together in one location ideally," he said, "and meet each other. It's such a wide spread =L. Like a going away party of sorts."

"Okay," Danny said, "let's put a limit on people involved to Tyler and I then. I don't think I'll be able to invent workable quantum teleportation quite that quickly =) ."

"I'm speaking more along the lines of my DC circle of friends," said Brad. "Jason Edwards, Toby Quaranta and his boyfriend, etc. I have a lot of potentially powerful friends.

"Can I tell you a secret," Brad said, suddenly, "since we are along the same thought lines? And for the love of science, don't tell Tyler =P ."

"As long as it won't get me hunted down and shot by marines, sure."

"My mind has been set for many, many years," Brad said.

"On?"

"That I'd do everything in my power to unite various groups of talented people together, and work out a way of building political momentum toward a seat in the senate, and possibly the presidency."

Brad explained that Tyler, along with most of his friends, didn't know the extent of his ambitions. "I'm only 21, remember =L ," he said. "But I deliberately put myself into situations (Don't ask, Don't tell is one of them) that can increase my political capital." He'd known he wanted to be president, he said, since he was thirteen.

Imagine, Brad said, the possibilities of a politician like Carl Sagan, with his brains and scientific outlook combined with his facility for clear communication. He would campaign passionately on two of the issues closest to his heart: scientific research and education.

"I'm trying to play off the civil rights card. Thus all the gay rights stuff on the side. My life goal is the expansion of human knowledge, and the elimination of the earth-moon system as the boundary of human influence. It's probably why I approach gay rights leaders in a 'hey, you're kind of cool, I'd like to talk about other stuff now' attitude. I intrigue them. They react in curiosity when meeting me. Here I am, 21, gay, obviously have some intellect, living under DADT, and, though the gay rights thing is interesting, I seem to have grander dreams in mind.

"Now I'm just being arrogant," Brad said, "which is fine, because I am, I guess."

Brad spoke to Danny with remarkable candor and an astounding lack of self-awareness—both hallmarks of immaturity. While he could open up around friends, he was no socialite and certainly not a charismatic leader of men; acquaintances, from classmates to coworkers, quite often found him irritating if not utterly forgettable. Yet he was unmoved by the obvious limitations that stood in his way. His ambitions were boundless, extending from Capitol Hill and the White House to literally beyond the moon and into outer space.

He was a young man, with a young man's dreams. Though he wasn't well suited for military life, he had an exciting future planned and every reason to believe that once out of the army he'd be presented with a host of good opportunities. He was driven by a benevolent passion for science and secularism—for, in his own words, "the expansion of human knowledge." In short, he had lofty goals reflecting an inflated ego, a bright future, and a purity of idealism that is rarely seen in older, more jaded, and more cautious individuals.

■ ■ ■

In mid-August, Tyler and Danny drove to Watertown to visit Brad—this was the first time Danny and Brad had met in real life. Over the next several weeks, Brad and Tyler visited each other regularly, and often Danny came along. Sometimes, Danny and Brad spent time together on their own; the development of their friendship was accelerated by the peculiar circumstances of their lives. They chatted online often, and when they were together Brad was on leave and thus free to spend long, languid weekends relaxing and talking about wide-ranging topics or nothing at all.

On one such weekend, they'd planned a kayaking trip but realized at the last minute that a recent pre-deployment vaccination Brad received forbade him from coming in contact with water. Instead, Danny and Brad took a last minute trip to DC. They spent the night at Debbie's house and took the metro downtown to Dupont Circle. Brad intended to show Danny around the district and introduce him to his friends and favorite bars. But the evening was hijacked when the sole of Danny's shoe came loose. The night turned into a wacky misadventure as the two of them, joking that Danny had "lost his soul," ventured around DC late at night with Brad leading the charge in search of glue to fix the shoe. They never made it to a bar, but, like good friends becoming great friends, they had a delightful evening nonetheless.

Shortly after the escapade in DC, Brad went up to Boston. He saw Tyler and spent time with Danny, who showed Brad around his favorite haunt, pika. Brad was thrilled by the place. He tended to be quiet and reserved in a group of strangers, but at pika, where smarts and quirks were celebrated in equal measure, he was instantly among friends. He explored the intricate house and took a bouquet of pictures: of the system of outdoor balconies, with a slide, fire pole, and tree house; of the madcap art throughout the complex ("Yo Ho, Yo Ho, a pikan's life for me," read one sign); and of the pikans themselves lounging and working in the detritus of their student lives.

This was a world Brad hoped to join once he got out of the army; it's no coincidence MIT was at the top of his list of dream schools. Immersed in computers, creativity, and a community of progressive thinkers, in Cambridge he'd seen another iteration of what home might look like.

He and Danny spent a good bit of time talking about the free software movement, which Brad supported if only in vague terms. He nursed a programmer's pipe dream: completely rewriting the C library "but 100 percent open source from top to bottom."

It was a highly ambitious goal. In layman's terms, Brad was suggesting building a car from scratch, but, rather than using industry standard parts, he'd build all of the parts themselves from scratch as well. Though the enterprise would probably have been impossible for him alone, redundant, and a lot more trouble than it was worth, it certainly showed a level of dedication to free software ideals. The parallel between Richard Stallman's GNU project is imperfect but plainly evident nonetheless.

"So what's rms [Richard M. Stallman] like?" Brad once asked Danny.

"Surprisingly easy to hang out with," said Danny. "Dunno, that's a hard question to answer about anyone. What are you like?"

"I'm like a sharp minded and aggressive twink," Brad said. ">rawr<."

Later in the same conversation Brad brought up Stallman again.

"Does the great rms know of my existence?" Brad asked.

"I don't think I've had cause to mention it. I'd ask if I could give him your email address for some kinds of questions, but I wouldn't want to get you in trouble. If you are ever around Boston when he is I'm sure we could go have lunch somewhere or something; he likes meeting random supporters." Brad volunteered his e-mail address and asked Danny to put him on the Free Software Foundation's mailing list.

■ ■ ■

It was a cool evening in early October, and Brad was back in DC to rest and see friends and family before deploying to Iraq. In days he would be in Kuwait and soon thereafter at Forward Operating Base Hammer, forty miles into the desert east of Baghdad.

Jason Edwards invited him to a quiet dinner at his friend Kevin's house near Logan Circle. Kevin had been at Berin Szoka's party the year before, but he and Brad never met.

Over a meal of soft-shell crab, tilapia, and roasted potatoes, the three had an uneasy conversation. Naturally, the topic of Iraq came up, and, though there was little disagreement between them, the talk was heated and awkward. Brad was on edge, and as he spoke about the war, the tenor of his speech grew agitated. A DC attorney with a sunny and engaging manner, Kevin tried to steer the conversation into less fraught territory. But, as Brad picked around the soft-shell crab—this wasn't a meal to his liking—he was clearly preoccupied with events in the Middle East. Repeatedly, his voice spiked in a near-yell, and Jason reminded to calm him down. Kevin was stunned that Brad, so small and with a disposition that oscillated that night between meek and confrontational, was soon to be going into a war zone. He would later describe Brad as very critical of the war, and Jason described the position Brad expressed that evening as equating the American occupation of Iraq to "pissing on a fire."

"He definitely left me with a sort of a jaded take on the whole affair. Like, what is this kid doing in the military, you know?" Kevin said.

Brad was anxious but trying to stay focused. He'd arranged to take classes online with the University of Maryland, so he could use his downtime constructively. "He told me he was a little afraid about going to Iraq," said his aunt Debbie, "and I told him anyone would be afraid, that I'd be frightened out of my mind. He was eager to go, though, and eager to be with his unit."

On Sunday, October 11, Tyler Watkins was with friends at the Washington Mall in a rainbow sea of roughly 200,000 people. His relationship with Brad was on the rocks and their respective experiences in an open relationship distinct—Tyler, the socialite, dating in Boston, and Brad, the soldier, isolated at Fort Drum. They had split temporarily in early September but reconciled in advance of Brad's deployment, and on this day, at the National Equality March in DC for gay rights, Tyler was unquestionably in Brad's corner. He wore a necklace with the phrase "ask, tell," and held a sign that read "Army Wife."

But Brad was not at the march with him; he had left DC the day before and was with his unit getting ready for war. By October 16, he was in Kuwait making preparations to cross the border into Iraq.

7
Shakoosh

"It's not gore, it's principle."

—Bradley E. Manning

orward Operating Base (FOB, pronounced "fahb") Shakoosh
appeared in a desolate patch of the Mada'in Qada, the southeastern portion of Baghdad province, forty miles due east from
the capital, during the violent spring of 2007. The region was a lattice-
work of hostility. Shia' insurgents in Moqtada al-Sadr's Mahdi Army
and Sunnis under the banner of al-Qaeda in Iraq targeted occupying
American forces while waging civil war on one another in a triangle
of violence that inflicted chaos upon the population of 1.2 million in
the area. Like other suburban areas encircling the Iraqi capital—the
"Baghdad Belts"—the Mada'in Qada had become a refuge and staging
ground for the various forms of insurrection that arose against the
US-led occupation. Following implementation of the Bush administration's "New Way Forward in Iraq," the strategic shift known commonly as "the surge," FOB Shakoosh was positioned at the empty
center of a handful of urban areas to secure the surrounding territory and thus Baghdad itself. In a matter of months, the once-empty

moonscape became a grid of dirt roads and tents surrounded by a large sand berm topped with concertina wire. Rumor among the troops held that the FOB's given name offended the local population, *shakoosh* being the Arabic word for "little hammer" and supposedly carrying an explicit connotation.[1] After the army completed construction, it renamed its new FOB "Hammer."

By October 2009, the Mada'in Qada was a relic of the battleground it had been. Violence across the country was down by 90 percent, and the rocket attacks that tormented FOB Hammer with "deadly accuracy" during the peak of American casualties in 2007 were now both rare and inaccurate. The FOB had developed into a more permanent settlement, a self-contained ochre world of plywood and aluminum, with shipping containers and low-lying buildings to house and supply up to four thousand soldiers. In the desolate sands fifteen miles from any major population center, FOB Hammer was a relatively safe outpost with a perimeter roughly equivalent to the distance of half a marathon, arising in an empty plain with lines of sight extending to the horizon.

Still, the carnage in Iraq was far from over. On the afternoon of October 25, 2009, a pair of bombings in Baghdad killed more than 150 people in the most deadly attack since 2007. Later that evening Brad Manning, waiting in Kuwait to make the final leg of his deployment journey, signed online and sent a message to Danny Clark. In days he would arrive in Iraq.

"At a staging area in Kuwait," he typed. "Starbucks Internet hotspot =P. It's how America fights its wars these days... =) ."

"Lols, you have Starbucks everywhere," Danny said. "Pikans are enjoying the fact you're in a Starbucks in Kuwait."

"Wait until they find out I'm at the Starbucks at FOB Hammer," Brad said.

---

1. An unofficial survey of Iraqi Arabic speakers indicates that shakoosh translates simply to "hammer" and carries no explicit connotation. If the name was offensive it seems attributable to the oppressive connotation of the word *hammer* rather than anything sexual.

"FOB Hammer?"

Brad gave his address. "That's my addy. Spread it around. Care packages welcome =P (especially Cambridge/Harvard/MIT items)."

They discussed the mechanics of how they could keep in touch during Brad's deployment and searched around online for free-as-in-freedom video chat software. Brad gave Danny his new e-mail address.

"Should we worry about encrypting things?" Danny asked, concerned about discussing gay-related topics while Brad was deployed under Don't Ask, Don't Tell.

"Not at all," Brad said. "Monitoring systems is technically infeasible. It's just military/government scare tactics. There's very little monitoring in place. That which is in place, is in place on those who are deemed a credible threat already," Brad said. Still, he'd be careful about what pictures and information he posted on Facebook, sent in e-mails, and so on. Security remained a concern. "130+ civilians died in Baghdad this afternoon (its 8 hours ahead)," he said, "so it's not exactly over or anything."

"Yeah, I heard this morning. It's disturbingly easy to become inured and just take stuff like that for 'normal' news."

"Going to be working on what happened tonight," Brad said. "Trying to figure out who, what, where, why, etc. And what it means for us now that we own 1/3 of the city, soon to be 1/2." Brad said he had to leave to grab some food.

"Be well," said Danny. "Glad I have your email now. I'll set up that program for later."

"Ok. Remember, send me stuff, preferably small tidbits, reminders of those who support me, etc. The weirder, wilder, or harder to find the better."

"Will do, Sir!"

"Ttys [talk to you soon]. Manning out!"

■ ■ ■

By October 29, Brad Manning's unit had arrived at FOB Hammer. Brad was surprised by how wet and cold the Mada'in Qada could get at night—he'd arrived in Iraq at the outset of the rainy season, after the temperature had dropped precipitously from the scorching summer months to the cool desert winter. Brad moved into his CHU (Containerized Housing Unit, pronounced "choo"), a shipping container separated into three separate rooms, and his war against the dust began at once. In his room he kept an iPod touch, his personal Macbook Pro, a microphone for video chatting, an external hard drive, and writeable CDs. His roommate, an enlisted army MP named Eric Baker, was openly homophobic and established early on that the two were not going to be friends, but their interaction was limited to requests like "turn off the light" and they never had any substantial conversation.

The sand at FOB Hammer was particularly fine-grained—soldiers stationed there called it moondust—and the persistent winds across the wide-open landscape conspired with the trucks moving in, out, and around the base to keep the dust clouds circulating. Exacerbating the air quality problem were the burn pit at the southern end of the FOB where trash of all varieties was incinerated, producing noxious fumes, and the smokestacks at brick factories in the town of Narwhan to the north, which emitted steady black plumes that seemed always to hover low over the ground in the area. The smog and stench lent an otherworldly feel to the outpost.

"One could easily feel stranded there," Dennis Carnelli, a soldier deployed with the brigade that built FOB Hammer, wrote in an e-mail, "as there were few (if any) terrain reference points and a bevy of former Iraqi military buildings, usually bombed out or falling apart, dotting the entire interior of the base. But for the 'surge' objective, it is likely that there would be limited, if any, human activity in the desert where Hammer was built."

Every so often a soldier at the FOB would commit suicide—multiple deployments and protracted wars had caused the suicide rate in the army to skyrocket, surpassing the rate in the civilian world in 2008. The suicides were greeted by most on the base with a mix of resignation and annoyance. The phone and Internet connections would be shut down for days at a time to prevent news of the death from leaking out before an investigation could be completed and the family notified. With long periods of boredom to fill, thousands of miles from friends and loved ones, these connections to home were precious.

Brad's first weeks at war in a hostile foreign land, thousands of miles from the futility of training and drills in army discipline in the safety of New York or Louisiana, were an adventure. Brad was feeling optimistic. He told Danny he'd been approached by the army's new cyberwarfare unit, a pioneering new unit based at Fort Meade dedicated to waging cyberwar under the then-under-formation United States Cyber Command—the Pentagon had recently acknowledged the online domain as a potential battlefield. Working out of Maryland, Brad could be near DC, the city he loved, enroll in college part time, and get experience working with the National Security Agency; maybe he'd stay in the army at the end of his enlistment after all, he thought.

Workdays at FOB Hammer were long and often tedious. Brad started his deployment assigned to the night shift, which started at 10 PM and lasted at least twelve and up to eighteen hours. He worked in a Sensitive Compartmented Information Facility (SCIF) with a conference room to one side and a main room with rows of computers surrounded by plywood walls covered in maps stuck with pins like pockmarks. From a workstation with two SIPRnet computers that he shared with a soldier who worked the day shift, Brad was putting his skills and substantial talents to use in the real world. As an all-source analyst in the S-2 fusion cell on the Shia' threat team, he was tasked with digesting huge amounts of information on Shia' insurgents. Using the raw data he mined from SIGACTS, as well as human intel from interrogators, imagery intel from satellites, information from the signals intel team monitoring cell phone and other communications traffic, and more, he used Excel spreadsheets and other computer tools to crunch numbers and find patterns in enemy activity. Concerned that the fusion cell was too narrowly focused on local events, a higher-up in Brad's company e-mailed the analysts with a link to the Net-Centric Diplomacy database and a suggestion to explore the non-password-protected repository of State Department communiqués. With his findings Brad would prepare "products"—often PowerPoint presentations—for officers, who depended on the information to make important decisions.

The SCIF was more secure in name than in reality. Any computer with a red cord coming out of it, it was widely known, was connected to SIPRnet, and though not everyone had official access to SIPRnet, those who did commonly kept a sticky tab on the side of the computer with the username and password for the machine. No one was supposed to be inside the SCIF without a reason to be there, but the regulation was regularly flouted. "I would go over there and hang out, whenever I wanted, just to say hello, even though I didn't work there anymore," said one soldier who worked with Brad Manning at FOB Hammer. Though the rules forbade anything personal from being inside the SCIF and called for strict control of data storage devices, in reality soldiers routinely moved data on unlabeled writeable CDs, which were often left scattered haphazardly in the main room. During shifts soldiers listened to music stored on their SIPRnet machines, watched pirated movies and played computer games stored on the shared hard drive, all against regulations.

The physical security of the Pentagon's information systems was excellent throughout most of the network. SIPRnet access was restricted to discrete sessions on unique computers with disabled USB and CD drives. But in the grand scheme of the Defense Department's organizational structure the FOB was effectively on the front lines, and the needs and wants of the moment, more than regulations implemented back in Washington, DC, dictated who had access to what computers. Information that was strictly protected at the Pentagon and on major military bases around the world was uniquely vulnerable at an outpost like FOB Hammer.

Brad's unit's primary focus was on preparing for Iraq's March 2010 parliamentary elections, upon which American hopes for democracy in the country hinged. But his activities weren't restricted to FOB Hammer's Area of Operation. He bragged to Danny that he played a small part in the November 2009 seizure of assets in the United States, which controversially included property occupied by four mosques of a foundation believed to be linked to the Iranian government. By mid-December Brad had been promoted in rank to specialist. It was a promotion based on tenure, but he was no less prized in the unit as the soldier most skilled with computers and lauded for his talent for deriving actionable information from large data sets. Though automatic, the promotion was still indicative of a young man doing his job to satisfaction.

The day-to-day reality of his responsibilities as a low-level analyst for the world's biggest employer (the United States Department of Defense), however, was fairly mundane. Much of the work done on the night shift was simply completing the day shift's unfinished tasks. Often, his job was simply to "take slides from subordinate battalions, change wording, improve spelling, replace battalion symbols with brigade symbols, disseminate throughout brigade and forward to division," he wrote. "Leaves a computer savvy guy a lot of time to pry around."

There were aspects of the job with which he was becoming uncomfortable. In training, abstractions like "enemy" and "ally" can appear simple and obvious, to be taken for granted. Intelligence analysis becomes routinized—information in, information out. But his experiences in the first weeks of deployment revealed a level of ambiguity, and a gravity, for which his training hadn't prepared him. In one instance, the Iraqi Federal Police had arrested fifteen Iraqis for spreading "anti-Iraq" propaganda, but the police weren't cooperating with the Americans, who wanted to know more about the what prompted the arrest. Brad was tasked with investigating and found that the supposed propaganda was a legitimate article tracing the corruption trail in the cabinet of Prime Minister Nouri al-Maliki. Brad hurried to a superior with the information—the Iraqi Federal Police were sometimes torturing captives—but, by his own account, Brad was told to "shut up and explain how we could assist the [federal police] in finding more detainees." In another instance an army unit, operating on information Brad provided, ambushed a suspicious meeting in Basra, and someone only tangentially connected to the meeting was killed in the operation. Brad felt a gnawing guilt. The reality of warfare, even in intelligence analysis, Brad found, wasn't as sanitary as it had seemed at Fort Drum.

Brad Manning was not the first soldier to reflect on the inherent uncertainties and difficulties of gathering and analyzing military intelligence. In *On War*, the nineteenth-century Prussian soldier and military theorist Carl von Clausewitz was speaking more to an analyst like Brad Manning than to a combat infantryman when he observed, "The general unreliability of all information presents a special problem in war: all action takes place, so to speak, in a kind of twilight, which like fog or moonlight, often tends to make things seem grotesque and larger than they really are." This and other selections from *On War* in its various translations have been conflated over time into the phrase "the fog of war," often used to describe the hectic and confusing nature of combat. But for Clausewitz, the fog of war was a strategic dilemma for the commanding officer and those who provided his information. On his deployment, Brad almost never left the FOB—when working, he rarely even left the SCIF—but the grim magnitude of the decisions he made every day, life-and-death determinations based on imperfect information, was present in his mind to a degree incongruous with his position far from the actual battlefield.

Life at FOB Hammer was a pressure cooker for the army's macho culture. Troops came and went from patrols through semi-hostile territory, and the occasional mortar rained down on an empty spot in the FOB, but the days of heavy combat were long gone. A malaise hung over the base, as soldiers spent long hours fending off boredom, playing video games; trading contraband pornography; playing volleyball, football, or baseball in the large open spaces; or standing around computers connected to SIPRnet watching "war porn," the often gruesome aerial attack video made suddenly ubiquitous in the digital era. For Brad, who wasn't included in the army camaraderie, the aimless hours were intensified.

In the cauldron of hypermasculine army life, Brad began questioning his gender. Whether attributable to a legitimate gender identity crisis or to a subconscious reaction to the blustering and aggressive expressions of masculinity that surrounded him, Brad took his feelings seriously. Not long after arriving in Iraq, he got in touch online with a gender identity counselor. He let loose a torrent of emotional unrest, blending his gender struggles with his morally conflicted feelings about the war in which he was now engaged. "I feel like a monster," he wrote.

■ ■ ■

On November 25, 2009, WikiLeaks published a massive database of messages sent on September 11, 2001, to the pagers of journalists, FBI and Secret Service agents, and officials from FEMA and the Pentagon. In real time, posting each message concurrent with its time stamp, WikiLeaks recreated the events over the twenty-four-hour period following the attacks. Brad, the voracious news consumer, took note. He recognized immediately that the pager messages were from a National Security Agency database. It was at this time, around Thanksgiving, that Brad Manning began reaching out to Julian Assange. WikiLeaks, it was clear, was dealing with legitimate, high-level sources.

On November 28, 2009, Brad was logged on to his SIPRnet computer when he searched Intelink-S—a search engine on SIPRnet—for the phrase "retention+interrogation+videos." This is the first record of a search done on his computer related to WikiLeaks. The phrase is consistent with what was, at the time, listed on the WikiLeaks website as one of the Most Wanted Leaks of 2009: "CIA detainee interrogation videos. While the CIA claims to have destroyed 92 of the videos, others are known to remain." The next day Brad searched the phrase again and, on November 30, almost certainly after first soliciting the information from WikiLeaks, he received a brief and impersonal message from the group: "You can currently contact our investigations editor directly in Iceland 354 862 3481, 24 hour service: ask for Julian Assange."

On December 1, for the first time recorded on his work computer, Brad searched Intelink for the keyword "WikiLeaks." From that day through the following spring he would search for the word at his workstation 119 times. On that first search, he turned up the

March 2008 counterintelligence report in which the army outlines its strategy for defeating WikiLeaks: "Successful identification, prosecution, termination of employment, and exposure of persons leaking the information."

Brad did not immediately begin leaking, or even collecting, classified information, but these first few weeks of December are when he got serious about turning his data mining skills to the task of finding information of interest to WikiLeaks. He searched for key phrases like "WikiLeaks" and "Julian Assange." Brad's first search for documents relating to JTF-GTMO, the military task force for extracting information from prisoners at Camp Delta in Guantánamo Bay, Cuba, occurred on December 8.

On December 18, Brad sent a message to Danny online. It was early in the morning in Boston, before sunrise.

"Good timing," Danny said, "giving a friend a ride to Logan this morning. What's up? Same as yesterday? ;-) ."

"Haha, >punch< =P ," wrote Brad. "I need to talk to you some time. Securely of course."

"Of course. I'll prepare the cone of silence. Oh I can go on Skype, I don't think we've got that working yet," Danny said.

"Can't, roommate is asleep."

"Just one roommate? Could be worse. By default I imagine a warehouse-like space filled with scores of less-than-twin sized 3-level-high bunk beds."

"Lol. Not quite. I'll take some pics at some point."

"Yeah that'd be cool if it wouldn't get you, you know, court martialed. By secure you mean like OTR plugin [Off the Record, a method of digital chat encryption] to Skype?"

"I mean secure as in TORified or in person," Brad said.

"What time is it for you over there? 1:14 p.m. is right?"

"Indeed. That's the correct time, Mr. Clark."

"Yes Sir, Private Manning."

". . . Specialist," said Brad, noting his recent promotion.

"Ah, k. How far away are you from [meeting in person] at the moment?"

"I don't know yet."

"Sanity-o-meter doing okay?

"I think sanity has dwindled drastically," Brad said.

"Ah, now that'll drive you insane :-p ."

"You familiar with TOR?" said Brad. "I don't trust these local national computer networks."

"Yes, [the Free Software Foundation] runs a node, but I think GnuPG or OTR [both methods of digital encryption] would make more sense. Perhaps combined with TOR for the super-paranoia-mode," Danny said.

"Sounds like a plan. We'll work it out. Email me the details."

"Cool. You have GnuPG key up on keyserver for your gmail?"

"Gmail not safe," Brad said.

They would sort details out later. Danny had to run out the door to get his friend to Logan in time for a flight. "Ttys! Happy holidays!" he said.

"Same to you," said Brad. "^_^ Merry Festivus."

Danny got to work preparing a care package for Brad. He'd already sent a postcard, which Brad had received, but now he had a bigger collection of items to mail, including the first three volumes of Neil Gaiman's ten-volume graphic novel series *Sandman*, the stress management standard *The Relaxation Response*, a few articles on managing PTSD, and an original Game Boy with Tetris—he had read that the classic video game was supposed to help ward off PTSD. Also included was a yellow paperback copy of *Free Software, Free Society: Selected Essays of Richard M. Stallman*, signed by the author. Stallman's note to Brad, according to Danny's recollection, was short and to the point: "Fight for freedom any way you can."

Later that evening, Brad showed up to work forty-five minutes late. He'd been chronically late throughout the deployment, and his supervisor, Specialist Daniel Padgett, had finally had enough. Though not yet a noncommissioned officer, Padgett was assigned by Sergeant Adkins to serve as the NCOIC (Noncommissioned Officer In Charge) of the night shift of the S-2 fusion cell. Due to his rank, Padgett lacked clear authority over Specialist Manning in the chain of command and had to receive special permission from Adkins to counsel the truant soldier.

On December 20, Brad was late again—he was preoccupied with something in his CHU. When Brad arrived at work Padgett took him into the SCIF's conference room, where they sat down on either side of a table to discuss Brad's inability to show up for work on time. Padgett explained to Brad that his "Commando Day," the one day a week he had off, was taken away until further notice, and he was required to report to Padgett's CHU in uniform every evening before work at 9:15 PM.

Brad, who had sat quietly through Padgett's admonition at first, suddenly began screaming. In a blind rage he stood up from his chair, gripped the table, and flipped it over, sending a computer sitting atop it crashing to the ground. Padgett put his arm on Brad's shoulder and tried to calm him down. Hearing the commotion, another soldier entered the room. To him it seemed Brad was about to lunge after the M-4 rifle hanging on the wall. The soldier grabbed Brad from behind and drew his arms up, locking his fingers together around the back of Brad's neck in a full nelson hold. Brad finally calmed down and worked for the rest of his shift.

The incident was clearly indicative of a young soldier dealing with serious psychological and emotional stress. Several soldiers, including Showman, who had been in the main room of the SCIF and rushed to see what the commotion was about, reported what had happened to Sergeant Adkins. Though many felt the event warranted a derog—a derogatory remark in a security clearance file—and that Brad's access to sensitive information ought to be rescinded, no action was taken.

■ ■ ■

Brad spent hours rooting around for interesting information in the classified networks to which he had access. He'd always been motivated by an instinctual inquisitiveness, and the secret truths revealed in classified reports he read were fascinating. He was, by now, disillusioned with aspects of the American occupation—not an uncommon state for American soldiers in Iraq in 2009—but he was not an antiwar ideologue. Brad was a ravenous consumer of information, and what seems to have troubled him was the information gap between what he read in the news and what he saw as an intelligence analyst.

One video Brad found was aerial footage of the US strike on the Afghan village of Granai, in the western province of Farah. Due to what the Pentagon labeled "some problems with tactics, techniques and procedures," a May 4, 2009, bombing campaign left scores of civilians dead in what human rights workers called "the worst episode of civilian casualties in eight years of war in Afghanistan," according to a report on the incident in the *New York Times*. Among the between 20 and 140 dead (the total death toll is disputed on several fronts) were a large number of children. The Pentagon has never released the Granai video, and it has thus never been seen by the public, but one can imagine that watching it might be gut-wrenching for someone who has read the civilian accounts of children's bodies ripped apart in the explosions.

On a Centcom server at MacDill Air Force Base in Tampa, Florida, Brad found the video with other documents from the Pentagon's fact-finding investigation into the attack. The video had been scheduled for release in mid-2009, but at the last minute the Pentagon declined to make it public.

This video is the first classified document Brad Manning sent to WikiLeaks. The particulars of the leak are unclear but completing the task would have been quite easy. It seems that around New Year's, Brad used his SIPRnet computer to burn a CD with the Granai strike video and the entire file on the investigation, which he then copied onto his personal Macbook in his CHU. By clicking a simple link on the WikiLeaks homepage—the phrase "Submit documents"—a menu popped up on the screen through which, as when attaching a document to an e-mail, he could select what file on his computer's hard drive he wanted to upload. On January 8, 2010, WikiLeaks tweeted, "Have encrypted videos of US bomb strikes on civilians [link to

Wired.com story about the airstrike controversy] we need super computer time [dead link]." The group was never able to decrypt the file and thus the video was never released.

Perpetrating this first leak would have required astoundingly little deception. Soldiers regularly left the SCIF carrying burned CDs with classified information to be shared with their Iraqi allies. And to have an aerial attack video—"war porn"—playing on one's computer screen in the SCIF was perfectly ordinary.

Indeed, Specialist Showman was being trained by a superior to be a target analyst, and as part of her professional development, she and a number of other soldiers gathered around computers to watch and discuss such videos. One clip in particular was watched several times over and became a topic of some discussion in the SCIF.

The footage is black and white, shot from a camera mounted on an AH-64 Apache helicopter flying high above the ground in a nearby southeastern suburb of Baghdad. The helicopter has been called in as reinforcement following a firefight between Americans and the Mahdi Army.

The camera scours the Baghdad skyline, zooming out over the city at first as the pilot searches for the zone where the fighting was taking place. Eventually, the camera locates a group of men walking down the street, some carrying weapons. The gunner on the helicopter receives permission to engage and opens fire, kicking up dust in a flurry of bullets fired from the Apache's chain gun, sending the men running for their lives. When the dust clears, bodies litter the ground. A man tries to crawl to safety and is cut down in a storm of gunfire. A van arrives to collect the wounded, and it too is shredded in a torrent of 30 mm caliber bullets designed to decimate vehicles, armored and otherwise.

Brad found the GPS coordinates and date of the incident, plugged them into Google, and found a headline from the *New York Times* glaring back at him: "2 Iraqi Journalists Killed as U.S. Forces Clash With Militias."

A bit more research down the rabbit hole—this was the kind of research Brad did for fun (and, not incidentally, for a living)—and he found that Reuters had been trying since 2007 to acquire a copy of the video under the Freedom of Information Act. The Pentagon denied its request, arguing that the video could not be released because it was classified. Then, in September 2009, *Washington Post* reporter David Finkel published a book that included an account of the attack. Finkel's recounting gave the impression that he'd watched the unreleased video, though Finkel would not confirm that he'd seen it. By accident, Brad had stumbled into the midst of a minor scandal. The government had a secret it refused to share with the press, though, as Brad could see, the secret didn't seem to include anything about ongoing operations. What Brad did see in the video, once he had some context, was a violent attack on a group of people who seem basically harmless in which a group of civilians, including children, are slaughtered. The video showed an "airstrike on Reuters Journos, some sketchy but fairly normal street-folk, and civilians," Brad would later say. The video was, crucially, merely embarrassing. And yet the army refused to let the public see it, despite the ongoing controversy about what exactly happened in the attack. Brad closed the video, but he filed the memory away.

Brad made a key decision on January 5, 2010. On this day he began downloading 400,000 SIGACTS from the CIDNE Iraq database, the reports that would one day come to be known as the Iraq War Logs. This was a decisive move, perhaps more important even than his earlier leak of the Granai video. The 400,000 SIGACTS from CIDNE Iraq represented his first en masse, nondiscriminating leak of classified information. He followed it up on January 8 by downloading 91,000 SIGACTS from CIDNE Afghanistan. The next day, he wrote a brief text file labeled "Readme." It was apparently a message to the intended recipient: WikiLeaks.

> Items of historical significance of two wars Iraq and Afghanistan Significant Activity, Sigacts, between 00001 January 2004 and 2359 31 Dec 2009 extracts from CSV documents from Department of Defense and CDNE database.
>
> These items have already been sanitized of any source identifying information.

You might need to sit on this information for 90 to 180 days to figure out how to best send and distribute such a large amount of data to a large audience and protect the source.

This is possibly one of the most significant documents of our time, removing the fog of war and revealing the true nature of 21st century asymmetric warfare.

Have a good day.

Brad moved the data to his personal computer and stored the files on an SD card (the kind of storage device used in many digital cameras). He did not, it appears, immediately send the information to WikiLeaks. It remains unclear when exactly the data was sent, but the possible time range includes the period Brad spent on leave in the United States. He may have saved the data and sent it to WikiLeaks from the United States, perhaps with help from friends, though no evidence has ever been produced to support the allegation. There is no indication that anyone at WikiLeaks knew the group was in possession of the logs until months later, though this may have been due to a backlog of submissions in their system.

The timing of Brad's early leaks is significant for two reasons. He'd been in Iraq for about a month when he began exploring the possibility of leaking state secrets and had apparently sent his first leak—the Granai video and related documents—by early January 2010. This, importantly, was before his return to the United States. There is no evidence that he required external inspiration to seek out Assange or any assistance from friends to download data and transmit it to WikiLeaks. Second, his initial interest in leaking came at a time when he was under significant pressure as an all-source intelligence analyst in Iraq but before the repeated episodes of profound emotional and psychological breakdown that began in mid-December and continued until his arrest. Incidents extending back to the spring of 2009 at Fort Drum, and farther back into his adolescence and childhood, revealed a person prone to manic outbursts. But the total psychological unraveling that began to manifest itself in December 2009 occurred in tandem with, not directly prior to, the leaking. This timeline would become essential many months later as the public sought to understand not just what Manning had done, but why he had done it.

Just as he was beginning what would become a several-month-long spree of leaks, the pressure was ballooning inside Brad's mind. Long workdays in the plywood box had become more arduous since he lost his one day off a week. He'd been talking to Tyler, and he'd begun to understand how differently the two saw their relationship. He agonized over his gender, which he'd come to feel was absolutely programmed female, even if the hardware was infuriatingly male. And he'd by now made the irrevocable decision to violate his security clearance by leaking the Granai video and downloading nearly half a million SIGACTS destined for WikiLeaks.

In the melodramatic myopia of young adulthood, thousands of miles from what small support network he had, Brad's emotional turmoil merged with the terrible reality of what he saw as an intelligence analyst in Iraq. The mystery was deeper, he believed, the tragedy more profound, than anyone knew. In his own mind, he was a fly on the wall in the central command of American foreign policy. In less tormented moments he was prone to measured analysis with shades of gray, but in this moment, on the morning of January 14, 2010, after a long shift in the SCIF, his world—his *whole* world—seemed to be tearing itself asunder. He felt abandoned by his friends and family, his country, the army, and by his love, Tyler. Brad had been building a home among friends in DC and Boston, in his identity as an intelligence analyst, in his boyfriend, and in a hopeful future as a veteran with a Top Secret security clearance. Now, one piece of home after another was collapsing in the twenty-two-year-old's frantic, heartbroken psyche. His life was cascading, it seemed, back into insignificance.

Brad signed online and sent a message to Danny.

"Hey," he said. It was two in the morning in Boston, and Brad got no response. He posted a status update to Facebook: "Bradley Manning feels so alone." Two hours later Danny responded to his message.

"*yawn*," Danny said. "Morning, EST."

"I know silly."

"Just getting back to your 'hey' from a few hours ago."

"I'm lost," Brad said.

"In Iraq? That's not good :-(I thought you were supposed to find people!"

"Figuratively. I don't know who I am, where I am, what I want."

"Ohhh in a metaphysical sense," Danny said.

"I'm tired. And alone."

":-(."

"And hopeless."

"Well the obvious hope is you are out in, what, one year and nine months?"

"No, it doesn't matter. I'm finally drowning. I have a bank account and social security number, nothing more."

"Dude, you are a great person and at least the alone part will pretty much instantly go away when you are back in the states, and will have a ton of time to post-process it, and many people to talk with when you get home." Danny hated seeing his friend so distraught and didn't understand where this was all coming from. He'd seen Brad upset, but not like this.

"No. I've seen too much, figured out too much. I can't seem to wiggle out, even just enough to breathe. No one has enough time to understand, and I can't find enough time to take a breath of fresh air."

"Please don't be afraid to share disturbing details with me; my uncle was a MD in Iraq. I doubt it could get more disturbing than his stories."

"It's not gore, it's principle."

Danny apologized for being out of touch. He'd left his position at the Free Software Foundation to start his own business, Freedom Included Inc., a consulting and customization firm, to infuse free software ideals into systems administration. He'd be around to chat more often from now on, he said.

"I've lost a lot of hope," Brad said.

"In humanity in general?"

"Indeed. Everybody is so busy scrambling to survive, and I'm wedged in the middle of this mess. I'm merely just a pawn in this game, like everyone else. They've run me into the ground."

Danny searched for a way to comfort his friend. "It would probably be lacking in wisdom to make overall judgments of humanity based on a war zone," he said. "In any case, care to share some incidents, or is this mostly the stuff you've shared with me before?"

"There's too much. I've tried putting on paper, but there's too much, and not enough time. I don't know what I'm coming home to. I don't know what home is."

"People here are mostly oblivious."

"I know."

"That hasn't changed."

"Indeed. I didn't want it to be this way."

"Have you considered an anonymous blog? Might be therapeutic."

"I've tried to avoid it. There's no such thing as anonymity. It doesn't matter what I do, I can't seem to win anything, let alone protect what little I have. I fell in love with Tyler, which was dumb, but I couldn't help it. But he doesn't have a clue. He says he does, but is no different from anyone else—oblivious. I'm overwhelmed."

"I would think anyone of good conscience would be."

"My past attempts at trying to put together a life, the ones I keep making every day—but I always end up in someone's pocket, and thrown out like nothing."

"But you shouldn't confuse what you do have with what you are likely to get. You seem to not have been lucky with a starting position in life, but your course seems very likely to become easier in a few years."

"What makes you say that?" Brad asked.

"You are smart, cute, a good person; once you have a job or are getting an education and have a stable location, I see no reason why you wouldn't quickly accumulate lots of friends, more close friends, and a boyfriend who respects you."

But Brad would not be consoled. "I'm incredibly lost. People want to help me, but they don't know how. And those who do try and intervene push me closer off the edge. I can't find stability. I'm about to crash right now and I don't know how bad it's going to be."

"Other than going AWOL to Canada or something it seems like at the moment there isn't much to do other than wait, but if you ever want to Skype or need anything please ask. Also I really hope to hang out with you when you get to the US."

"I'll try," Brad said. "No one has a clue. Everyone only sees a tip of the iceberg, not realizing how big it is. But I'm pretty damn hopeless right now. I don't know what I want anymore. I'm not suicidal but I've certainly thought about putting my hands up and refusing to be someone's bitch, say exactly what's on my mind."

"With regard to commanding officers?"

"Officers in general. My head hurts."

Danny continued offering solace. "What, edited for legality, would you like to tell some officers?" he asked, offering his friend an outlet for frustration.

"I'm fed up with everything: personality differences getting in the way of the job at the micro level; living under a policy that leaves me unable to talk about my problems, and effectively being punished for not saying anything at the micro level; keeping important information out of the public sphere at the macro level; being betrayed by congress, the public and the president at the macro level over freedom I'm supposedly fighting for at the macro level; being completely unable to know who I am, and being so psychologically compartmentalized for survival at the personal level. The pressure builds and builds and builds, and I'm surrounded by it 24/7 =L ."

"Well I guess if it really gets to be completely unbearable you do have an out—purposefully getting discharged. Also, have you looked into orgs that help people in your situation? I would think something must exist."

"They suck. They're just as bad, and getting discharged is damaging. Especially how I would do it. I wouldn't keep it under the rug. No matter how hard they tried to keep it quiet. I've kept in contact with journalists."

"That would be a positive in the eyes of some employers/colleges."

"True, but I'd also be broke and in more debt."

"You could try to find a college that would give you a scholarship. In some ways I wish I was still with IBM; I'm really not in a position to help financially at the moment."

"Lol." Brad finally laughed, if only virtually. "I'd spend another few months here, and then face a board when we got back, so it wouldn't solve much. I'd probably get out at the 3 year mark in October."

"If you want to share a shopping cart, refrigerator box, and under-bridge steam grate, I'm there! ;-) ," Danny said. He talked excitedly about his new business venture, but Brad quickly refocused the conversation on his own problems. "Hmm. I wish my life were nice and simple," he said. He was in a self-centered spiral of angsty depression. "I've got all this .gov.mil mess around me =(."

"Eh, you'd get bored, just like me."

"It's my own fault. I wish I had a boyfriend I could come home to, and maybe even settle down with."

"So stuff with Tyler is :-(?"

"He's 'dating,' so we talk, but I got too hopeful."

"Your life situation has always just been tough, but your decisions are hard to dispute."

"How so?" Brad asked him.

Their conversation continued in much the same vein over the next twenty-five minutes, Danny trying to encourage Brad with reminders of the life that awaited him outside of the army, Brad, in a fit of exhaustion, nurturing his own sadness. Finally, around 3:30 PM in Baghdad, Brad went to sleep.

■ ■ ■

Brad was lying on the ground at Baghdad International Airport on the evening of January 22, 2010. He was on his way home and, at the moment, chatting online with Danny through the rather mundane occurrence of a far-off mortar attack, which at this point felt more like a duck and cover drill than a defensive maneuver amid enemy fire.

"All clear sounded, and internet stayed up," Brad said. "Shia extremists target our bases, but don't aim to hit, they just aim at empty lots. They're playing a dangerous game." His mood was greatly improved from the fit of depression just days before. "They're trying to make the locals think that they are driving America out of Iraq . . . while also not blowing us up and keeping us here longer."

Danny invited Brad to an MIT party happening that Sunday, but Brad said it was doubtful he could make it. His long trek home was on an uncertain schedule, he explained, and he had a couple errands to take care of in DC before heading up to Boston to visit Danny and Tyler.

The two chatted for a while about Tyler. Brad missed him and wondered how he was—Tyler, it seemed, was going through personal drama of his own but keeping Brad fairly distant. "He's vague about our relationship status," Brad said. Still, Brad was feeling better about the relationship, as well as life in general.

Brad told Danny that his commander was trying to get him into West Point. It was a long shot, he knew, but the school had a marvelous reputation, and Brad didn't mind the idea of spending several extra years in the army as an officer. Hell, maybe he would take the education and use Don't Ask, Don't Tell to his own advantage, like Dan Choi did, he said. Out of the doldrums of depression, the old Brad was back, bold and audacious as ever.

He continued on the subject of Dan Choi. "Great West Point program, then deployed, cushy job during the toughest deployment of the war, forced into position where he had to be a captain or go national guard, went national guard and then outed himself. He was basically given free college, an easy job during an infamous unit deployment—my unit, 2007—and great national publicity. Bastard," Brad said, cheekily. "You want to know what he actually DID?"

"Maybe not over insecure channels (?)," said Danny.

"Sat in a bunker all day, signing paperwork. Hey, I do that. Except, inside of a tin and plywood building. If a rocket makes a direct hit I'd be shredded to pieces by wooden shrapnel," Brad said. "Everyone knows what he did at his unit, but god he was smart. Yet, not bright like me. I'm beyond sinister. I'm after the presidency. End DADT? Fuck that. I want to live in the most bumpin' house in DC."

"=P - bumpin' ?" Danny said.

"I think were going to be ok, me and Tyler. I think we'll be ok =) ."

":-) ."

8
Collateral Damage

Keith Rose walked into room 328 on the third floor of the Sha-
piro Student Center at Brandeis University and saw Tyler Watkins surrounded by a group of friends—chatting, effusive, very
much the leader. Tyler was the pride coordinator for Triskelion, the
umbrella group for Brandeis University's LGBT/queer community.
Sitting alone and sullen in the corner of the room was Brad Manning.
When Keith caught Brad's eye, the young soldier, back in the United
States for a brief respite from Iraq, lit up immediately.

The two met the year before at a dance in Boston. The first time
Keith saw Brad he was grinding erotically with Tyler, carefree on the
dance floor. Keith sat next to Brad in the back of the bus on the way
back to Brandeis after the dance that night, and he asked Brad the
question that often came up when Brad told people he was enlisted.

"I asked him why he would be in an organization that had committed atrocities, that had discriminated against gay men and dis-
respected atheists, and the first thing he said was that he wanted to
serve his country and, you know, be a soldier. And he also said that
he wanted the benefits—I mean, you can go to school afterward on
the GI Bill."

Brad was just trying to impress him, Keith figured, when he
started talking about the access to privileged information he had as
an intelligence analyst. "If you had any idea what goes on over there,"
Keith recalled Brad saying, "you would certainly be against the war."

On this cold evening in late January much had changed since their first meeting. Brad had experienced the stresses of life as a soldier in Iraq. Away from the strictures of military life he had tried out life as a woman. Wearing a dress, a wig, fake breasts, and a turtleneck to cover his prominent Adam's apple, he went out in public in Washington. He stopped at a gas station to buy cigarettes and went to two of his favorite establishments, Starbucks and McDonald's. "The first thing I learned was that chivalry isn't dead," Brad would later write. "Men would walk out of their way and open doors for me." He even rode the train from DC to Boston in female dress, and, despite a few speed bumps when he had to show his driver's license, he felt at ease living as a woman.

When Brad arrived in Boston he could see that his relationship with Tyler wasn't as he'd left it. At the Triskelion meeting, Brad was sulking in quiet disappointment while his boyfriend—or the guy he'd thought was his boyfriend—was entertaining others. This was not the homecoming he'd expected after making the several-day trip from Baghdad to Kuwait to Germany to Atlanta to Washington, DC, and finally to Boston. Here he was, a war hero on an all-too-brief visit to the man he loved, and Tyler, it seemed, could hardly be less impressed. When Brad saw a friendly face enter the room he was elated.

"So I walked up to Brad and sat by him and asked him what was going on. He was really depressed and said he didn't really understand where he was in this relationship," Keith said. "Tyler was in the middle of Boston, and he's really a social butterfly, and he was surrounded by all the fish in the sea, whereas Brad was in the middle of Iraq."

For Tyler, the relationship was all but over, but actually breaking up with a soldier on deployment was a step too far; Tyler let the issue fester, stringing Brad along, and Brad wasn't getting the message. "You have to realize that Brad's situation was a lot more desperate than Tyler's," said Keith.

While Keith and Brad talked in the corner, Tyler and the others started playing a game, and the noise grew too loud for a conversation. Brad and Keith left the room and sat together in the atrium of the building. "He gave me a two-hour earful of all the things in the relationship that he just didn't understand. He felt really bad that he had been gone in the military and he came back and he didn't have his relationship anymore. So it was kind of like an e-mailed Dear John letter."

It was in this spirit that Brad called Danny on Wednesday afternoon, January 27, after a fight with Tyler, to ask if he wanted to hang out. Of course he did, Danny said, but he'd already committed to attending the open house of a new hackers club his friend David House had started at Boston University. Should be an interesting night, Danny said. He was giving a few friends a ride to the event, and he suggested Brad meet him there.

■ ■ ■

David House arrived to a wintry Boston in January 2008, with two suitcases and a chip on his shoulder. Boston University was just across the Charles River and a short walk over a snow-covered bridge from Cambridge and his dream school, MIT. Leaving behind his life as a movie theater projectionist in Florence, Alabama, he scrounged together the money from parents and scholarships and enrolled at BU at midyear, but he pined for the world on the other side of the river.

In his first semester he focused hard on his classes in geometric and algebraic algorithms, Russian literature, and introduction to Arabic. He got a position as a research assistant and spent the summer of 2008 learning to write code by doing it as he constructed a computer program to track in-vitro cell growth. A hacker who'd worked for years saving money and taking classes in order to make it out of northeastern Alabama and into an elite university, David was living at a fevered pace to avoid returning home a failure. His enthusiasm clashed with the indolent culture he found at BU.

"So I started coming here, to MIT, and I met kids who are just eccentric, like fire in their eyes, like, 'Free software! And here's why!'" David said.

With new friends, he embarked on urban adventures through buildings abandoned and otherwise. He climbed around the exterior of

MIT campus structures, explored underground tunnels, and sneaked into abandoned factories. It was real-life, real-time, urban hacking, and exactly what he'd been looking for: "This manic energy [at MIT], of passion and overcoming, which, to me, was really in line with how I got here."

David's life was bifurcated. His classes and his residence were in Boston, but his passion—his ambition—was on the north bank of the Charles, in Cambridge and the pioneering creativity of MIT. In the spring of 2009 he sought to bring the two worlds together.

"My subversive goal was actually to infect BU with this free software and hacker culture," he said, "but the teachers will get upset with me if I call it the Hacker Club. So I'll call it the ACM." The Association for Computing Machinery, or ACM, is a respected computer science society with chapters for students and professionals all over the world. But David never registered BU's ACM chapter with the official organization—as far as he was concerned, the name was a front. In reality, the club would be a place to nurture hacker culture at BU. In its first meeting, David gave a lesson in lockpicking to the few who came. At later meetings, as the gatherings grew in size, they talked about topics as practicable as finding security vulnerabilities in BU's student ID assigning algorithm or as abstract as figuring out the amount of plywood it would take to build a roller coaster.

While working on a project in the backyard of pika, David was introduced to an older young man named Danny Clark who, though he did not live at pika, was an important and often-present member of the community. Danny suggested to David that he might apply for pika's summer residency program—be a "summer random" in colloquial pikan. David lived at pika over the summer of 2009, and he was inspired by the experience to take the culture of unchecked creativity further once he was back at BU for the semester.

But the ACM lacked a space its members could devote to hackish pursuits. In fall 2009, the club secured an unused and untidy room in the basement of the computer science building, with permission to paint the walls, cause a racket, and generally make a mess. David and others in the club set out to build, in secret, their university's first hacker space: BUILDS, short for "Boston University Information Lab & Design Space." Work began immediately to prepare the space for an open house in January 2010.

■ ■ ■

Brad made the several-mile journey with his large camouflage backpack from Brandeis into Boston proper. After a frustrated search around the BU campus he got further directions from Danny and finally found the computer science building and the BUILDS open house in a room in the basement. It was a kooky affair and just what he needed amid the tension with Tyler.

The space had been transformed from a leaky, unwanted cavern into a hacker haven, and when Brad walked in it was buzzing with creativity—David House called it "a nexus of energy." Mural art, paintings, and LED lights covered the walls. There were tools and electronics of all sorts strewn about tables and four network server towers in a corner next to open computers where one and all were encouraged to code, play, explore, whatever. Eric Schmiedl, a friend of Danny's from TOOOL, the Open Organization of Lockpickers, did a presentation on ethical lockpicking. Representatives from the Free Software Foundation gave a talk about free software ideals. The entire evening was a coming-out party for the hackish scene at BU. David loved the wild eccentricities in Cambridge, the MIT hackers with fire in their eyes. With his help, the fire had finally jumped the river.

In part, the night was a celebration of the long effort to create a space for hackers at BU in both cultural and temporal terms. David's hacker-front club, the ACM, had created controversy on campus long before the night of BUILDS's open house. Shortly after founding the club, David and friends acquired two thousand Boston University student ID numbers and posted them online, without names or other identifying information attached. The idea was to crowdsource the hack to find security weaknesses in the ID-assigning algorithm. And find a weakness they did—the numbers were not as anonymous, according to David, as most students believed. It was, at heart, a classic gray-hat hack. The stunt drew the ire of the administration and earned ACM the attention of a cowboy boot–wearing information security expert. Eventually the authorities were convinced of the BU hackers' good intentions, and all parties to the dispute made peace.

On opening night David was in the limelight. In a hacker space of his own creation, surrounded by other creative types, he moved around the room like a frenzied gentleman hacker, wearing a black T-shirt, damp with sweat, and a black top hat cocked back on his head. He was pulled in different directions, but when David talked to someone he gave them his full, engaged attention. When, amid his humming around the room, a very short friend of Danny Clark's was introduced to him, he stopped to talk.

Danny introduced Brad Manning to David House, and the two exchanged pleasantries. Over the course of the brief conversation, Brad dropped the hints—jargon and subtleties—to indicate that he was at home in this culture. It was clear to David he wasn't a hacker, just a guy who had some familiarity with computers and information security. The talk was short, pleasant, and forgettable.

After the event, Brad piled into Danny's car with two other friends of Danny's. He and Eric Schmiedl had a brief if interesting conversation about their mutual interest in cryptography before Danny dropped Schmiedl off at MIT. The group then stopped by pika to hang out and have dinner. Later, Danny drove Brad to the Amtrak station. They said good-bye, and Brad walked toward his train, lugging an oversized backpack with a Velcro "Manning" nametag on his small, lean frame, en route back to Tyler's place at Brandeis. As Brad disappeared into the building, Danny looked on. In not too many days Brad was heading back to Iraq, but Danny was mostly worried about the same thing Brad was: the relationship with Tyler. Brad was helplessly caught in act three of a relationship that he never wanted to end. It was the last time Danny and Brad saw each other outside of a brig.

To make it easier for them to communicate securely about DADT-sensitive issues like Brad's relationship with Tyler and his conflicted gender identity, Danny helped Brad set up a GnuPG key, the GNU project/free software equivalent of PGP. An acronym for Pretty Good Privacy, PGP is an encryption system that includes a personalized, public "key," a unique series of characters associated with a particular e-mail address used to authenticate a person's identity over the Internet. Brad and Danny had already switched to encrypted chatting, and PGP would allow them to communicate via encrypted e-mails when the other wasn't sitting at the computer. In the end, Danny and Brad hardly used PGP at all. "The only thing I remember him sending using PGP was that 'test' picture of himself in DC in male-to-female dress," Danny said.

Shortly after Brad got back to Washington, the first inches of the blizzard the media would dub "Snowmaggedon" began falling on the capital. With electricity out across the region and transportation in frozen gridlock, he waited out the last days of his deployment quietly at his aunt's house. On February 8, just before leaving DC, he wrote on his Facebook wall: "Bradley Manning is hopefully returning to his place of duty over the next few days."

■ ■ ■

After their speaking engagement at the Chaos Computer Conference in Berlin, Julian Assange and Daniel Domscheit-Berg returned to Iceland in early January 2010. Though WikiLeaks' website was still offline, the group was operating at the same furious pace as before. Living out of a crowded apartment on the fourth floor of a monolithic, gray Reykjavik hotel near the harbor and working out of rented warehouse space used by local activists, the team organized support for the proposal to turn Iceland into a haven for transparency. The close living quarters and frenetic working pace were straining personal relationships in the group, principally that between Domscheit-Berg and Assange.

On February 4, 2010, after being on strike since December the year before, WikiLeaks announced it had met its minimum fundraising goal of $200,000. The next day, Domscheit-Berg left Iceland, alone. "Before I completely lost my shit, I booked a flight home," he wrote. He continued working remotely with Assange and others, but he wouldn't see Assange in person again.

Two weeks later, on February 18, the group published its first leaked document since the strike, a diplomatic cable written by the American chargé d'affaires, Sam Watson, whom Assange had met at the Reykjavik cocktail party in December. The cable described the American embassy's role in negotiations among Iceland, the United Kingdom, and the Netherlands over demands that the Icelandic government reimburse British and Dutch citizens for the money they lost in the collapse of Landsbanki bank's "Icesave" program during the global financial crisis. The release caused a minor stir in Iceland and helped shore up the Icelandic people's support for the transparency movement at a crucial time just days before a first-step parliamentary vote on the Icelandic Modern Media Initiative.

Assange left Iceland for a brief trip through Scandinavia, including a stop at an investigative journalism conference in Oslo. During the trip he determined he was being tailed by US agents and said so publicly on Twitter. By the time he returned to Iceland in late March, the Eyjafjallajökull volcano had begun spewing ash into the atmosphere which would create a noxious cloud over a swath of the Northern Hemisphere and disrupt global travel patterns for months. Back in Reykjavik, Assange rented a small, century-old cottage blocks from the cold North Atlantic waters of Faxa Bay under the pretense of being a journalist there to document the volcanic eruption. The house became WikiLeaks' chaotic headquarters while the group worked on a its latest venture, codenamed "Project B"—a grainy, black and white video of a 2007 Apache helicopter attack in Baghdad. *New Yorker* writer Raffi Khatchadourian spent a week at the Reykjavik house working on a profile on Julian Assange, in which he described the scene: "The house, as far as he was concerned, would now serve as a war room; people called it the Bunker. Half a dozen computers were set up in a starkly decorated, white-walled living space. Icelandic activists arrived, and they began to work, more or less at Assange's direction, around the clock."

■ ■ ■

The temperature around Baghdad bottoms out in January and quickly begins its steep rise to the searing summer heat. By the time Brad returned to Iraq in mid-February his roommate had gone on leave and he had the room to himself. He began an accelerated bout of data mining and leaking over the spring. On February 14, immediately after his return, he downloaded the army counterintelligence report on WikiLeaks that he'd come across during his first Intelink search for the group's name the past December. He uploaded it to WikiLeaks that day, though it didn't appear on the website until a month later. On February 15, Brad sent WikiLeaks a single diplomatic cable dealing with the Icesave fiasco. Known as Reykjavik-13, the document had been purloined from the State Department's Net-Centric Diplomacy database to which Brad had access through SIPRnet. The same day, he sent WikiLeaks the July 12, 2007, Apache airstrike video that would one day be known as "Collateral Murder." WikiLeaks tweeted on February 21 that the video file had been decrypted.

On March 5, Brad attempted unsuccessfully to download a group of documents related to the military prison at Guantánamo Bay, Cuba. The following day he installed a program called Wget onto his computer. A product of the GNU Project easily procurable for free online, Wget is a barebones data mining tool, allowing the user to automate the downloading of large amounts of information. Using the program's command line interface (recall the pre-graphical user interface world of MS-DOS) requires some facility with computers. Brad set up a system whereby Wget helped him procure the Guantánamo files. On March 8 he succeeded in burning them to a CD and transferring them to his personal computer before uploading them to the WikiLeaks site.

Having erased his hard drive in the meantime, on March 27 Brad downloaded Wget again. Beginning the following day and working in irregular spurts during his shifts over the next week and a half, he downloaded well over a quarter million records from the Net-Centric Diplomacy database. The bulk of these documents would later be published by WikiLeaks under the project title "Cablegate." Spanning from December 28, 1966, to February 28, 2010, Cablegate did not include all of the cables Brad purloined from the Net-Centric Diplomacy database. He'd continued downloading cables, albeit less intensively, up to May 3, but the files dated after February 28 became corrupted and were never released. The downloading of such enormous quantities of data had created problems with his computer.

Note that some of the first leaks Brad Manning perpetrated—the SIPRnet documents—represented the sort of en masse leaking that Julian Assange had prescribed for the world when he created WikiLeaks. Though in some cases Brad picked out certain files for leaking, like the combat videos and the Pentagon memo, very soon after he decided to become a whistleblower he began carrying out leaks of unprecedented scale. Brad was outraged by much of what he saw in Iraq, but he departed early on from the whistleblowing tradition of leaking particular pieces of damning information. Instead, inspired by his outrage, he leaked massive troves of secret information. As he said in the early message to WikiLeaks, the Iraq and Afghanistan SIGACTS were "historical documents" intended to help dissipate "the fog of war" and reveal "the true nature of 21st century asymmetric warfare." The target of his actions was not, in the end, individual people or policies. It was secrecy itself.

While the complete story of Brad Manning's communications with Julian Assange has yet to be revealed, bits of detail about them can be inferred from the information available. Brad would later describe aspects of the relationship. "I'm a high profile source," he wrote, "and I've developed a relationship with Assange. But I don't know much more than what he tells me, which is very little." Brad describes communicating directly with Assange via OTR encryption and says Assange offered him a job with WikiLeaks, which he declined. After first making contact with WikiLeaks shortly after Thanksgiving, Brad took months to ensure that the person he was communicating with over the Internet was indeed Assange. Verification of the WikiLeaks chief's identity finally came only after the Reykjavik-13 leak—Brad describes intensively questioning Assange about the surveillance he was under by American officials during his travels in Scandinavia while they tried "to figure out how he got the Reykjavik cable."

Investigators later found at least fourteen pages worth of chat logs between Manning and Assange. Only snippets of the logs have been made public.

"Anyway I'm throwing everything I've got at JTF Gitmo at you now," Manning said in one exchange, communicating through the OTR client Adium under the moniker "Nobody." "Should take a while to get up though."

"Ok great," replied "Nathaniel Frank," presumably an alias of Assange's. The Wikileaks chief apparently chatted with Manning under two different handles, dawgnetwork@jabber.ccc.de and press association@jabber.ccc.de, both hosted on the server of the Chaos Computer Club in Berlin.

"Upload is at about 36 percent," said Manning.

"ETA?"

"11-12 hours guessing since it's been going 6 already."

During a chat that took place on March 8, it appears Brad asked Assange for help in cracking the password on his SIPRnet computer in order to browse the classified network anonymously. "Any good at [LAN Manager] hash cracking?" asked Manning.

"Yes," said Assange. "We have rainbow tables [for cracking LAN passwords]."

As *New Yorker* writer Raffi Khatchadourian noted in a blog post a year after his Assange profile was published, Brad Manning told Adrian Lamo during their chats, "*New Yorker* is running a 10k word article on WikiLeaks on 30 May, by the way." The article had yet to be published or publicized, and Khatchadourian did not interview Manning for the piece—the only reasonable explanation for his knowledge of the piece is that someone at WikiLeaks, presumably Assange, told him. Additionally, the Reykjavik-13 cable was released amid intensive negotiations regarding the Icesave scandal and just weeks before a key national referendum on the issue, all while the WikiLeaks cadre was working hard to create momentum for the Icelandic Modern Media Initiative. While it is not outside the realm of possibility that Brad Manning unilaterally chose to send Assange a single diplomatic cable that addressed issues central to the Icesave dispute, including the upcoming national referendum, a bit of nudging from Assange to Manning during their tentative early stage online chats is at least as likely.

The question of how much and what kind of communication occurred between Brad Manning and Julian Assange is not a merely academic point. In the American legal tradition, media outlets in the past have been protected from prosecution for publishing state secrets so long as they are the passive recipients of leaks. If an organization is found to have solicited or helped facilitate a leak it may be held liable, having crossed the thin but sheer line between publishing a leak and helping perpetrate one.

Nothing in the record indicates decisively that Assange directed Manning in the leaking of documents, though it is possible that some such thing took place. One can more confidently surmise what Brad must have felt during his conversations with Assange. It's easy to imagine the young private, isolated at an army post in the Iraqi desert, lonely, and upset about his experiences in the war, talking with starry eyes to the already somewhat-famous rebel, Julian Assange. For such a young man, with so little of his own in the world, to have the ear and the interest of a celebrity like Assange must have been exhilarating—and in equal measure, perhaps, intoxicating.

By April, Baghdad is often more than 90 degrees Fahrenheit and the winter moisture disappears rapidly. As the days grew warmer and drier, the sands around FOB Hammer more scorching with every sunrise, Brad Manning's emotional state deteriorated even further.

"I remember my primary emotions," Danny later wrote, "being concern about his ability to get through his service combined with a pretty firm belief that he'd slog through it and be much happier going to college somewhere in around a year and a half (which probably seemed much closer to me than it did to him)."

"What I kept hearing over and over and over was that he couldn't survive, he wasn't going to make it through, he wasn't going to make it out," said Jason Edwards, "and I kept repeating to him, 'Just get through this, this will end, you'll get out of there and your time of duty will be over.'" Jason interpreted Brad's messages as a cry for help and potentially suicidal. He would return to the computer to find the troubling messages Brad left for him while he was away. But Jason was by now in a new relationship and emotionally invested elsewhere. The friend he and Brad had in common, Toby Quaranta, was also in a serious relationship and hadn't spoken to Brad in many months. For many of the people to whom he considered himself closest, Brad Manning was out of sight, out of mind.

"The last thing I really remember Bradley saying to me," Jason said, "was on AOL Instant Messenger, and he said, 'You're going to hear some news that's going to shock the world.' I don't recall any conversations after that."

■ ■ ■

On April 5, 2010, Julian Assange held a press conference at the National Press Club in Washington, DC, steps away from the White House. Standing behind a lectern, wearing a dark brown blazer and a bright red tie over a black shirt, Assange gave the public its first viewing of the aerial video footage of the Apache helicopter attack over Baghdad that killed two Reuters journalists in 2007. The footage had been edited significantly from the raw video Brad sent WikiLeaks more than a month earlier. Cut down to nearly eighteen minutes and titled "Collateral Murder," it had been given additional flourishes, like a George Orwell quotation at the opening and introductory text that highlighted the presence of children among the victims and identified the targets of the attack as civilians. Assange told the reporters that the leak of the video "sends a message that some people within the military don't like what is going on."

Public reactions to the video were predictable and extreme. WikiLeaks' allies insisted it showed clear evidence of war crimes, while the Pentagon and its defenders criticized WikiLeaks for presenting an image of combat "as seen through a soda straw," in the words of Defense Secretary Robert Gates. As is often the case, the truth was more difficult to sort out than the impassioned parties on either side would admit.

Long before the video was released, the Pentagon had conducted an internal investigation that concluded the unit in question acted properly. Yet the video evokes troubling questions.

After the first attack, the gunner in the Apache is eager to kill an injured man who is trying to crawl to safety—the man, not incidentally, turns out to be the journalist Saeed Chmagh and not a combatant at all. "All you gotta do is pick up a weapon," says a voice in the video while crosshairs hover over Saeed. Killing a combatant who has surrendered or is no longer a threat due to injury is illegal under the rules of engagement. Willfully targeting a noncombatant is a violation as well—most societies call it murder. But Saeed wasn't identified as a journalist, and the soldiers in the helicopter mistook his camera for a rocket propelled grenade, which, importantly, can be used to take down Apache helicopters. In a revealing moment, the gunner on the Apache, bound by the rules of war despite an obvious desire to rack up another kill, does *not* fire on Saeed as he's crawling on the ground.

The Apache then reports that a van has arrived to "pick up the bodies." Another voice over the radio confirms the van is "picking up the wounded." The Apache requests permission to engage.

Under the Geneva Conventions, it is unlawful to target those caring for wounded combatants, without regard for allegiances. However, the assumption in the treaty, which was first put to paper while the American Civil War was still raging, is that medical personnel are identified as such. The minivan in the July 12, 2007, Apache attack is a common, unlabeled van. Inside were a little girl and a little boy on their way to school.

The Apache helicopter receives permission to fire on the van and strikes. A sudden barrage of bullets tears into the vehicle as the driver throws the van into reverse and slams into a building before coming to a stop.

After the Apache attack, ground forces arrived on the scene, and Specialist Ethan McCord ran to the van. Inside he saw the little girl, four years old, with an injury to her stomach, and the eight-year-old boy with wounds covering his body. McCord, who would later speak out in support of whoever had leaked the video of the attack, rushed the two children to safety. The children survived their injuries. Saeed Chmagh and others were killed in the attack.

Defense Secretary Gates defended the Apache units. "They're in a combat situation. The video doesn't show the broader picture of the firing that was going on at American troops. It's obviously a hard thing to see. It's painful to see, especially when you learn after the fact what was going on. But you talked about the fog of war. These people were operating in split-second situations."

This is indisputable. WikiLeaks' edited version of the video gives the impression that a helicopter, unprovoked and largely for sport, has attacked a group of innocent civilians. But the record shows that the area had been the site of raging gunfights all day long. Though by no means conclusive evidence that the men killed were combatants, the weapons found at the scene, which included RPGs, at least vindicate American troops who thought they were dealing with hostile forces.

Disagreement about exactly what happened in Baghdad on July 12, 2007, and the legal and moral implications of those events, will probably never be resolved to everyone's satisfaction. Nonetheless, two truths can be gleaned in reflecting on the leak of the Apache video and the debates that followed.

First, more was gained than lost with the public airing of the video. There were no vital secrets revealed to the enemy and no tangible damage done to the United States or its allies as a result of the leak. But the debates the video provoked placed the Iraq War, and fundamental questions about the nature of modern warfare, at the forefront of the national conversation. If only briefly, an American public that had largely stopped thinking about Iraq was confronted with gruesome images that made urgent again the grave life-and-death questions that the soldiers we task with fighting our wars confront in the course of a day's work.

Second, what damage the video did to the prestige of the United States was a direct result of the lack of publicly available information about the day's events. The grainy and short video was indeed, to paraphrase Secretary Gates, a view of the July 12 attack as seen through a soda straw, but when WikiLeaks posted it online, it was also the only view of the attack available to the public. The absence of more information allowed the impression to take hold for many that the Americans targeted unambiguously harmless civilians in an otherwise peaceful neighborhood, rather than suspected enemy soldiers amid a daylong bout of combat. The Pentagon's unwillingness to release the video for two years despite Reuters' repeated requests generated a cloud of suspicion. When the video revealed no essential secrets, it was doubly damning.

The video gave the American public a glimpse of the cold and awful nature of modern warfare being conducted at its behest—the United States is, after all, a democracy. It would not have been unreasonable for the Pentagon to have released the video immediately, noting that war is ugly, the American military is strong, and this sort of mistake happens when it is tasked with defeating an urban insurgency. But a culture of secrecy prevented the Pentagon from doing so, instead moving reflexively into a cover-up. Ultimately it was secrecy, not the video, that, in this instance as in many others, tarnished the reputation of the Pentagon and the country it serves.

Back in Iraq, Brad was exhilarated by the airing of "Collateral Murder."

"He would message me, 'Are people talking about it? Are the media saying anything?'" said Tyler Watkins. "That was one of his major concerns, that once he had done this, was it really going to make a difference? . . . He didn't want to do this just to cause a stir. . . . He wanted people held accountable and wanted to see this didn't happen again."

At FOB Hammer, CPT Casey Martin, an intelligence officer who oversaw Brad's unit, watched the "Collateral Murder" video online. Martin liked to engage her troops on current events—especially Private Manning, who was more interested than most—and in mid-April she started a discussion with the group about the video's release.

"I asked the group if they had seen the video, because obviously it does not make the military look very good, how that affects us in an environment," she later said. "[Private Manning] came up to me and said he thought it was the same video from the share drive. I said no way, that's not the same video, it's definitely shorter in duration from what I saw."

To prove to her that the video was the same as the one that SPC Showman had been watching on her computer in the SCIF, Brad sent CPT Martin an e-mail with a link to the original video file in the shared drive in SIPRnet next to a link to the video online. It was reckless and brazen—Brad was acting as though he wanted to get caught.

Two days after releasing the "Collateral Murder" video, WikiLeaks posted to its Twitter feed: "Raised >$150K in donations since Mon. New funding model for journalism: try doing it for a change." In forty-eight hours the organization had raised almost as much money as it had during the month and a half spent on strike. The tenor of the tweet is revealing. After going on strike for lack of support, Assange and company had their swagger back, flush with new secrets. Nearly every document WikiLeaks had published since the strike was provided to them by Brad Manning—and the biggest cache of all was yet to come.

Meanwhile, under the pressure of leaking secrets, being socially isolated, and struggling with a gender identity crisis, Brad was unraveling psychologically.

According to an army investigation, portions of which were provided to the *Washington Post*, Brad Manning "started to exhibit 'bizarre behavior' at work, including showing 'blank stares when spoken to' and stopping in mid-sentence." The odd behavior only "increased in 'frequency and intensity' and gave 'an impression of disrespect and disinterest' to his superiors." Brad was advised by his superior, Master Sergeant Paul Adkins, to visit the chaplain—Adkins, who had been worried about sending Brad to Iraq back in August the year before.

On the evening of May 7, at around 10:00 PM just before shift change, Sergeant Adkins found Brad huddled on the floor of the SCIF's storage room. He was sitting upright in the fetal position next to a chair, with a knife at his feet. The vinyl of the chair had been cut repeatedly spelling out the words "I want." When Adkins asked

Brad if he was all right, Brad told Adkins he felt like he wasn't there, like he had no personality. He described his inner self as an onion, with layer upon layer concealing his core identity. SPC Showman, who saw Brad curled in a ball speaking with Adkins, commented to her superior, "Be ready for something to happen again," as she later recalled.

Later that night Brad was at work playing a game on a computer in the SCIF. An officer had been looking through the computer system for an intelligence product she needed but couldn't find—Brad helped her look for it but he couldn't find it either. The one person who would definitely know where to find the report was SPC Showman, who was then asleep in her CHU after a long shift at work.

Showman was tired and irritated at having been woken up when she walked into the SCIF around midnight. She saw Brad playing a computer game and became furious. Showman started berating Brad for goofing off on a computer game while she had to be roused to locate a file he couldn't find. Brad told her to calm down but the argument rapidly escalated and Brad lashed out. Surprising both himself and Showman, he punched her in the face, whereupon the much stronger woman body-slammed Brad to the ground.

"I'm tired of this! I'm tired of this!" Brad started screaming, pinned beneath the much brawnier woman on top of him. "I'm tired of everyone watching!" he yelled.

Thereafter, all artifice of stability in Brad's life disintegrated. The brigade psychiatrist diagnosed him with an "occupational problem and adjustment disorder with mixed disturbance of emotions and conduct," and recommended he be discharged. Command had the bolt removed from his rifle and demoted him from specialist back down to private first class.

Brad broke down in an e-mail to Sergeant Adkins, trying to explain the cause of his distress: he was a woman struggling to exist in the physical and social confines of life as a man. "This is my problem. I've had signs of it for a very long time. I've been trying very, very hard to get rid of it," he wrote. He'd thought joining the military would help but it hadn't. "It's the cause of my pain and confusion, and it makes the most basic things in my life very difficult." He was terrified, he wrote, of being found out and punished. "It makes my entire life feel like a bad dream that won't end." He closed the letter with a sort of apology. "Everyone's concerned about me, and everyone's afraid of me. And I'm sorry."

Brad was reassigned to work in a supply room unconnected to the SCIF. In switching from intelligence to logistics work his duties became significantly more humdrum. He was untrained in logistics work and at the bottom of the chain of command. Where he once analyzed enemy activity, he now spent his days moving boxes. But the supply room was also outfitted with a SIPRnet computer, and, despite the demotion and his manifest emotional instability, he'd still retained a TS/SCI security clearance. And Brad wasn't done helping WikiLeaks just yet.

The day of his altercation with Specialist Showman, WikiLeaks posted the following to Twitter: "We would like a list of as many .mil email addresses as possible. Please contact editor@wikileaks.org or submit." They were asking for all of the military e-mail addresses they could get. Using the SIPRnet computer in the supply room, Brad used Microsoft Outlook to gather as many military e-mail addresses as he could. He eventually collected thousands, though it seems he was never able to send the addresses to WikiLeaks.

Brad continued communicating with Danny regularly in encrypted online chat. Though he had a loyal friend in Danny, Brad's loneliness was a void too large for one friend to fill. He tried to call Jason Edwards on the telephone but got no answer. He tried Toby Quaranta, also without success. He called up his old friend Jordan Davis, but Jordan missed the call. As he had done in the past with Zach Antolak and Danny Clark, Brad sought out a sympathetic ear in a stranger online.

He'd sent a Facebook friend request in mid-March to Jonathan Odell, a Minneapolis-based novelist who has written about growing up gay in conservative, deeply religious Mississippi and whose Facebook presence is a running log of progressive political commentary. On May 9, Brad joined hundreds of Odell's friends in wishing him a happy birthday with a public post on his Facebook wall. He also sent Odell a private message.

Brad told Odell he had a story that needed to be told in book form. Odell asked if it was about being gay in the military. Through Brad's Facebook wall he could see the soldier's very public descent into heartbreak. In the space of two hours on April 30, Brad had put up a series of brazen Facebook posts: Bradley Manning "is utterly lost and confused over Tyler's relationship status"; Bradley Manning "feels much better =)"; Bradley Manning "is now left with the sinking feeling that he doesn't have anything left . . ."; and, "Anyone want to be my official 'next of kin'?" The next day: Bradley Manning "is livid: first lectured by ex-boyfriend despite months of relationship ambiguity; then personally attacked by uncle over 'ex-"boyfriend"'—with scare quotes—and 'lifestyle.'" Days later: Bradley Manning "is beyond frustrated with people and society at large." Then: Bradley Manning "is not a piece of equipment."

No, it was much bigger than that, Brad said. Facebook, he said, "doesn't even touch the surface." According to Odell, Brad said he'd been involved in some "'very high-profile events,' albeit as a nameless individual thus far."

"He was highly dramatic," Odell wrote later, "and doing a very public display of his broken heart, crying out for consolation from anyone." Odell never heard from Brad again.

On May 19 Brad sent an e-mail to Eric Schmiedl, the lockpicker he'd met during his visit to Boston months earlier. Though most of their exchanges were PGP encrypted, this bit mistakenly was not. Later, it would be uncovered by investigators.

"Are you familiar with WikiLeaks?" Brad asked.

"Yeah, I am," Schmiedl said.

Brad responded, "I was the source of the 12 July 07 video from the apache weapons team which killed the two journalists and injured two kids =l"

■ ■ ■

Near the end of his senior year of high school, in Florence, Alabama, David House was with friends in the back of a bookstore flipping through a copy of *2600: The Hacker Quarterly*. His friend, Margaret, was curious. "Who are the great hacker names?" she asked him.

"Well, there aren't really any great hacker names," he said, reflecting that most computer hackers use aliases. "But the public ones are, you know, Kevin Mitnik," the world's most famous fugitive hacker. He continued flipping through the magazine and came to a reference to an occasional contributor, Adrian Lamo, the "homeless hacker," who'd been recently prosecuted for breaking into the *New York Times*' network. "Adrian Lamo," he said next.

"Oh God!" a voice behind him gasped theatrically. He turned and saw his friend Michael, tall and looming over David's thin, blond-headed frame.

Michael explained that several years earlier, he'd met Adrian Lamo in an online chat room. They started talking frequently and quickly became friends. When Adrian ran into trouble with the law, the FBI came to school one day and pulled Michael out of class for an interrogation. Since that time Michael and Adrian had been in intermittent contact, sometimes communicating through intermediaries.

Michael asked David to pass a message on his behalf, a word document with a recipe for gingerbread cookies and, after scrolling down several blank pages, a note to Adrian. David complied and e-mailed Adrian Lamo the document.

David's e-mail piqued Adrian's interest, and he wrote back. "Who are you?"

■ ■ ■

Adrian Lamo grew up in Boston, San Francisco, and the DC suburb of Arlington, with a short stint in Bogotá, Colombia, in his early teens. In high school he started phone phreaking, using tones and various devices to manipulate the telephone system, but it was generally a lonely time for the budding hacker. He eventually dropped out and got his GED. He worked briefly in the San Francisco LGBTQ non-profit world and then hit the road, beginning life as a nomad.

Unlike many hackers, Adrian was not a programmer. While traversing the country, crashing on the couches and floors of friends and, when necessary, abandoned buildings, he'd use the web browser on computers at Kinko's copy shops for his hacking sorties. Rather than manipulating code, his hacks involved guesswork and cleverness. Adrian exploited plain-sight vulnerabilities in a corporation's network architecture—like obvious, standard-issue passwords—to penetrate the internal systems of such firms as Yahoo!, MCI WorldCom, and, most infamously, the *New York Times*. It was this last exploit that finally ended his career as a hacker.

Adrian was a vigilante thrill seeker operating in the ethical borderlands, the archetype of the gray hat hacker. He didn't hide his identity, and he always alerted his victims to the vulnerabilities he exploited, sometimes even helping them patch the hole, as it were.

But to say he did no harm misses part of the picture. After hacking into a secure network, like MCI WorldCom or AOL, he had a practice of publicly announcing the intrusion, humiliating network administrators. He never stole money (and he could have), but he surreptitiously edited news stories on Yahoo!, adding false information, effectively committing vandalism.

In the hacker world, the homeless hacker had become a beloved, if mythologized, character. Ed Soulkis, a computer security expert quoted in a 2003 *SF Weekly* profile by Matt Palmquist, put it best: "In the computer underground, he's very well-regarded," he said. "He's sincere, passionate, smart, with a good track record. Getting in and getting out without getting busted—wow. And the thing that stands out about Adrian is that he's very open about the fact he's breaking the law. I don't want to get into his head, but he seems to think he's OK because he follows the spirit, if not the letter, of the law. And you know what? Maybe there is some validity in the way Adrian does his thing, because his targets don't seem to disagree."

His reserve of charm didn't last forever.

After penetrating the *New York Times'* internal network in 2002, Adrian added himself to the database of op-ed contributors and made off with private information—social security numbers, addresses, and phone numbers—of high-profile contributors to the *Times'* op-ed page. As before, he announced the hack to the world. He contacted Kevin Poulsen, a convicted-hacker-cum-journalist at *SecurityFocus*, and told him about the hack. Poulsen called the *New York Times* to confirm the story.

Unlike Adrian's past targets, the *Times* was neither amused nor grateful. Whereas WorldCom opted to praise the hacker for notifying them of the gap in their security, through which the private networks of WorldCom's clients, including Bank of America, CitiCorp, and JP Morgan might have been compromised, the *Times* chose to prosecute. In the end, Adrian was sentenced to six months of house arrest and two years of probation with restricted computer use and saddled with $64,938 in restitution, to be paid in monthly installments of 10 percent of his income.

The once-brazen hacker was humbled by his confrontation with the law. In federal court he spoke with contrition about his actions.

"Since all this started, I have had a great deal of opportunity and time to see many of the effects of the things that I have done, how they have harmed the companies that I compromised, how they harmed me, how they harmed my family, how really they have harmed so many people around me," he said. "I've hidden behind a facade of words in some of the statements that I have made and some of the things that I have said, and for me really it's been an alternative between seeming flip or walking around in constant gloom," Adrian said. "This is a process I want no further part in. I want to answer for what I have done and do better with my life."

Adrian had long used pharmaceutical drugs to help fuel his adventures, online and otherwise. (In 2001, he overdosed on amphetamines.) "Substances that disassociate you from your senses have played a big part in my life," he was quoted as saying in 2003. "Drugs are not an indispensable part of my life. But there are times when I'd rather stay up until the next bus comes instead of curling up and finding my backpack gone when I wake. There are times I don't want to feel the pain." In the aftermath of his downfall, he became depressed, and his drug use accelerated. In addition to a cocktail of antidepressant, antiseizure, and antipain meds, he took powerful antianxiety medications, Xanax and Lorazepam, sometimes hitting up friends for drug money.

The years after his conviction were quieter than those preceding it. As a condition of his court-ordered rehabilitation from a life of hacking, he enrolled at the American River College, in Carmichael, California, where he studied journalism until 2005. Having become famous for his crimes and martyred by his trial, he spent the last half of the decade cashing in on his reputation, but his hacking days were over. He worked occasionally as a journalist, gave media interviews as the famously fallen homeless hacker, and worked as a threat analyst helping private companies identify vulnerabilities in their computer systems. He got married and divorced and, as always, maintained relationships with old friends and reached out to new ones online—people like Nadim Kobeissi, the founder of the ethical hacking net-work Anapnea, and David House.

In 2009, Adrian joined a group of computer security experts operating since 1996 under the name Project Vigilant. According to the group's founder and director, Chet Uber, the ultra-secretive legion of hundreds of volunteer professionals monitors web traffic for 250 million IP addresses in the United States, compiling and analyz-ing data on potential threats (much as the NSA does with interna-tional communications) as a kind of vigilante domestic intelligence agency. Serious questions about the group's legitimacy notwithstand-ing—due to its self-imposed secrecy virtually everything known about Project Vigilant comes exclusively from Chet Uber, and some in the cybersecurity industry have wondered if the suddenly famous group isn't a publicity stunt—Adrian developed a personal relation-ship with the director.

While volunteering with a group of ostentatiously patriotic cyberdefense vigilantes, Adrian was also a keenly interested fol-lower of WikiLeaks' progress. He donated money to the transparency activists and even became a source in one of the stranger episodes in the organization's brief history.

In February 2009, Julian Assange hurriedly e-mailed a list of fifty-eight former WikiLeaks donors, asking them for more money, but he forgot to put the e-mail addresses in the "bcc" (blind carbon copy) space. Instead, he e-mailed the entire list of donors with their e-mail addresses visible to every recipient. Testing the mettle of an organization with a stated dedication to radical, equal-opportunity transparency, Adrian Lamo leaked the list of donors back to WikiLeaks. Presented with a leak of its own internal secrets and a promise to provide a platform for whistleblowers without regard for ideological bias, WikiLeaks dutifully published the leak of its own donor list.

Though he left his criminal past behind, Adrian never gave up his itinerant ways. He traveled regularly and widely, visiting friends across the United States. On one such sojourn, in late February 2010, mere weeks after Brad Manning's visit to Tyler and Danny, Adrian Lamo arrived in Boston with a friend. While in town he intended to connect with a number of friends, including David House. Though they'd never met in real life, years had passed since their first virtual meeting, and they had become friends chatting online. David was looking forward to meeting his famous, and by now old, friend.

While working on a project at BUILDS one evening, David got a call from Adrian. He headed out in the frigid February night to find Adrian and his friend sitting beside the BU Bridge, which spans the Charles River connecting Boston to Cambridge. According to David, Adrian stood up and waved and then stumbled through traffic as he walked toward him. His speech was slurred. To David, he seemed seriously intoxicated. The meeting was brief and underwhelming.

Adrian Lamo's drug use was by then a matter of record, but it had fluctuated significantly over time, and early 2010 was a period of particularly high usage. His abuse of prescription pharmaceuticals got so bad that, in April, his father called the Sacramento County sheriff's department three times in three days to tell them his son was over-medicating. Adrian was subsequently arrested and spent nine days involuntarily committed to a psychiatric ward. On May 7, he left the hospital having been diagnosed with a mild form of autism known as Asperger's syndrome.

Geek syndrome. Engineer's disorder. Asperger's sufferers tend to be physically and socially clumsy, have difficulty interpreting social cues or expressing empathy, and exhibit sustained, intense focus on narrow minutiae, like sports statistics, weather patterns, or, as is often the case, computer code. Unlike more severe types of autism, a person with Asperger's is generally high functioning in most areas of life; there is substantial overlap between the syndrome's symptoms and mere eccentricities. The 1990s and 2000s saw an explosion of Asperger's diagnoses, particularly in techie hubs like Silicon Valley where nerds were meeting, and, one can surmise, copulating with other nerds at theretofore unseen rates.

It was a curious diagnosis for Adrian Lamo, who was renowned for his skill in social engineering, an activity the nonhacker world might simply call artful manipulation and which would seem to require a rather advanced ability to read social cues. Though often, but not always, over the computer, Adrian had developed intense friendships with people all over the country. Friends and friends-turned-enemies alike described him as exceptionally charismatic, convivial, and adept at winning the trust of new allies.

An Asperger's diagnosis had, by the late 2000s, become somewhat fashionable among hacker types. For a community that prized obses-sive working habits, technical prowess, and strict meritocracy, and eschewed societal convention and social courtesies, the disorder could serve as a kind of validation, an official confirmation of hackish charac-teristics. Bill Gates is often assumed to have undiagnosed Asperger's. Prominent hacker Nadim Kobeissi claims to have the syndrome. A number of hackers facing prosecution have used an Asperger's diagno-sis in their legal defenses.

Adrian Lamo's longtime contact in journalism, Kevin Poulsen, wrote an article for Wired.com's Threat Level blog on May 20, 2010, describing Adrian's ordeal in the mental institution and diagnosis with Asperger's. In the piece, Adrian dismisses the idea that the diagnosis mitigated his guilt for his hacking crimes, insisting that Asperger's might explain his adeptness at hacking but not his decision to hack. "I have always maintained that what I did isn't necessarily technical, it's about seeing things differently," he said.

But the Asperger's article wasn't the only press Adrian Lamo received on May 20. Earlier the same day, Poulsen published an article about the leak of a 2003 documentary, *Hackers Wanted*. Narrated and produced by Kevin Spacey, the film set out to differentiate between the purity of the hacker ethic and the malicious cybercriminals the media had come to label "hackers"—the black hats or "crackers," in traditional hacker parlance. Much of the movie follows the exploits of a much younger Adrian Lamo during his run from the FBI after his digital break-in into the *New York Times*. The film had gone unreleased because of disputes between the partners involved in creating it but had been leaked online that day. Poulsen quoted Adrian in the article: "It's ironic that a film about overcoming barriers, about new technologies, about thinking differently, had to come to the public eye by being hacked out of the hands of people who, after making a film about the free flow of information, tried to lock away that information forever," he said. "The truth tends to itself."

The day the two articles were posted online, Adrian Lamo received an e-mail that had been encrypted using an old PGP public key to which he no longer had the access code. He could not decrypt the e-mail, and it went unread. It was a message from Brad Manning.

■ ■ ■

Adrian Lamo was working on his laptop in Carmichael, California, the Sacramento suburb where he was living after having been released from the psychiatric hospital into his parents' care. Shortly before two in the afternoon on May 21, he received an unsolicited instant message from a complete stranger.

"Hi."

It wasn't uncommon for Adrian to be contacted at random by strangers online. His minor fame had brought him many such messages over the years, often from hackers or would-be hackers bragging about their exploits. And in the community he trafficked in—hackers, programmers, geeks, what have you—sending a message online to a person one had never met was not uncouth.

"How are you?" asked the person with the screen name bradass87. "I'm an army intelligence analyst, deployed to eastern Baghdad, pending discharge for 'adjustment disorder' in lieu of 'gender identity disorder,'" bradass87 said. In Bagdhad, the time was near midnight.

Adrian did not respond. Minutes passed. "I'm sure you're pretty busy," bradass87 said. "If you had unprecedented access to classified networks 14 hours a day 7 days a week for 8+ months, what would you do?" he asked.

"Tired of being tired," came the response. Adrian was away from the computer, and his auto-response function had answered for him.

"?" bradass87 typed.

Several hours later Adrian responded. "What's your MOS [Military Occupation Specialty]?"

Hours passed before the answer came. "Re: 'What's your MOS?'—Intelligence Analyst (35)F)."

"Tired of being tired," came Adrian's auto-response.

They'd been missing each other, separated by a ten-hour time difference, but by the next morning (California time) they were both at their computers at the same time. After a quick, superficial reintroduction, bradass87 opened up a more serious discussion.

"So yeah. I'm in a sticky situation," he said. "It's nice to meet you by the way. Only starting to familiarize myself with what's available open source."

"Open source or OSINT [Open Source Intelligence]? ;P ." asked Adrian. "Pleased to meet you."

"Same deal. I'm kind of coming out of a cocoon. It's going to take some time, but I hopefully won't be a ghost anymore."

"You mentioned gender identity, I believe," said Adrian.

"I've had an unusual, and very stressful experience over the last decade or so."

They treaded cautiously through the next several minutes, as the talk centered on sexuality. The Don't Ask, Don't Tell policy was in effect, and it was natural for the stranger Adrian was chatting with to be a little paranoid about divulging too much.

"I'm a journalist and a minister," Adrian said. "You can pick either, and treat this as a confession or an interview (never to be published) and enjoy a modicum of legal protection."

The cagey exchange continued, as they spoke in ambiguities about DADT issues and the enigmatic worlds of hackerism and military intelligence, trading unspecific bona fides. Adrian Lamo's identity was known to bradass87, but Adrian did not yet know that bradass87 was Brad Manning—he'd only inferred that bradass87's first name was Brad.

Brad alluded to the real reason he'd messaged Adrian Lamo out of nowhere. "This is what I do for friends," he said, sending a link to the WikiLeaks article in Wikipedia. ">sigh<," he said. "Living such an opaque life has forced me never to take transparency, openness, and honesty for granted."

"I've been a friend to WikiLeaks," Adrian said. "I've repeatedly asked people who download *Hackers Wanted* to donate. And donated myself."

"I know. Actually how I noticed you, during my usual open source collection (Twitter, news.google.com, etc.). >nod< They've got a lot of ammunition. It's the support they need from the public in publishing the material coming through soon."

This was a dangerous dance. Adrian was worried this bradass87 character was a "false flag"—a military term for a covert operation undertaken in disguise to fool the enemy, the public, or both. He feared he was being entrapped. Brad was afraid of saying too much for obvious reasons, but he felt compelled to talk. He *needed* to talk to someone.

"I'm not really sure where this is going, apart from awkward weirdness," Brad said.

"I apologize if I've made you feel awkward," Adrian said.

"No it's me. I said too much too fast," Brad said. "Am I coming off too quick? I've closed myself off for awhile, so I thought I'd reach out to someone who would possibly understand."

Brad went on to tell his life story to Adrian, complete with bootstrap embellishments to his Horatio Alger tale. He recounted a family brawl in which his father attacked him in a drunken stupor. After he broke his dad's nose, Dad chased him out of the house with a shotgun, letting off a couple poorly aimed shots that damaged the house. The incident earned him a lashing from his father, he said, "for making him shoot up the house." The story was remarkably detailed for having been completely fabricated.

"I'm very isolated at the moment. Lost all of my emotional support channels. Family, boyfriend, trusting colleagues. I'm a mess," Brad said. "I'm in the desert with a bunch of hyper-masculine trigger happy ignorant rednecks as neighbors and the only safe place I seem to have is this satellite Internet connection." His professional life had fallen apart, he explained, and he was in limbo waiting to be discharged.

"And little does anyone know, but among this 'visible' mess there's the mess I created that no one knows about yet."

Adrian didn't press Brad for details at first; the young soldier was forthcoming on his own. Adrian asked how, in such a state of emotional tumult, Brad Manning could have been given a security clearance. "I enlisted in 2007. Height of the Iraq War, no one double checked much," Brad said, "Background checks are jokes anyway." Brian Manning would later say that neither he nor anyone he knew was ever contacted regarding his son's security clearance.

After dropping hints throughout the conversation, Brad Manning, rather suddenly and unsolicited, began his detailed confession.

"I've been penetrating .smil.mil networks for over a year, as well as .sgov.gov [second-level domain names for the army and State Department classified networks, respectively]. I've created a massive mess, and no one has a clue, because 95% of efforts are on physical security of classified networks and managing OPSEC on unclassified networks."

"Want to go to the press? :) ," Adrian asked.

"No. There's an issue with that."

"Open offer."

"Hypothetical question," Brad said. "If you had free reign over classified networks for long periods of time. Say, 8-9 months, and you saw incredible things, awful things, things that belonged in the public domain and not on some server stored in a dark room in Washington, DC, what would you do? Or Guantanamo, Bagram, Bucca, Taji, VBC for that matter," Brad said, listing off US Army installations around the world. It was a subtle but telling insight—information that once might have been stored in a dark room in Washington, DC, was now stored on a server connected to army outposts the world over.

"Things that would have an impact on 6.7 billion people," Brad continued. "Say, a database of half a million events during the Iraq War, from 2004 to 2009, with reports, date time groups, lat-lon locations, casualty figures? Or 260,000 state department cables from embassies and consulates all over the world, explaining how the first world exploits the third, in detail, from an internal perspective?

"The air-gap has been penetrated . . . =L ." Brad said. The "air gap" is a network security term for a physical separation designed to insulate one part of a system from a wider network.

"How so?" Adrian asked. Minutes of silence passed. "You there?"

"I'm here. Let's just say *someone* I know intimately well has been penetrating US classified networks, mining data like the ones described and been transferring that data from the classified networks over the 'air gap' onto a commercial network computer, sorting the data, compressing it, encrypting it and uploading it to a crazy white-haired Aussie who can't seem to stay in one country very long =L ."

"Depends. What are the particulars?" Adrian asked, intrigued and not a little bit troubled. Was this kid serious?

"Crazy white-haired dude = Julian Assange," Brad said. "In other words. I've made a huge mess :'(I'm sorry, I'm just emotionally fractured. I'm a total mess. I think I'm in more potential heat than you ever were."

"Not mandatorily," Adrian said. "There are always outs."

At Adrian's request, Brad described the contents of the files he claimed he had leaked. They revealed, he said, "crazy, almost criminal political backdealings. The non-PR versions of world events and crises," including inside information on the build-up to the Iraq War and damning details about the American-Pakistani relationship. "There's so much. It affects everybody on earth," Brad said. "Everywhere there's a US post, there's a diplomatic scandal that will be revealed. It's open diplomacy. Worldwide anarchy in CSV format. It's Climategate with a global scope and breathtaking depth. It's beautiful, and horrifying. And it's important that it gets out. I feel, for some bizarre reason, it might actually change something."

The insight contained in the phrase "worldwide anarchy in CSV format" deserves a moment for special consideration. An acronym for Comma Separated Value, CSV is an elegantly simple text format designed for easy search and tabulation. Earlier in the conversation Brad had said diplomats would "have a heart attack" when they discovered that "an entire repository of classified foreign policy is available in searchable format to the public." This fact—that the information he'd leaked was digitized and searchable—is essential to what made Brad Manning's leaks groundbreaking.

A leak of this scope was unlikely but not impossible in a predigital era. Certainly the opening of the Soviet archives after the fall of the USSR was a moment of even greater en-masse exposure. But the information Brad had given to WikiLeaks *came digitized*. The point may seem technical and mundane at first, but it is central to what made the leaks revolutionary. No scholars would have to pore over hard-copy documents and index them to make them useful—this was the Soviet archives with a search engine. Journalists with access to the leaked documents could find stories hiding within them at speeds impossible in an earlier era. This level of efficiency in research would have urgent and dramatic effects on unfolding global events in the months that followed.

Brad and Adrian continued chatting, and Adrian learned the full identity of the young man he was talking to. "Oh! You're the PGP guy. I'm an idiot," Adrian had said, upon realizing that Brad was the person who sent him the indecipherable e-mail the day before. The two had exchanged several e-mails back and forth but Adrian couldn't read them due to the obsolete encryption key and suggested they connect via instant message. Brad sent Adrian a few pictures to help establish his bona fides, and they became friends on Facebook; "You're kinda cute," Adrian told Brad.

Long after midnight in Iraq, Brad decided to turn in for the evening. Adrian had gone silent for half an hour. "It's getting awfully late. Need sleep," Brad said.

"Sorry. I'm just swamped today. I'll be more talkative in the future," said Adrian. "Keep your chin up. For me. *re-hug*."

In divulging his unprecedented breach of state security, Brad Manning had put Adrian Lamo in a very difficult position, but not without help from Adrian himself. When their conversation began, both men were reticent, and Adrian offered himself as a "journalist and a minister" to assuage Brad's concerns. When Brad lamented that he was violating WikiLeaks' security procedures, Adrian said, "Not really. 2600 is an ally of WikiLeaks," referencing the hacker magazine he was involved in producing.

"How old are you?" Adrian then asked Brad.

"22. But I'm not a source for you. I'm talking to you as someone who needs moral and emotional fucking support :'(."

"I told you, none of this is for print," Adrian assured him.

But Adrian was torn. The leak Brad had described was so vast that it seemed irresponsible by its very nature. One couldn't predict the ramifications of unleashing such a massive repository of state secrets as was held in 260,000 State Department cables; one person couldn't even be reasonably expected to have read all of the documents. Lives were threatened by this leak, Adrian felt.

On May 23, while it was nighttime in California, Brad Manning spent the day lathered in sunscreen traipsing around the hot sand at FOB Hammer. No longer an intelligence analyst, Brad's demotion had left him with tasks such as these, setting up preparations for a barbecue and a group of visiting cheerleaders for the Minnesota Vikings NFL team.

"How are you feeling today?" Adrian Lamo asked after he and Brad started chatting again at about 7:20 in the morning California time.

"I'm feeling a little better," Brad said. "I had a lot on my mind, keeping to myself." He told Adrian about setting up for the cheerleaders. "Ran a barbecue but no one showed up. Threw a lot of food away," he said. "I'm sunburned and smell like charcoal, sweat and sunscreen. That's about all that's new."

Adrian Lamo may have supported the work of WikiLeaks, but what bothered him about Brad Manning's leaks was exactly what made them the first leaks to truly exemplify WikiLeaks' principles. The ideas Assange had set forth before founding the organization called for mass leaking on a global scale without regard for ideology and with an allegiance only to the truth. As the group matured over the course of several years, the purity of that vision occasionally came out of focus—WikiLeaks and its supporters hadn't always toed that line—but for Julian Assange, the ideal never faded. Adrian Lamo himself gave the world its best example of Assange's adherence to his own principles when he leaked WikiLeaks' donor list back to WikiLeaks. But confronted with an example of the WikiLeaks philosophy taken to its logical extreme, Adrian buckled. He saw grave danger in the leaks and felt compelled to turn in the perpetrator to the authorities, perhaps, as he has said since, in order to give the US time to prepare for the blow.

In the months after Manning's arrest, Lamo was often abstruse as to why exactly he did what he did. He suggested he was simply a witness to a crime and felt a civic responsibility to report what he'd seen. He knew little more about the contents or possible effects of the leaks than anyone else. He may, as he suggested, have felt that turning Brad in could help the United States stop the leaks from being published. Adrian seems to have felt that Brad posed an ongoing threat—Brad told Adrian he was no longer doing intelligence work but had retained a security clearance—and may have hoped to prevent further leaks. It is possible that Lamo felt he was in legal jeopardy under the principle of *misprision of felony*, the crime of concealing a crime in American law, but nothing he has said indicates this is the case. The motivation he repeated time and again in the years that followed was concern about the damage Brad Manning's leaks might cause.

And yet the perpetrator was a troubled young man who had confided in him in search of guidance and comfort. "He was lonely and wanted somebody to talk to," Adrian said. "It's the most painful part of it—the fact that he had such a simple and pure intent, and it had to be me." Over the years many hackers had told Adrian about their crimes, and he'd never turned one of them over to the law. But this case was different. "I felt a responsibility as a witness to a crime, essentially," Adrian would later say, "to go forward to the right people who would know how to do the right thing. This is my first espionage investigation. I had no real idea what to do."

What followed was one of the more bizarre episodes in the life of a hacker who had once been on the run from the FBI. Adrian contacted a friend who had worked in army counterintelligence, who advised him to go the authorities immediately. He also consulted Chet Uber, his colleague at Project Vigilant, and Uber told him the same thing. Each of those individuals then contacted the U.S. Army Criminal Investigation Command to tell them what he had learned about the leaks. Over the ensuing days, the former hacker undertook his greatest social engineering project yet: keeping Brad Manning talking while the authorities closed the net. "Did I, in the end, keep him talking so he wouldn't be spooked by my sudden disappearance? Yes, at my own volition," Adrian Lamo later said. "This wasn't some episode of whatever cop drama is popular these days, where you know who the bad guys are and get moral certainties. It was real life. I don't know that I did the *right* thing. I did the *necessary* thing."

Many of their conversations over the next several days revolved around WikiLeaks and the "data spillage" Brad claimed to have committed, but Brad also discussed his plans for life after being discharged from the army. He said Assange had offered him a position with WikiLeaks, but he wasn't interested. He intended to head back to the United States and move between Boston and DC, freelancing and looking for steadier work while undergoing his medical transformation from a man into a woman. He'd already started setting up a web presence for his female identity in the form of a Twitter account for "Breanna Manning," the name he intended to take once his transgender switch was complete.

Having had his own troubles with federal authorities in the past, Adrian was extremely anxious in advance of his first meeting with federal investigators, set to take place on May 25. The day before his scheduled meeting, he contacted Kevin Poulsen and told him the vague summary of what was going on—he'd been contacted by someone claiming to be an army intelligence analyst who confessed to having turned over classified information to a "foreign national." Adrian didn't think, at the time, it would be much of a news story, but he was terrified that he'd meet with Army CID and get pulled into the net of a federal investigation, not to be heard from again. "He was very paranoid," Poulsen said. "He was going into a meeting with the feds, and he wanted to make sure that if it boomeranged on him somehow and he was incommunicado, that the story would get out." Poulsen asked Adrian for logs of his conversations with the intelligence analyst, but Adrian turned him down.

Over the course of their ensuing conversations, Adrian pressed Brad for details, and Brad obliged with copious statements that would, after his arrest became public, become a wealth of insight into his motivations. He described his experience with the Iraqi detainees who'd been arrested for circulating a scholarly critique of corruption in the country. "Everything started slipping after that," Brad said. "I saw things differently. I had always questioned the way things worked, and investigated to find the truth, but that was a point where I was a *part* of something. I was actively involved in something that I was completely against."

"What would you do if your role with Wikileaks seemed in danger of being blown?" Adrian asked.

"Try and figure out how I could get my side of the story out," Brad said, "before everything was twisted around to make me look like Nidal Hasan [the US soldier who'd been charged the previous November in the mass shooting at Fort Hood]. I don't think it's going to happen," he said. "I mean, I was never noticed. Regularly ignored except when I had something essential, then it was back to 'bring me coffee, then sweep the floor.'"

Brad Manning was not an ideologue or a partisan—"I don't have a doctrine. Socialism and Capitalism are the same thing in practice."—but he was fervently interested in global affairs. His words while talking to Adrian Lamo, which would be some of his last statements uttered before being placed under arrest, made it clear that he had acted out of conscience. He believed he was making a better world.

"I don't know, I'm just weird I guess," he said to Adrian. "I can't separate myself from others. I feel connected to everybody like they were distant family. I . . . care? [This picture] sums it up for me," Brad said. He sent Adrian a link to a photograph taken in 1990 by NASA's Voyager 1 at the suggestion of Carl Sagan, one of Brad's heroes. After the spacecraft had traveled four billion miles from its launch pad, the Voyager team turned the camera around to take a few parting shots of our solar system. Among the resulting images was one with the dark vastness of space in the background, a column of orange refracted sunlight in the foreground, and midway down the column of light, a tiny speck of blue: planet Earth. Sagan borrowed the image's name, "the Pale Blue Dot," for the title of a book, in which he wrote in its opening pages:

> Look again at that dot. That's here. That's home. That's us. On it everyone you love, everyone you know, everyone you ever heard of, every human being who ever was, lived out their lives. The aggregate of our joy and suffering, thousands of confident religions, ideologies, and economic doctrines, every hunter and forager, every hero and coward, every creator and destroyer of civilization, every king and peasant, every young couple in love, every mother and father, hopeful child, inventor and explorer, every teacher of morals, every corrupt politician, every "super-star," every "supreme leader," every saint and sinner in the history of our species lived there—on a mote of dust suspended in a sunbeam.
>
> The Earth is a very small stage in a vast cosmic arena. Think of the rivers of blood spilled by all those generals and emperors

so that, in glory and triumph, they could become the momentary masters of a fraction of a dot. Think of the endless cruelties visited by the inhabitants of one corner of this pixel on the scarcely distinguishable inhabitants of some other corner, how frequent their misunderstandings, how eager they are to kill one another, how fervent their hatreds.

"I get that," Adrian said.

"Get what . . . that connection?"

"Yeah," he said. "Which is why I'm sad for the people I sometimes have to hurt."

Brad was partial to dramatic gestures, and the Pale Blue Dot was certainly a poetic way to express his worldview, which had changed in an important but perhaps not at first obvious way. Though he was critical of the operation, Brad was not convinced that the effort to rebuild Iraq was entirely a folly. He was distraught by the violence he saw, but he wasn't a pacifist—he'd never been one to take such a wholesale position. A clear and logical strain of thought in the violent oscillations of his emotional, youthful idealism is not immediately obvious, but it is there.

Brad had moved away from what in political science is called the state-centric paradigm. He had ceased to interpret global events through a lens that held governments to be the primary actors on the world stage. He'd lost faith in the state's ability to benevolently guide human affairs by regulating the flow of information, the foundational principle behind government secrecy. His insight, both prescriptive and descriptive, was that mere individual humans are the primary actors driving world affairs and ought to be recognized and respected as such—a democratic notion in the most literal sense.

"I want people to see the truth regardless of who they are," Brad said, on the afternoon of May 25, Baghdad time, while discussing his decision to leak the "Collateral Murder" video. "Because without information, you cannot make informed decisions as a public. If I knew then, what I knew now kind of thing. Or maybe I'm just young, naive, and stupid."

"Which do you think it is?" asked Adrian.

"I'm hoping for the former. It can't be the latter, because if it is we're fucking screwed as a society. And I don't want to believe that we're screwed."

About twelve hours later, in the early morning hours of May 26 at FOB Hammer, Brad was lamenting the terrible state of information security at the base.

"It's sad," he said. "I mean what if I were someone more malicious? I could've sold to Russia or China and made bank."

"Why didn't you?" Adrian said.

"Because it's public data."

"I mean the cables," said Adrian.

"It belongs in the public domain. Information should be free."

Information should be free. The sentence was a variation on a slogan in the hacker community, "Information wants to be free," and inside this oft-misquoted catchphrase are two ideas central to understanding Brad Manning's leak.

In 1984, in response to the publication of Steven Levy's book *Hackers: Heroes of the Computer Revolution*, the writer and countercultural icon Stewart Brand organized a "Hackers' Conference" to get the people Levy had described under one roof. During a session hosted by Levy, Brand commented, "On one hand, information wants to be expensive, because it's so valuable. The right information in the right place just changes your life. On the other hand, information wants to be free, because the cost of getting it out is getting lower and lower all the time. So you have these two fighting against each other."

Levy writes in his update to *Hackers*: "The entire quotation neatly encapsulates the tension that has defined the hacker movement over the last quarter-century—an often heated battle between geeky idealism and cold-hearted commerce. Hackers want information to be free—not necessarily free as in free beer, but free as in freedom, to quote Richard Stallman."

In quipping "Information should be free," Brad was aligning himself with the hackers' free software ideal. Whether it be the source code to a computer program, scientific data, or basic facts about the conduct of a country's foreign policy, information ought to be widely available and exchangeable in the spirit of open, transparent mass collaboration and competition.

Packed into the phrase is its second meaning, evident in the original quotation whence the slogan comes. Brand was describing the natural tendency of information toward freedom by metaphorically assigning it a motivation: desire. Information *wants* to be free because its nature is to spread—because it is so valuable and, as Brand stated, "the cost of getting it out is getting lower and lower all the time." In the digital age the spread of information is easier than ever, and the more valuable the information, the greater tendency it will have to spread.

Brad Manning's decision to leak state secrets was clearly made with altruistic motivations. The whistleblower described feeling morally conflicted about the war machine he was supporting, citing specific instances in which he felt betrayed by his superiors. He said he had perpetrated the largest leak in American history—very likely world history—because of a belief that information should be free for the betterment of all mankind. And, though he doesn't appear to have intended it when he said, "Information should be free," Brad Manning's leak illustrated the futility of wanton state secrecy in a digital age. Mass classification of information is a self-defeating proposition. Secrecy makes information scarce, increasing its value to those who don't have it. On the other side of the veil, overclassification dilutes the well of state secrets, making the information less valuable to those who do have it. In a digitized world designed to spread information widely and cheaply, this is a system designed to break down. Secrecy destroys itself.

■ ■ ■

On May 26, Adrian called Kevin Poulsen to tell him he had another meeting with federal investigators scheduled for 4:00 PM the next day. Poulsen asked again for the logs of the chats between Adrian and the intelligence analyst, and Adrian relented, again worried he might be silenced after meeting with investigators. He had two conditions: that

Poulsen drive to Sacramento to pick up the logs in person (transferring them electronically was not secure and out of the question, Adrian said), and that Poulsen not publish the chats until Adrian gave him permission.

The next morning, May 27, Poulsen drove to Sacramento to pick up the chat logs from Adrian. They spent several hours together, as Adrian gave Poulsen a more fully detailed version of events, including the name of the intelligence analyst: Bradley E. Manning. He also described, for the first time, the vast scale of the leaks the soldier claimed to have perpetrated. At 3:00 PM, Poulsen drove back to San Francisco with the chat logs loaded onto a thumb drive. An hour later, Adrian had his second meeting with authorities, at a Starbucks near his home in Carmichael.

On the morning of May 28, Adrian called Poulsen and told him that two days earlier, on May 26, Brad Manning had been arrested at FOB Hammer, the prime suspect in what was the largest breach of state security anyone could remember. On June 1, Adrian gave Poulsen permission to publish the logs, and Poulsen set about verifying the bizarre story. The soldier was on his way to the brig at Camp Arifjan in Kuwait.

9
WikiLeaked

Julian Assange was scheduled to appear beside Daniel Ellsberg, the famous leaker of the Pentagon Papers, at a conference in New York on Thursday, June 3, 2010. But by Tuesday that week something was amiss. Assange wrote to the conference organizers: "I have received urgent advice that it is unsafe for me to travel to the US and am canceling all my plans there. . . . I am not happy, but this is what happens when a country stops following the rule of law. Sorry I don't have more notice." He appeared instead via Skype video link from Australia.

Later that evening Assange was riding in a car with reporters from the Australian Broadcasting Corporation's *Foreign Correspondent* program, eating cold leftover risotto and drinking a can of Coke. As recounted by Andrew Fowler in *The Most Dangerous Man in the World*, "We had strict instructions to drop him off on a nondescript stretch of road. Julian Assange disappeared down the street; he was going into hiding with a bag full of secrets."

■ ■ ■

The repercussions of Adrian Lamo's decision to release logs of his chats with Brad Manning to Kevin Poulsen are easily understated. The Pentagon didn't publicly acknowledge Brad's arrest until the day after Poulsen's story broke the news; the army spokesman Poulsen spoke to while reporting the story either wouldn't or couldn't confirm the investigation even existed. The Lamo chats gave the public a rare glimpse into the thinking of a young whistleblower and became, with a couple exceptions, his only public statements for well over a year after his arrest. On June 5, at Brad's direction, his aunt Debbie posted a message to his Facebook account: "Some of you may have heard that I have been arrested for disclosure of classified information to unauthorized persons. See http://collateralmurder.com/," but what, or when, the general public would have learned about Brad Manning had Adrian Lamo not contacted Kevin Poulsen, we will never know.

"I only contacted Kevin as a sort of insurance policy," Adrian said later. "Because of my previous dealings with the FBI, I was hesitant to contact federal authorities. I knew they didn't always play fair. I wanted to make sure the story got out if I didn't come back for any reason. That may sound a little paranoid, but you have to remember, they said I was paranoid before, but it turns out they really were out to get me."

The fact that the extent of the leaks was now public knowledge led to a schism in WikiLeaks itself, as the pressures of its sudden wealth of secrets fomented what might be called WikiLeaks' second civil war.

On news of Brad Manning's arrest, WikiLeaks' core leadership was presented with a moral quandary: to publish or not to publish, now that the likely source had been compromised. Disagreements ensued between the partners. But initial concerns about publishing any more of Brad's leaks, lest they worsen his plight—at this point only the "Collateral Murder" video, the Reykjavik cable, and the army counterintelligence memo on WikiLeaks had been released—were soon overwhelmed by the temptations of the trove of secrets. WikiLeaks ultimately decided that it makes a commitment to a source that it will publish that which is leaked to it, come what may. After all, in the WikiLeaks world, information wants to be free.

Assange was in possession of some of the most valuable information in the world, and some of WikiLeaks' cadre felt he was going rogue as he began unilaterally cutting deals with other media organizations without so much as a consultation with others in the inner circle. The rift that would eventually separate Birgitta Jonsdottir, Julian Assange, Daniel Domscheit-Berg, and others had its roots here.

Accounts differ of how WikiLeaks' deal with its media partners came about, but according to David Leigh at the *Guardian*, it wasn't until his colleague Nick Davies read portions of the chat logs published by *Wired*, in which Brad describes the astounding scope of the leak, that Davies thought to suggest a collaboration between WikiLeaks and his employer. *Guardian* reporters were dispatched to locate Assange, which was no easy task. The Australian was then traveling surreptitiously in Europe, perhaps, as some suggested, the most eagerly hunted man in the world. In his possession, if the chat logs were to be believed, was by far the biggest leak of military secrets in the history of the United States and very possibly the world. Only after journalists from the *Guardian* tracked Assange down did negotiations for the WikiLeaks partnership with the mainstream press begin in earnest.

On June 16, after he read the Lamo chats *Wired* had released, Davies e-mailed Assange. "Hi Julian, I spent yesterday in the *Guardian* office arguing that Bradley Manning is currently the most important story on the planet. There is much to be done, and it will take a little time. But right now, I think the crucial thing is to track and expose the effort by the US government to suppress Bradley, you, WikiLeaks, and anything that either of you may want to put in the public domain." He asked if the two could speak further on the subject of Brad Manning and WikiLeaks. Assange replied with a rote press release about the Icelandic media haven initiative. More e-mails were exchanged, and Assange eventually put Davies in touch with several of his WikiLeaks associates. Connecting with Assange would take a bit more effort.

A few days later, Davies got an anonymous tip that Assange was flying into Brussels for a press conference. Another *Guardian* reporter tracked Assange down, and, after days of missed connections and tentative discussions, he and Davies finally sat down with Assange for a six-hour negotiation in the courtyard café of the WikiLeaks spokesman's hotel.

Since Brad Manning's arrest, Assange had been on the run with his extraordinary cache of classified documents. According to the *Guardian*'s account of the meeting, Assange said he'd been prepared for weeks to post the documents online, but concerns about the legal implications for the recently arrested army private had kept him from doing so. Davies suggested that a collaboration with his newspaper, an established, respected brand, would lend moral credibility to the entire WikiLeaks enterprise. "We are going to put you on the moral high ground—so high that you'll need an oxygen mask. You'll be up there with Nelson Mandela and Mother Teresa," Davies said. "They won't be able to arrest you. Nor can they shut down your website." Assange was convinced.

The partners decided to bring the *New York Times* in on the deal. An American publication, particularly one with a history of publishing official secrets and standing up to an enraged American government, would help protect WikiLeaks and its source from charges of espionage. The German newsweekly *Der Spiegel* formed the final part of the team. The resulting collaboration was extraordinary in certain respects. WikiLeaks had worked with partners in the mainstream media before but never on so massive a trove of digitized secrets— never before had anything comparable existed. As Sarah Ellison wrote in *Vanity Fair*: "One of the oldest newspapers in the world, with strict and established journalistic standards, joined up with one of the newest in a breed of online muckrakers, with no standards at all except fealty to an ideal of 'transparency'—that is, dumping raw material into the public square for people to pick over as they will."

As afternoon turned to evening, Assange and the reporters continued their conversation in an Italian restaurant. With the partnership in the works—the *New York Times* and *Der Spiegel* would still have to be approached—the discussion turned to how they could securely move the documents back to the *Guardian*'s office in the United Kingdom. Assange said he would set up a website through which the files pertaining to the war in Afghanistan could be downloaded. It would be encrypted using PGP, he said, scribbling a password on a napkin.

■ ■ ■

Sunday, July 25, 2010, was a watershed moment in world history. On this day, WikiLeaks and its media partners, the *New York Times*, the *Guardian*, and *Der Spiegel*, began publishing the set of field reports from Afghanistan leaked to them by Brad Manning, which they titled the Afghan War Logs. The onslaught of classified information that was to come would eclipse the memory of those first leaks in the popular narrative, but at the time the Afghan War Logs were published they were like nothing the world had seen—the beginning of the information age exploding upon itself.

"These war logs—written in the heat of engagement—show a conflict that is brutally messy, confused and immediate," the *Guardian* wrote in its introductory report. "It is in some contrast with the tidied-up and sanitised 'public' war, as glimpsed through official communiques as well as the necessarily limited snapshots of embedded reporting."

The *New York Times* focused on the confirmation in the reports of long-rumored Pakistani treachery. "The behind-the-scenes frustrations of soldiers on the ground and glimpses of what appear to be Pakistani skullduggery contrast sharply with the frequently rosy public pronouncements of Pakistan as an ally by American officials, looking to sustain a drone campaign over parts of Pakistani territory to strike at Qaeda havens."

US authorities were prepared with a raging response. The leaks, said a statement from the Obama administration, "could put the lives of Americans and our partners at risk, and threaten our national security." With predictable lines about the irresponsibility of the leak and how it hindered the war effort, the statement included a telling dodge. The administration went to pains to point out that the documents covered the period from January 2004 to December 2009, the month a then-still-fresh President Obama instituted his new strategy for the war.

The bulk of the furor directed at WikiLeaks related to claims that Afghans who cooperated with US authorities were named in the documents and were thus endangered by their public release. "Mr. Assange can say whatever he likes about the greater good he thinks he and his source are doing, but the truth is they might already have on their hands the blood of some young soldier or that of an Afghan family," said Admiral Mike Mullen, chairman of the Joint Chiefs of Staff.

But the lesson that became clearest after the publication of the Afghan War Logs was that analyzing the effect of such a massive document leak was an impossibly daunting task. The *Times*, the *Guardian*, and *Der Spiegel* did not even agree among themselves about what the reports revealed; the *Guardian* rejected the very logic that led the *Times* to its lead story on Pakistani intelligence. And all involved— WikiLeaks, the press tripartite, and the US government—were induced to overstate their cases.

Though care was taken, the press partners insist, to redact the names of at least some informants, and some of the documents were withheld because their release was deemed too dangerous, WikiLeaks came under attack even from former allies, like Amnesty International, for endangering the lives of ordinary Afghans. The Taliban announced that it was combing through the documents in search of "spies," but no evidence was produced that a Taliban enforcer ever gleaned the identity of an Afghan informant from the Latinized version of a Pashto or Dari name mentioned in the logs. In the fog of the Afghan war, in which Afghans cooperating with NATO forces had been executed by Taliban for years, to prove that WikiLeaks was to blame was a complicated errand to say the least. Proving that WikiLeaks was not to blame for any informant deaths was, in a familiar logical conundrum, probably impossible.

WikiLeaks and its press partners reported that the logs included evidence of collusion between Pakistani intelligence and the Taliban, previously unreported civilian and friendly-fire casualties, and a clear trend of increasing violence in the country, adding up, in the words of the *Guardian*, to "a devastating portrait of the failing war in Afghanistan." And yet, observers with more distance from the leaks concluded that they ultimately confirmed what we already knew about the war: "that it was going badly," to borrow from Blake Hounshell writing for

Foreign Policy's Passport blog. The *Washington Post* reported, "The disclosure of what are mostly battlefield updates does not appear to represent a major threat to national security or troops' safety, according to military officials." The administration and its cheerleaders sought to downplay the significance of the leaks by highlighting how benign they ultimately were, and they were right. The leak was, it turned out, mostly harmless, which was the most damning revelation of all.

The Afghan War Logs represented the world's first true glimpse into what a new WikiLeaks era might look like: mass, largely nondiscriminating leaking of state secrets in the effort to achieve a more just world. But our peek behind the curtain of government secrecy turned out to be far less sensational than we had imagined it would be. The question that went too often unasked in the wake of the War Logs and the leaks that followed was the one that should have troubled us most deeply: why was all this information secret?

Clearly there was good reason to keep secret *some* of what was included in the logs Brad Manning leaked. Publicizing the names of Afghan informants may well have put innocent lives at risk. And in the short term, of course, the army requires secrecy in its communications in order to wage war. But taken on the whole, the logs were profoundly, troublingly boring, of interest primarily to journalists and historians. Much of the information in them proved to be harmless but useful for helping the public understand the complex and messy war being waged on its bill and by its members. Had the Pentagon revealed most of the information in the logs responsibly, it's difficult to imagine what "serious damage to national security" would have resulted, as required for information to be classified at the Secret level.

■ ■ ■

His name was now associated with the largest leak of military secrets in history, but to most of the public Brad Manning remained a mystery. During the months of June and July, after making an initial splash following the publication of Poulsen's article, the name Bradley Manning receded from the headlines. The young soldier was in a detention facility at Camp Arifjan in Kuwait, making no public statements.

WikiLeaks spent the summer coordinating with its media partners on publication of the War Logs and defending itself from the growing anger of the American establishment. Assange and a cohort of allies, most prominently Glen Greenwald at Salon.com, lashed out at Kevin Poulsen and Adrian Lamo with accusations that they colluded with US authorities to ensnare Manning. WikiLeaks' Twitter feed that summer often featured defensive posts, most likely from Assange, lambasting the group's critics and decrying a supposed "covert smear campaign." An inexperienced media handler who was prickly and arrogant to begin with, Assange's under-siege mentality made him seem paranoid and imperious to many journalists covering the story. What little coverage there was of the Bradley Manning story was relegated to second-tier media outlets and online discussion boards. Manning was eclipsed in stories that centered on Assange's strange personal style and the Assange/Greenwald versus Poulsen/Lamo sideshow. Even at the *Guardian*, the paper that initiated the collaboration with Assange based on Manning's statements in the chat logs, the Manning story went quiet and its subject remained an enigma. But the calm didn't last for long.

After the Afghan War Logs' publication on July 25, the name Bradley Manning reentered the public mind. On August 3, Rep. Mike Rogers (R-Mich.) called for Brad's execution. Lamenting what he called a "culture of exposure" in government, Rogers said, "If they won't charge him with treason, they ought to charge him with murder." And yet still little was known about Brad Manning. On August 8, Ginger Thompson, writing for the *New York Times*, produced the first substantive profile of the young private and set the tone for much of the media coverage that was to follow.

The tenor of Thompson's article reflected Brad's tormented mental state at the time of his chats with Adrian Lamo. Drawing on reporting from Oklahoma, Boston, DC, and Wales, the writer painted a decidedly agonized portrait of Brad's life, with an emphasis on bullying and sexuality. She then theorized, through a familiar journalistic guise ("others" or "sources" or, in this case, "friends") about what made him do it.

"And now some of those friends say they wonder whether his desperation for acceptance—or delusions of grandeur—may have led him to disclose the largest trove of government secrets since the Pentagon Papers," Thompson wrote. "'I would always try to make clear to Brad that he had a promising future ahead of him,' said Daniel J. Clark, one of those Cambridge friends. 'But when you're young and you're in his situation, it's hard to tell yourself things are going to get better, especially in Brad's case, because in his past, things didn't always get better.'"

But Danny did not wonder if desperation for acceptance or delusions of grandeur led Brad to disclose anything. He felt his quote had been taken profoundly out of context.

Danny had decided to speak to Thompson in order to publicize the fund-raising effort for Brad's legal defense. While he was talking to the reporter, he sent an e-mail to other Bradley Manning supporters. "New York Times reporter physically in Boston now who would like to talk to people (in boston now as in she is sitting 10 feet away from me). She claims she is trying to do a story that will help to humanize Brad more, and also said she'd put in a link that would get to the fund-raising effort. I get a good vibe from her, but who knows. She's fine with giving quote review/approval, talking with people on anonymous background, etc."

When Danny asked her why no mention was made of the legal defense fund, he said, "She was like, 'Oh, the editors have a policy of not allowing links to fund-raising sites,' which, like, and you didn't know this? Just such obvious bullshit." Danny became more reticent about talking to the media and would eventually stop almost completely. "That was sort of the beginning of my 'talking to reporters is a losing game,'" he later said.

Many of Brad Manning's friends and associates found the piece to be a shallow characterization of the young man they knew. The profile was not inaccurate, just incomplete while presenting itself as authoritative. Informed by the emotional breakdown Brad displayed in his most recent Facebook posts and the Lamo chats, the writer took an uninformed leap into hypothesizing about his motivations. The profile drew a straight line from bullying to delusions of grandeur and desperation for acceptance, with the implicit message that the leak was a malicious attempt to get back at the army. Thompson's profile had introduced Brad to the world in an unequivocally negative light and wrote him into a suspiciously convenient narrative.

After growing steadily throughout the 2000s, the country's preoccupation with bullying spiked in the summer after Brad's arrest and before Thompson's profile appeared (a simple review of the term "bullying" in Google's search trends will verify the fact). Additionally, earlier that year the president announced in his State of the Union address that he'd make an effort to repeal Don't Ask, Don't Tell. The issue was hot in American politics—mere months later Obama would sign the act repealing the policy. Suddenly, Brad Manning was a touchstone for two of the issues at the forefront of the American zeitgeist. To the far right, he was clear evidence that gays were unfit for military service. And in the American mainstream, the leaks were explained away as the actions of a disaffected homosexual who had come to hate the army after being bullied into madness.

The narrative took hold among pundits on the right-wing fringe. Ann Coulter riffed off the *Times'* caricature of Brad Manning to argue against the imminent repeal of DADT: "Look at the disaster one gay created under our punishing 'don't ask, don't tell' policy. What else awaits America with the overturning of a policy that was probably put there for a reason (apart from being the only thing Bill Clinton ever did that I agreed with)?" Others in the right-wing blogosphere echoed Coulter's sentiment. "The record shows that Manning allegedly betrayed the United States because of anger over what he perceived to be the army's failure to accommodate his peculiar 'sexual orientation,' which he advertised on Facebook," read a column in *Accuracy in Media*. "I believe Ginger Thompson's article was spot on," said another typical column, this from a blogger for *Red County*. "Once PVT Manning embraced the gay lifestyle he became deeply disturbed. His acceptance of the gay lifestyle and the friends he made both in and outside the military led him to what he is today—a traitor to his country."

Thompson's profile in the *Times* had a more far-reaching effect than inspiring right-wing bloggers. Assange was incensed by the Manning profile, complaining that it "removed all higher-level political motivations from him and psychoanalyzed him down to problems in his childhood and a demand for attention." The incident planted the seed that would result in Assange's falling out with the *New York Times* and eventually the complete dissolution of the fragile alliance between WikiLeaks and its original old-media partners.

In the weeks after the Afghan War Logs went live online, the pressure mounted on WikiLeaks. The Pentagon and the US Department of Justice launched an official probe into the possibility of criminally prosecuting Assange for playing midwife to the leaks. While girding itself for further leaks, the Pentagon created a special task force in which 120 officials worked around the clock in an effort to stop Assange. The WikiLeaks Task Force's unfortunate acronym said more than any public affairs representative could about the American government's stunned reaction to Brad Manning's leaks.

On Wednesday, August 11, Assange flew from London to Stockholm to seek a safe haven in Sweden. He'd come to Sweden at the invitation of Anna Ardin, a thirty-one-year-old political activist, to speak at a conference of the Brotherhood, the faction of the Swedish Social Democratic Party to which Ardin belonged. But Assange also intended to apply for residence and work permits in Sweden. Some of WikiLeaks' servers were based in the country, and an offer of aid had come from the Swedish Pirate Party, the oldest of a group of political parties built around hacker ideals such as free exchange of information, personal privacy, and transparent government. Even more enticing for Assange were Swedish source protection laws, under which it is not only unlawful to compel a journalist to reveal a source but forbidden for a journalist to reveal the identity of an anonymous source at all. Assange would have to become a legal resident of Sweden to register WikiLeaks as a Swedish organization and come under the protective scope of the law.

Ardin arranged for Assange to stay at her flat in a Stockholm suburb while she was out of town. She was set to come home on Saturday, the day of Assange's scheduled lecture, but she returned a day early. The encounter would have a far-reaching effect on the future of WikiLeaks.

According to Ardin, she and Assange were at her home on Friday evening having a quiet cup of tea when he began stroking her leg. Though Ardin welcomed the attention at first, Assange turned aggressive, and she became resistant. Assange pulled off her clothes, breaking her necklace in the process, while Ardin tried in vain to put her clothes back on. Ardin later told the Swedish police "she didn't want to go any further but that it was too late to stop Assange as she had gone along with it so far. She says that she felt she only had herself to blame, and so she allowed Assange to take off her clothes." Ardin reported that when she realized Assange intended to have unprotected sex with her she tried to "wriggle her hips and cross her legs to stop penetration" and reached for a condom. Assange asked what she was reaching for, she said she wanted him to wear a condom, and he put one on. However, Ardin reported to the police that Assange had "done something" that caused the condom to rip and ejaculated inside of her unprotected.

Details of Assange and Ardin's sexual encounter—and the several days that followed—are disputed. Much depends on how one defines consent and on the subtleties that accompany intimate relations between the sexes. What is undisputed is that the morning of Assange's lecture to the Brotherhood, he and Ardin were seen together at the lecture hall. Ardin organized a crayfish party in Assange's honor at her flat that evening, and Assange spent the next several nights in her bed, though they did not have sex. Ardin posted enthusiastically to Twitter the night of the party, "Sitting outdoors at 2am, hardly freezing, with the world's coolest, smartest people. It's amazing!" She also expressed substantial discomfort with Assange, who had "been violent" and "exceeded the limits of what she felt she could accept," according to one friend.

At his lecture, on Saturday before the crayfish party, Assange met a twenty-five-year-old fan, Sofia Wilen, with whom he spent much of the day and to whom he made several apparently welcome sexual advances before returning to Ardin's apartment that night.

Assange was busy applying for Swedish residency on Monday and Tuesday, during which time he continued staying with Ardin. On Tuesday, August 17, he spent the night at Wilen's apartment fifty miles from Stockholm. Wilen would tell Swedish authorities that the night had been deeply unpleasant. She sent frantic text messages to a friend indicating that "there had been bad sex and Julian had not been nice," according to the recipient. By her own account, Wilen awoke in the morning and Assange began ordering her around, sending her out to buy breakfast, which she did despite finding his behavior piggish. She returned with food and cooked for him, and they had sex again, with a condom. After breakfast the two fell asleep, and Wilen awoke surprised to find Assange atop and inside of her. "Are you wearing anything?" she asked. "You," Assange said. "You better not have HIV," she said. "Of course not," replied Assange. The unprotected sex is undisputed, but Assange described Wilen as merely "sleepy" at the time and insists that Wilen made him breakfast only after the incident.

Assange returned to Ardin's flat on Wednesday. The woman said she'd had enough of Assange's presence at her place and wanted him out. According to the police, "Assange suddenly took all the clothes off the lower part of his body and rubbed [her] with his erect penis. [She] says she thought this was strange and unpleasant behavior. She no longer wanted Assange to live in her flat, which he ignored."

Though the truth of the entire multiday episode remains murky, one certainty emerges from the muddled accounts: Julian Assange is not a gentleman. The undisputed record reveals Assange to be clumsily sexually aggressive, predatory, and infantile in his approach to women. But neither woman accused Assange of the violent, forcible, nonconsensual penetration that the word *rape* connotes in most of the world.

Nonetheless, Wilen and Ardin spoke shortly after their unhappy dalliances and agreed to go together on Friday, August 20, to the Swedish authorities. Further complications and inconsistencies accompanied the bungled investigation, but when news broke that

Julian Assange was accused of rape and of "sexual molestation," based on his odd, pantsless proposition to Ardin, the story took off across cyberspace.

The allegation of "rape" was based on an accusation that would not likely merit even an investigation in American courts, and "molestation" was simply a gross mistranslation from Swedish, repeated by journalists who were either vindictive or lazy or both. But a fantastic scandal had been unleashed into the echo chamber of the Internet. The complex situation was simplified and crucial details overlooked. In the court of public opinion Assange was an accused rapist and molester, the latter moniker carrying, at least in the United States, undertones of pedophilia.

On August 31, Assange met with Swedish authorities and was formally told of the allegations against him. Sometime not long thereafter, Assange left Stockholm for London. On October 18 his application for Swedish residency was denied.

Daniel Domscheit-Berg had been vacationing with his wife and young son in Iceland when the news broke of the rape allegations against Assange. He flew back to Berlin the next day, where he sat inconsolable in his apartment, logged on to the internal WikiLeaks chat room for days on end. Relations among WikiLeaks' internal cadre had been increasingly difficult ever since Brad Manning's arrest, and Domscheit-Berg could feel the organization—the cause to which he had devoted years of his life—coming apart.

Assange apparently learned before Poulsen's story came out that Brad Manning had been arrested, but he didn't immediately share this knowledge with others in the WikiLeaks core. He moved solo around Australia and then Europe, carrying with him the cache of classified documents and unilaterally discussing deals with media organizations like the *Guardian* and the *New York Times*. Some of his colleagues felt he was becoming dictatorial. The trouble had been brewing for months.

Over the summer, WikiLeaks had been the scene of a pseudo-insurrection. An anonymous group—ostensibly but unverifiably more than one person—calling itself the "WikiLeaks Insiders" posted a letter on John Young's Cryptome website, denouncing financial mis-management at WikiLeaks and calling for a full audit from the Wau Holland Foundation, the hacker nonprofit that managed WikiLeaks' funds. "Illuminated by the spotlight of global publicity, Assange and [Domscheit-Berg] are trying to attempt to divert the WIKILEAKS donor base from the fact that there is no day to day accounting at WIKILEAKS. The LIMITED DISCLOSURE from the Wau Hol-land Foundation is no substitute for a fully audited disclosure of WIKILEAKS operating cash flows and current financial position." By the time the rape allegations were announced, many of those inside the organization felt Assange was already severely discredited. Ami-cable relations between him and Birgitta Jonsdottir had deteriorated, and when Assange lashed out following the rape accusations, blaming them on a US-led conspiracy against him, Jonsdottir publicly called for him to step aside as the face of the organization. Others echoed her call in private.

According to Domscheit-Berg, he and two of WikiLeaks' chief technical employees, the Technician and the Architect, pushed back against Assange's increasingly autocratic style. "Ultimately, of course, it was Julian who made the decisions," Domscheit-Berg wrote. "The rest of us were too indecisive and skittish or simply lacked the resolve to set any limits for him. Julian thus became the autocratic head of WL, accountable to no one and tolerating no challenges to his authority. This had emerged as a problem when Bradley Manning was arrested, and clearly it was going to continue to be a problem in the weeks to come. The investigations in Sweden would prove to be the wedge that finally broke up our team." On August 25, Domscheit-Berg, the Architect, and the Technician switched the WikiLeaks system into maintenance mode and shut Assange out of its Twitter and e-mail accounts. "We were trying to shake Julian up," he said. Assange called their bluff and closed down the entire WikiLeaks system. "We caved almost immediately, restored the wiki, and gave him the passwords," Domscheit-Berg wrote.

A report in *Newsweek* the following day described growing dis-affection within WikiLeaks. Domscheit-Berg opened a chat with

Assange intending to discuss the proposed release of the classified Iraq war documents several weeks hence. But Assange was intent on conducting an inquisition regarding the anonymous source who'd spoken to *Newsweek* about WikiLeaks' internal drama. Assange asked Domscheit-Berg repeatedly if he was responsible for the leak, Domscheit-Berg denied it, and Assange asked again and again. The discussion finally reached a breaking point.

"If you do not answer the question, you will be removed," wrote Assange.

"You are not anyone's king or god. And you're not even fulfilling your role as a leader right now," said Domscheit-Berg. "A leader communicates and cultivates trust in himself. You are doing the exact opposite. You behave like some kind of emperor or slave trader."

"You are suspended for one month, effective immediately."

"Haha. Right," wrote Domscheit-Berg, by all appearances literally incredulous. "Because of what? And who says that? You? Another ad hoc decision?"

"If you wish to appeal you will be heard on Tuesday."

"BAHAHAHA. Maybe everyone was right and you really have gone mental, J. You should get some help."

"You will be heard by a panel of peers," wrote Assange. "You are suspended for disloyalty, insubordination and destabilization in a time of crisis."

If some felt Assange was being imperious, it was at least in part because, as far as WikiLeaks was concerned, he was effectively an emperor. Domscheit-Berg ridiculed Assange's unilateral suspension of him, but the move was a success in some respects. Domscheit-Berg, along with the Technician and the Architect, were shut out of their WikiLeaks e-mail accounts, for all practical purposes barring them from participating in the organization. Domscheit-Berg characterized the episode more as a defection than a suspension, but whichever it was there can be no question as to who, in the end, was in charge of WikiLeaks. Assange had been the ideological progenitor and undisputed spokesman from its earliest days, and when the two top-tier WikiLeaks insiders had a schism, Assange took the organization with him.

But Domscheit-Berg was no amateur player. The German programmer, along with the Technician and the Architect, had been central to setting up and managing the WikiLeaks system, and Assange was beginning to look to some like the emperor with no clothes. When they left weeks later, they took the contents of a WikiLeaks server with them, including the password-protected file Assange had tucked away to allow David Leigh of the *Guardian* to download the State Department cables.

Troubled days lay ahead for the Australian. Hunted by an increasingly enraged superpower, he was on the run and now more isolated than ever, with sexual misconduct allegations complicating matters.

■ ■ ■

Getting the Iraq War Logs published proved to be a trying experience for the team at the *Guardian*. Assange had expanded the group of media partners to include the likes of Al-Jazeera and the new London-based Bureau of Investigative Journalism—groups the original old-media partners, according to the *Guardian*'s David Leigh, considered "riff raff." When Assange requested that the Iraq War Logs publication date be postponed, Leigh used the opportunity to get the real jackpot out of Assange: the more than 200,000 State Department cables he had in his possession, according to the logs of the chats between Brad Manning and Adrian Lamo. Assange offered half of the documents, but Leigh held firm. He wanted them all. Eventually Assange capitulated. While he and Leigh sat together, Assange set up the PGP encryption for the file and temporary website from which Leigh could download the documents, which were hidden in a subdirectory on a WikiLeaks server. On a scrap of paper Assange wrote a phrase: *ACollectionOfHistorySince_1966_ToThe-PresentDay#* .

"That's the password," he said. "But you have to add one extra word when you type it in. You have to put in the word 'Diplomatic' before the word 'History.' Can you remember that?"

"I can remember that," said Leigh. The *Guardian* had the gold.

On October 22, WikiLeaks and an expanded cohort of media partners released the Iraq War Logs, 391,832 classified field reports from US soldiers in Iraq written between 2004 and 2009. This cache dwarfed the Afghan War Logs and alone represented the biggest leak of military secrets in US history.

Coverage of the Iraq logs provided a more clearly unflattering depiction of an American occupation than the previous batch of leaks. The website Iraq Body Count found around 15,000 previously unreported civilian deaths in Iraq. The logs documented copious instances of security contractors—what in an earlier era would have been uncontroversially called mercenaries—acting recklessly and indiscriminately, sowing chaos in and out of combat. The leak also disproved the Pentagon's repeated assertion that the US military doesn't conduct body counts on enemies and civilians. Through the logs the public learned of the now-notorious "Frago 242" (short for "fragmentary order"). Issued in June 2004, Frago 242 explicitly directed coalition troops in Iraq not to investigate violations of the laws of war not committed by members of the coalition. The order amounted to official permission for the Iraqi authorities to employ torture. On evidence were hundreds of reports of detainees who suffered from "abuse, torture, rape and even murder by Iraqi police and soldiers whose conduct appears to be systematic and normally unpunished," according to the *Guardian*.

As before, the *Washington Post* wrote an editorial condemning the leak, arguing that it, like the "dump of documents on Afghanistan in the summer, mainly demonstrates that the truth about Iraq already has been told." In his politically motivated dissemination of leaks, Julian Assange, the *Post* asserted, "offered abundant evidence that there is no secret history of Iraq or Afghanistan."

Again, in general terms the *Post* got it right: the leaks largely confirmed the narrative of a complex and messy war that had been widely reported in the mainstream press. But in its apologia for the government's position, the paper inadvertently highlighted the most important question the document leak raised (though it was all too seldom asked by members of the media): why did the heretofore-unknown details in these documents remain secret for so long? The timing of the leak created a political crisis in Iraq's nascent democracy, complicating negotiations to form a new government. But the Iraq War Logs compromised no ongoing operations, nor, apparently, did they reveal vital technological, scientific, or urgent military secrets. (On this round, all parties involved were careful to redact the names of innocents who might have been harmed by the revelations.) For the most part the leaks merely confirmed what was already assumed or asserted, and evidence that the government had lied—claiming not to know how many civilians were killed in the course of its combat operations, for example—was more damning than any single revelation. That the war logs were scandalous was due more to fact that they held information the public should already have had access to than to any specific facts they contained.

Days after the Iraq War Logs went public, the *New York Times* ran a profile of Julian Assange written by veteran correspondent John F. Burns. The piece portrayed the founder and face of WikiLeaks as erratic, arrogant, and dismissive of any who dared question his authority or the efficacy of his leadership. Burns quoted from a chat between Assange and a twenty-five-year-old WikiLeaks volunteer from Iceland. "I am the heart and soul of this organization, its founder, philosopher, spokesperson, original coder, organizer, financier, and all the rest," said Assange, who Burns portrayed frequently dangling the threat of excommunication over his subordinates. The profile quoted sources inside WikiLeaks who described widespread disillusionment with their increasingly isolated chief and over a dozen defections in addition to Domscheit-Berg.

The profile infuriated Assange, who described it as a "smear hit piece" with "errors in it from top to bottom." Others, including journalists and top-tier academics, joined the chorus of denunciation, and Burns said he could not "recall ever having been the subject of such absolutely relentless vituperation." With the Burns piece coming on the heels of the *Times* profile of Brad Manning, which Assange had called "absolutely disgusting," Assange broke off the relationship with the *Times*, intending to cut them out of future collaborations, including the upcoming release of the State Department dispatches that promised to be more sensational than anything WikiLeaks had released yet. In the end, the team at the *Guardian* provided the cables to the *Times*, leading to their own rift with WikiLeaks and its increasingly isolated leader.

A Stockholm court approved a request on November 18 to detain Assange for questioning in regard to the sexual assault allegations, and two days later, the Swedish police issued an international arrest warrant. But for Assange, then living in hiding in London, the rape charges were an annoying sideshow. The greatest leak he was ever to release— his magnum opus, in a way—was days away from publication.

■ ■ ■

WikiLeaks and its media partners started publishing a trickle of leaked diplomatic cables on November 28, 2010. The full collection totaled 251,287 cables from 271 American diplomatic stations around the world and included communiques spanning from December 1966 through February 2010 (with the preponderance from the most recent three years). Cablegate, as WikiLeaks came to call the diplomatic cable release, was larger in terms of the amount of information exposed than both the Afghan and Iraq War Logs collections. By itself, in terms of the secrets revealed, it almost certainly represented the single biggest leak in American history. Unlike the ground-level snapshots of the wars in Iraq and Afghanistan, the diplomatic cables were detailed dispatches between diplomatic posts around the globe, offering a never-before-seen, candid view of American diplomacy.

Again, the stories the cables exposed were too many even to summarize in these pages. The *New York Times* called the leak "an unprecedented look at back-room bargaining by embassies around the world, brutally candid views of foreign leaders and frank assessments of nuclear and terrorist threats." Rather than shocking revelations, most of the news from the leak came from shocking corroboration. Rumor and conjecture was confirmed, as in the case of the covert war against al-Qaeda in Yemen, sanctioned by the Yemeni government;

what a former ambassador called the "appalling greed" of people close to the king of Morocco, a key US ally in North Africa and the Middle East; vast, insidious, and growing corruption among the Tunisian ruling elite; and proof that US diplomats determined the 2009 ouster of the president of Honduras was an "illegal and unconstitutional coup," though the Obama administration refused to publicly call the action a coup d'état and moved quickly to normalize relations with the new Honduran regime. The leaked cables also exposed a list compiled by the State Department of sites deemed vulnerable to terrorist attack.

Unlike in the case of the war logs, there was little question as to why the diplomatic cables were classified. This was not transparent diplomacy but opaque diplomacy conducted under the assurance of secrecy, suddenly revealed. Diplomats writing in private to one another offered frank and often unflattering descriptions of foreign leaders and of the inner workings of American diplomatic affairs. In the controlled release that began in November 2010, WikiLeaks and its partners redacted the names of informants whose lives or livelihoods might be threatened were their identities to be publicized. But months later, these efforts at mitigating harm would be undermined by the very people who had worked so hard to bring the documents to light.

In February 2011, after the initial cables' release, the *Guardian's* David Leigh came out with a book, *WikiLeaks: Inside Julian Assange's War on Secrecy*, in which he detailed the scene where Assange handed him the password for the PGP-encrypted cables. Believing the password had become obsolete, he used the entire phrase as the epigraph of a chapter.

In the meantime, Domscheit-Berg had returned to Assange the contents of the file he'd taken, but somewhere along the chain of custody the file with the cables made its way online. With the file in circulation and the password published in a book written by one of the key characters in the WikiLeaks drama, it was only a matter of time before someone put the two bits of information together. In late August 2011, someone did. Domscheit-Berg highlighted the leak while speaking to a reporter to support his claim that Assange and WikiLeaks practiced poor operational security. (He'd by now started a rival project, OpenLeaks.) In response, WikiLeaks released the unredacted file on its own, citing the need, if intelligence agencies could now open the file, for people identified as informants in the cables to have access to documents as well.

The names of informants who had spoken to State Department officials under promise of anonymity were suddenly vulnerable, and many feared lives were in danger. The United States claimed hundreds of sensitive sources had been compromised, and a State Department spokesperson called the release "irresponsible, reckless and frankly dangerous." But a review by the Associated Press of sources identified as most sensitive found that none of them was endangered by the release—many, in fact, were surprised to find that a casual, innocuous interaction with a foreign service officer had landed their name in an official communique with an order to "strictly protect" their identities. The United States said several of those named in the cables had to be relocated for their safety but wouldn't provide specifics, and a number of those identified were dismayed by the release, including a German party official who was named as a source for the State Department. But in the end only one person—an Ethiopian journalist who fled his country after his name was revealed—was known to have been endangered by the dissemination of the unredacted cables.

The lives of more American officials than foreign informants were changed by the cables' exposure. The US ambassador to Mexico resigned his post when his unflattering assessment of Mexican security forces was made public. (Some speculated that he'd already soured his relationship with the Mexican government by dating the daughter of an opposition party leader.) Ecuador expelled its US ambassador, the charge d'affaires to Turkmenistan was reassigned to Russia, and the ambassador to Libya was recalled at a critical moment—January 2011, months before the country erupted into civil war. No doubt these shakeups complicated American diplomacy.

In the United States the preponderance of coverage of Cablegate focused on Assange and the presumed damage to American prestige wrought by the leak. The federal government reacted with pathetic, blundering rage. After the release of the cables, the State Department maintained its position that they were classified and tried to prohibit their dissemination despite their widespread availability on the Internet. The White House sent a message to employees throughout the federal government warning them not to read the cables on work computers, personal computers, smartphones, or other devices. At the urging of a federal official, the School of International and Public Affairs at Columbia University warned students against reading, discussing, or posting links to the cables on social media sites. Veteran Foreign Service Officer Peter Van Buren, the author of a book critical of America's occupation of Iraq, was suspended from his State Department job and had his security clearance revoked after linking to WikiLeaks cables on his blog. All despite the fact that anyone in the world with an uncensored Internet connection could search the entire repository of cables at any time.

Taken on the whole, the cables released by WikiLeaks portray an American foreign service working hard and faithfully to promote American interests in a complex and dangerous world. But most of the reactions from government highlighted presumed damage done to American stature and the increased difficulty American diplomats said they would have in gaining the trust of potential informants abroad. Government commentators and apologists generally failed to note that the mistrust foreign sources would henceforth have for American operational security was, the case of WikiLeaks confirmed, warranted.

Defense Secretary Robert Gates, ever the thoughtful statesman, took the long view in his assessment of the overall impact of the WikiLeaks disclosures. "Now, I've heard the impact of these releases on our foreign policy described as a meltdown, as a game-changer," he said. "I think those descriptions are fairly significantly overwrought. The fact is governments deal with the United States because it's in their interest, not because they like us, not because they trust us, and not because they believe we can keep secrets." The American position in the world, Gates insisted, was resilient enough to withstand even a dose this ample of unwanted transparency. "Some governments deal with us because they fear us, some because they respect us, most because they need us. We are still essentially, as has been said before, the indispensable nation. So other nations will continue to deal with us. They will continue to work with us. We will continue to share sensitive information with one another. Is this embarrassing? Yes. Is it awkward? Yes. Consequences for US foreign policy? I think fairly modest."

Still, condemning WikiLeaks—and either explicitly or by extension its chief source Brad Manning—was a nearly universally held position among American political elites. It was WikiLeaks' fate to receive the support of only fringe politicians. While some mainstream politicos cautioned against overreacting, only one legislator, a perennial rogue, consistently and forcefully took the contrarian position in support of the whistleblowing operation.

Rep. Ron Paul (R-Texas) made frequent public statements in defense of WikiLeaks and Brad Manning. "If we have an American citizen that is willing to take the consequences and practice civil disobedience and say, 'This is what our government's doing,' should he be locked up in prison?" Paul asked a crowd of supporters while Brad Manning sat in jail awaiting trial. "No!" they shouted back. "Or should we see him as a political hero? Maybe he is a true patriot who reveals what's going on in government."

On the floor of the House of Representatives, Paul delivered a tough, unequivocal speech in which he posed many of the key questions the WikiLeaks saga presented but the political establishment was too timid or indifferent to ask. "Number one. Do the American people deserve to know the truth regarding the ongoing wars in Iraq, Afghanistan, Pakistan, and Yemen?" Paul asked rhetorically. "Number two. Could a larger question be, how can an army private access so much secret information? Number three. Why is the hostility directed at Assange, the publisher, and not at our government's failure to protect classified information? Number four. Are we getting our money's worth of the eighty billion dollars per year spent on intelligence gathering?" Paul's list continued for nine points total and covered some of the central issues being left out of the public debate. He closed with a final question: "Was it not once considered patriotic to stand up to our government when it is wrong?"

■ ■ ■

The focus of the story in the United States on the peculiarities of the messengers Assange and Manning, and on the damage done to American prestige, reflected a failure to appreciate the impact the release of the cables was having abroad. Indeed, the most significant impacts Cablegate would have on the world would be outside the country WikiLeaks ostensibly targeted with the leak. Again we are faced with effects spread too far and too wide to be accounted for entirely in these pages.

The leaked cables provided incontrovertible proof that, like in the case of the Honduran coup d'état, the United States had in some instances acted dishonestly and against the interest of good governance. Many riveting revelations, however, related only tangentially to the United States but carried important implications for people most Americans didn't know existed. Such was the case with the Western Sahara, to cite just one example.

America's closest ally in North Africa, the Kingdom of Morocco, had been engaged in a decades-long struggle with the Polisario Front over a stretch of largely desolate terrain to the northeast of Mauritania known as the Western Sahara. The territory was a Spanish colony until 1975, but after independence Morocco asserted a historical claim to the land, and fighting began between the kingdom and the local inhabitants, Sahrawis, under the banner of the Polisario Front. Tens of thousands of local Sahrawis were forced into refugee camps in neighboring Algeria, beginning one of the most protracted refugee crises in the world. In 1991, armed conflict gave way to a ceasefire and public relations war, but the standoff continued, with around 100,000 refugees residing in Polisario-administered camps. (Like most aspects of the dispute, the actual population of the camps is a matter of contention.) While the Polisario accused Morocco of committing war crimes in an illegal occupation and violently suppressing peaceful demonstrations, Morocco accused the Polisario of holding the Sahrawi people captive in its camps in the Algerian desert, among a litany of other sins. The post-9/11 era brought accusations that the

Polisario allowed al-Qaeda to recruit and smuggle goods in the refugee camps. The entire issue is notoriously fraught with obfuscation, but when WikiLeaks released a confidential dispatch from the American embassy in Algiers, a rare bit of unpolluted light was cast on the ongoing debate. Members of al-Qaeda, according to an American diplomat, "perceive the Sahrawi people as too close to the West and not pious enough, in part, these contacts believe, because Sahrawi religious leaders have encouraged Western NGOs to participate in seminars on inter-faith dialogue and women's issues." For most of the world the revelation went unnoticed. But for thousands of African refugees living in decades-long limbo in remote Algeria to be publicly acquitted of complicity with the world's most notorious terrorists was a breath of not-inconsequential fresh air.

The most dramatic—and disputed—illustration of how the leaked cables affected the course of human affairs was probably in the case of Tunisia and the ensuing Arab Spring. When the publication of leaked cables relating to Tunisia's ruler, Zine El Abidine Ben Ali, coincided with a popular uprising against the kleptocratic regime, many wondered if the cables inspired the revolution. After an unofficial survey of contacts throughout the country, the Washington director of Human Rights Watch wrote: "The candid appraisal of Ben Ali by US diplomats showed Tunisians that the rottenness of the regime was obvious not just to them but to the whole world—and that it was a source of shame for Tunisia on an international stage. The cables also contradicted the prevailing view among Tunisians that Washington would back Ben Ali to the bloody end, giving them added impetus to take to the streets. They further delegitimized the Tunisian leader and boosted the morale of his opponents at a pivotal moment in the drama that unfolded."

Others echoed that analysis. "WikiLeaks came at the right moment," one prominent Tunisian activist told the Institute for War and Peace Reporting. "The regime did not have any internal popular legitimacy. . . . WikiLeaks taught the Tunisian people that even foreign diplomats from the West, among them the Americans, were not on good terms with the regime," he said. "When Tunisians realized that their suspicions had grounds and were even well documented by foreign diplomats, there was no longer any excuse—the regime had to change." As revolution spread from Tunisia to Egypt, Syria, Libya, Yemen, and Bahrain, WikiLeaks released cables in tandem with developments on the ground, intending to inspire further revolt. Regimes as intractable as that of Hosni Mubarak were toppled, and it seemed to some that WikiLeaks had been the spark that catalyzed the season of upheaval that remapped the geopolitical landscape like few events in modern history.

When WikiLeaks released a fund-raising commercial playing off MasterCard's much-parodied "Priceless" advertisements, featuring a video of the Egyptian popular uprising that credited WikiLeaks for changing the world, a cacophony of observers cried foul. An Egyptian writer, reflecting on the leaks' effect on the Arab Spring, told the *New York Times*, "For Tunisia, I don't know. Information flow there was much more controlled, and the leaks did include major gems. But for Egypt, not at all. What was common knowledge already exceeded WikiLeaks, [which] had absolutely no impact." Dan Murphy, who spent five years as an Egypt correspondent, wrote in the *Christian Science Monitor*, "The problem with the ad's climactic assertion, of course, is that it isn't true. The Egyptian revolution came after a decade of bubbling protest, of political organization at great cost and risk to the few who got involved. The Egyptian left had spent years trying to create a strong independent labor movement (independent unions were outlawed under Mr. Mubarak)." Murphy closed his article with a quip: "So here's my own Mastercard take: 'Hundreds of thousands risking their lives to face down a tyrant? Expensive. Taking credit for it from a London mansion? Cheap.'"

Murphy's disdain for WikiLeaks was a common sentiment among those who disputed the group's influence on the Middle East uprisings. An organization run by Westerners taking credit for revolutions that were won through tremendous sacrifice on the part of local African and Middle Eastern activists struck many as cynical and patronizing. While WikiLeaks' allies celebrated what they believed to be its revolutionary global impact, activists in Tunisia, Egypt, and elsewhere defended their hard-won revolutions from opportunists trying to cash in on their successes. The truth about what effect the WikiLeaks cables had probably lay somewhere in the uninspiring middle.

No one in Tunisia or Egypt—certainly no one prone to take to the streets in protest—needed American diplomats to tell them their ruling regimes were corrupt. Those revolutions were spearheaded by courageous activists who spent years doing the dangerous and often tedious work of political organizing, and what inspiration was needed was at hand long before an Australian computer science student dreamed up his idea for radical transparency. Indeed, by the time WikiLeaks began publishing cables relating to Egypt, the uprising was well under way, and furthermore, very few of the documents were ever translated and widely disseminated for an Egyptian audience.

But to assign the causes of the Arab Spring only to local conditions is to deny its essential character as a season of cascading revolutions. The uprising in Tunisia heartened revolutionaries in Egypt, whose defeat of Mubarak encouraged Libyan rebels, whose violent overthrow of Muammar Gaddafi inspired Syrians under a brutal crackdown from their own dictator, and so on. Drawing a straight line through each event is, of course, a gross oversimplification, but it is clear that local actors were influenced by events beyond their national borders and were heartened by the spirit of democratic insurrection reverberating back and forth around the world. Later in the spring, Spaniards took to the streets in mass protests reminiscent of the symbolic occupation of Cairo's Tahrir Square during the Egyptian uprising. That summer, the Canada-based magazine *Adbusters* issued a call for a Tahrir-like protest in the United States, in which activists were asked to "Occupy Wall Street." The Occupy movement subsequently emerged in cities across the United States and then the world. Posters and slogans in support of both WikiLeaks and Brad Manning were not uncommon at Occupy gatherings around the country.

At most, the WikiLeaks cables helped inspire the Tunisian uprising and gave fodder to Egyptians during their revolution, setting off the chain reaction that sparked or fueled revolt the world over. At least, the cables contributed to a spirit of upheaval and a sense among activists that a world dominated by powerful governments and corporations was not invulnerable to change. One has a difficult time imagining diplomatic cables from any other country in the world having such a profound impact on world affairs. In the final summation, the effects of the WikiLeaks cables were a testament to the enduring moral authority and political influence of the United States despite deeply troubling revelations within them.

When President Obama announced in late 2011 that the last American soldier would leave Iraq by the end of the year, one of WikiLeaks' greatest victories was hidden within the story. The decision to remove all US troops from Iraq came after the collapse of negotiations between the US and Iraqi governments over renewing the Status of Forces Agreement for 2012. The talks had been severely complicated after WikiLeaks released a cable corroborating the stories Iraqi locals had long told about a vicious attack on civilians perpetrated by American troops in 2006.

American officials had denied anything inappropriate occurred and impeded investigations into the incident, but the cable WikiLeaks made public included details from a UN-led probe that told a different story. The UN investigator found evidence, corroborated by autopsies, to support the account locals had long told: in March 2006, American troops in the perilous town of Ishaqi, near Baghdad, entered a home after a firefight at 2:30 AM, handcuffed at least ten occupants, including four women and five children all under the age of six, and executed each of them with a gunshot to the head. The Americans then called in an air strike to cover up evidence of the crime.

The UN findings had been made public earlier, but the cables' release cast new attention on the story. In the 2011 negotiations over troop levels, the Americans insisted their soldiers maintain legal immunity in Iraq, but Iraqis, outraged over the Ishaqi murders, demanded that American troops be subject to Iraqi laws and Iraqi punishment. The disagreement proved intractable, and when talks fell through President Obama announced, "After nearly nine years, America's war in Iraq will be over." It is overly simple but not altogether inaccurate to say that WikiLeaks—or rather, Brad Manning—helped end the Iraq War.

Since nearly all of the classified material WikiLeaks released in 2010—certainly all of its most significant material—came from Brad Manning, the question of how great an impact WikiLeaks had on global events is really a question of Brad Manning's impact. The specifics remain in dispute, but the simple answer is indisputable: he had a far greater impact on the world than any single individual, particularly a troubled US Army private from rural Oklahoma, could ever reasonably hope to have. Those who maligned Brad for having "delusions of grandeur" profoundly misunderstood the situation. He saw the wealth of secret information available to him, understood the importance of its being digitized and searchable, and envisioned a way to make it public with maximum political impact. Against the better interest of his own future he carried out history's biggest leak of official secrets, and in so doing he changed the world. What one thinks of Brad's dangerous decision to become a whistleblower is irrelevant to the issue at hand. Brad Manning may have seen grandeur in his power to effect change by leaking, and if he did there was nothing deluded about it.

■ ■ ■

Though WikiLeaks was making headlines and shaping global events, things were not well for Julian Assange or his organization. Assange had turned himself in to British authorities on December 8, 2010, and been remanded to house arrest at a manor in the English countryside while awaiting resolution of his legal troubles in Sweden. Fearing the Swedes intended to extradite him to the United States, where politicians had been calling for his arrest and worse, Assange fought efforts to force him to appear in person for questioning on the sexual assault charges.

But Assange's legal troubles were not the greatest challenges facing WikiLeaks. Beset by defections and a financial blockade, wherein companies like PayPal, Visa, and MasterCard refused to process donations to the group, the organization was more fragile than ever. Making matters worse, the departures of Domscheit-Berg, the Architect, and the Technician left the website unable to accept leak submissions.

A great wave of publicity and upheaval had accompanied the release of Brad Manning's leaks, beginning with Reykjavik-13 and ending with the full, unredacted cache of State Department cables. But as the wave subsided many wondered: what was the future for WikiLeaks and radical transparency?

10
Saving Private Manning

The Acetarium 2.0, according to its website, "is a dynamic and highly exclusive living, working, dining and recreation space . . . a intellectually charged space that occupies the intersection of technology and culture—art and science."

The Acetarium 2.0, in reality, is the apartment of a friend of Danny Clark. There is nothing official about its name or tongue-in-cheek website that includes a faux quote from Paris Hilton: "The Acetarium is the place to be in Boston this year. It's totally hot!" Located in the gentrifying artist-haven neighborhood of Davis Square, it's a social hub of Boston's free software community. On Saturday night, June 5, Danny was at one of the many parties hosted there when he received a surprising phone call.

It had been over a week since Danny had heard from Brad, and he was growing concerned. They tended to keep in fairly close touch, and such a long stretch without Brad signing online was unusual. Their last conversation had been on May 25, and on May 30, Danny posted on Brad's Facebook wall: "Hi, are you okay? Haven't seen you on IM for a while. Posting here in case others worry as easily as I :-) ."

On the afternoon of Wednesday, June 2, Danny had received a call from Adrian Lamo. Though they had never spoken before, Danny knew Adrian by reputation; David had told him about his own meeting with the famous Adrian Lamo, and Danny noticed a few weeks earlier that Brad and Adrian became Facebook friends. On the call,

Adrian said he was worried about their mutual friend, "saying, did I know anything, and he was also concerned," Danny said later, "and to stay in touch. He sort of encouraged me to look into it more. And I thought it was sort of odd, but besides knowing that he had a drug problem I had no reason to believe that he was a bad guy, and if he and Brad did know each other somehow I certainly didn't want him to worry."

Immediately after the call, Danny e-mailed Brad's aunt Debbie. "Hi, it's Danny—I met you and stayed over at your house (thanks!) briefly a while ago, just before Brad went to Iraq," he wrote. "Brad hasn't been contactable for about a week (since 5/26), and I'm a bit worried, so I'm just wondering if you have heard anything; I just want to make sure he's alright." He attached a photo of him and Brad together and left his phone number, in case "that would be more appropriate."

"I haven't really been hearing from Brad," she wrote back immediately. "This is troubling. When he is posting on Facebook, I know he's okay but now that you mention it, I haven't seen any recent posts. If I hear from him I will let you know. Please do the same if you hear from him." Danny suggested that Brad's parents or sister, as next of kin, might know if something had happened to him, and Debbie promised to tell him if she heard anything.

They were dancing around the deepest fear of those with a loved one at war; Brad's friends and family feared he was dead.

On that Saturday night, at the Acetarium, Danny's phone rang, and again it was Adrian Lamo. "He said that Brad was coming out as the person who was doing the WikiLeaks," Danny later said, "and that he, Adrian, was doing public relations for Brad." Confusion and a peculiar sense of relief fought for space in Danny's mind. "I think I was more relieved to hear that Brad wasn't dead, and the whole impact of what this would mean was lost on me," Danny said. "And so [Adrian] starts talking, and he says he wants to have Brad painted as a good guy and humanize him." He asked Danny if he would talk to Kevin Poulsen at *Wired*, who was then working on the story that would publicly break the news of Brad Manning's arrest.

Poulsen was still trying to verify that Brad Manning had been arrested at all—at this point all he had were chat logs from Adrian Lamo and a Facebook post from Danny Clark indicating that Brad had gone missing. Poulsen had asked Lamo for the phone number of the friend who'd posted on Brad's wall.

Danny went to a quiet bedroom, away from the rest of the party, and jotted down some quick notes for the interview. There were two possible scenarios, he wrote: either he knew Brad was guilty and wouldn't comment, not yet knowing what his defense would be, or he didn't know anything and thus couldn't say anything. "In any case," he wrote, "I'm not going to comment on that subject at this time." The conversation went roughly according to Danny's script.

"In the course of interviewing Clark," Poulsen later wrote in an e-mail, "it became clear that Lamo had already talked to him on the phone without revealing that he was the one who turned in Manning, so I elected not to use the interview." Danny was thus never quoted in the story. The next evening, June 6, an article was posted on Wired .com's Threat Level blog under the headline: "U.S. Intelligence Analyst Arrested in Wikileaks Video Probe." And with that the Bradley Manning story burst onto the world stage.

The next day, Tyler Watkins sent a message online to Danny, asking what he knew about Lamo. Danny said he'd heard about Lamo's past drug problems and cautioned Tyler against talking to him. "Friends I trust say he's good at using social engineering to get results he wants, so unless you have good reason to trust the results he wants are the same as the results you want, be careful," Danny said. "That said, I appreciate him coordinating media coverage, and the main editor at Wired he works with seems to have edited other pieces that are balanced and not full of shit."

Tyler said he had no plans to talk to Lamo. He added that it would be typical of Brad to open up to someone when he shouldn't.

Thereafter, Tyler declined to speak to the media and, like many of Brad's friends, distanced himself as much as possible from the dicey situation. But Brad was not left entirely on his own. While he was being ferried to a military jail in Kuwait and his friends and family were scrambling for more information, a formerly American anarchist in Bratislava, Slovakia, was rushing to Brad's aid.

■ ■ ■

Mike Gogulski grew up in Orlando, Florida. He started studies in computer science at the University of Central Florida in 1990 but partied his way out of school by the second semester. Like many others of his generation, studies in computer science would have been redundant anyway—soon he was making a hefty income as a network administrator. He was, according to the personal bio on his website, on a "meteoric career path, going from hobbyist hacker to megabucks consultant" when the dot-com bubble burst and his career trajectory swerved. He became a permanent traveler and set up a home base in Slovakia.

Mike, who describes himself as an anarcho-capitalist, was critical of US foreign policy at the time of the first Bush administration, and by the time George W. Bush invaded Iraq he'd become disgusted. In a matter of years he was so thoroughly disillusioned that he felt obligated to live wholly according to his anarchist principles. With his home in Slovakia, he renounced his American citizenship and officially became a stateless person. Mike had seen WikiLeaks' "Collateral Murder" video, and when news broke that Brad Manning had been arrested for the leak, it took him no time to determine that Brad was a hero. On June 10, he registered bradleymanning.org and began organizing a movement to support the accused.

Back in Cambridge, Danny Clark was mobilizing too. He registered the domain name bradleyemanning.org, set up e-mail and Facebook accounts for the support effort, and began exploring options for "a charitable trust for [Brad], as whatever happens I doubt he'll be able to take advantage of the GI Bill to go to college when it's over," he wrote in an e-mail to his friend Eric Schmiedl. "The reality," Schmiedl wrote back, "is that Brad won't have to worry about getting an education for quite a while if they convict him." It was a good point. And the consensus among his supporters held that if Brad was to get the most vigorous defense possible, he would need a civilian attorney—and someone would have to pay the bill.

The last few weeks of June were harried and confused, but the Bradley Manning Support Network, along with a fund for Brad's legal defense, took shape around the network Mike Gogulski formed. Danny contacted Mike, and, after proving he truly was a friend of Brad's from before the arrest, he and Mike combined efforts. Others were brought in, including Nadim Kobeissi, the Montreal-based, Lebanese-born hacker, freedom of information activist, and former friend to Adrian Lamo; Rainey Reitman, a San Francisco–based progressive activist; and David House. Jeff Patterson, former marine and the head of Courage to Resist, a group that helps defend conscientious objectors, took over the fund-raising for Brad's legal defense. Daniel Ellsberg became one of Brad Manning's most prominent defenders. And thus, out of a hectic and disorganized genesis, the effort to save Bradley Manning became a movement.

Meanwhile, Brad was alone in a cell in the military detention facility at Camp Arafjan in Kuwait. He was distraught but exercising his right to remain silent and to not cooperate with the investigation. Not that the state needed his help—the army's Computer Crimes Investigation Unit was busy gathering evidence on its own. Though he took some precautions, such as e-mail with PGP encryption, OTR chatting, deleting files, and at least one full erase of his personal computer's hard drive, for all his intelligence training Brad's information security precautions were almost nil. Dissecting the various SIPRnet machines he worked on, and his personal computer, digital forensics teams uncovered records of his searches in Google and Intelink. He'd left a clear trail using Wget to download the Guantánamo documents and the Net-Centric Diplomacy cables. Detectives searched his old room in the basement of Debbie's house, and on their second try they found the SD card on which Brad had saved the Iraq and Afghanistan SIGACTS accompanied by his "removing the fog of war" message to WikiLeaks.

Brad's aunt Debbie became the family's point person for his case—his mother was in Wales, debilitated by a stroke, and his father at first chose not to get involved. A lawyer herself, Debbie spoke with

Brad's military-appointed JAG attorney, CPT Paul Bouchard, about the possibility of getting Brad civilian representation. Bouchard spoke to Brad, who said he was interested.

The support network gathered the names of a number of possible attorneys, including another JAG officer in the army reserve, a lawyer for the Electronic Frontier Foundation, and a former president of the National Association of Criminal Defense Lawyers then representing Guantánamo detainees. On her own, Debbie spoke to fellow lawyers and assembled a list of possible names. CPT Bouchard also had a couple suggestions. One of them was David Coombs.

A native of Boise, Idaho, a golfer and a fisherman, David Coombs spent twelve years on active duty in the Army JAG Corps before leaving to go into private practice in 2009. He had tried well over a hundred cases, most famously on the defense team for Hasan Akbar. Days before the invasion of Iraq was to begin, in 2003, Akbar, a Muslim who claimed he acted on religious grounds, threw grenades and opened fire on his fellow American soldiers while at a rear base in Kuwait, killing two and injuring fourteen. He was a difficult client. During his trial, Akbar smuggled scissors out of a conference room and repeatedly stabbed an MP in the neck. Akbar was sentenced to death, but the case cemented Coombs's reputation as a vigorous and principled defense attorney. Coombs taught at the Roger Williams School of Law near his home in Rhode Island, and at the military's JAG school in Charlottesville, Virginia.

Manning was charged on July 5 with moving a classified video, fifty State Department Cables, and a classified PowerPoint presentation onto a nonsecure computer. He faced up to fifty-two years in prison, but these were merely preliminary charges; more serious charges were to come.

On July 29, "because of the potential for lengthy continued pretrial confinement given the complexity of the charges and ongoing investigation," according to an army press release, Brad was transferred from Kuwait to the military jail at Marine Corps Base Quantico in Virginia. Once Brad was in Virginia, he and Debbie considered the candidates for his civilian representation. They settled on Coombs.

■ ■ ■

The July 2010 HOPE Conference (Hackers on Planet Earth) at the historic Hotel Pennsylvania in midtown Manhattan promised to be an exceptionally stirring affair. Themed "The Next HOPE," the conference was the eighth that *2600* magazine had put on since 1994. But the two years since the last gathering had been some of the most tumultuous in hacker history. WikiLeaks was busy injecting the hacker ethic into mainstream global affairs, and the topics over which hackers obsess—institutional transparency, personal privacy, freedom of information, and information security—were never more urgent. Unlike other computer-related conferences, HOPE was purely a hacker's affair. "There are other conferences that relate on certain themes [to HOPE], but most don't hit the politics/anarchy/ hacking all at once. It's actually a pretty rare combination," said one conference organizer.

That year's conference was likely to include plenty of internecine drama as well. Though the preponderance of hackers seemed to support WikiLeaks, a prominent *2600* insider, Adrian Lamo, had turned Brad Manning in to the authorities, and Lamo's status in the community was transformed overnight from lower demigod to Judas. Adding spice to the mix, Assange was set to give this year's keynote address, though the recent intensification of US efforts to bring down WikiLeaks threw those plans into question. The conference was sure to be crawling with feds.

Boston certainly was. Investigators visited the home of Danny Clark (he wasn't there and left them a voice mail with instructions to contact his lawyer) as well as pika, Tyler Watkins, David House, and others in the area. Even people only tangentially related to the situation, such as the lockpicker Eric Schmiedl, whom Brad met at BUILDS the previous January, were given special attention by investigators. David was not alone in his belief that he was under twenty-four-hour surveillance, and a spirit of paranoia spread among the Cambridge hacker community. Schmiedl would eventually uproot to Germany, where he held dual citizenship and where he continued to report CIA tails, attempts to drug and kidnap him, and a host of other paranoid machinations.

The caravan of Boston hackers was thus abuzz with a defiant spirit when the group set out for New York City on Friday, July 16, to attend the HOPE Conference. "It was exciting, a thrilling time," David House recalled. "Nobody knew what was going to happen, there were feds everywhere, and everyone knew they were feds. This was before WikiLeaks got hammered in the press so we had this untouchable moral high ground. And then Lamo's presence there was this huge splinter."

Adrian had been trying to endear himself to Danny Clark since their conversations in June, and they had remained in contact though his role in Brad Manning's arrest was now public knowledge. For Danny, Lamo was still the best of very few sources of information regarding the ongoing investigation. For Lamo, Danny was a mark.

After turning Manning in to the authorities, Lamo became a confidential informant for the government. He was not paid for his services, but the federal government covered travel and other expenses on his behalf. As a result of one of Lamo's tips, in July investigators caught up with a physicist at a Department of Energy laboratory named Jason Katz, who had been working with WikiLeaks in the effort to decrypt the Granai attack video.

Danny hoped that by meeting Lamo in person he'd learn something new about the still-mysterious situation his friend Brad had gotten himself into. They arranged to talk at the HOPE Conference, and Lamo said he had a place Danny could sleep for the weekend. This was New York City after all, and a space to spend the night for free was useful.

Danny drove himself to the conference, but before he got to New York he was already having car trouble. The alternator was nearly dead by the time he reached the Hotel Pennsylvania. He unloaded the Free Software Foundation materials from his car and helped set up the booth and then spent most of the evening busily talking to passersby. When Lamo stopped by they could talk only for a moment. Lamo, it turned out, didn't even have a place to stay for himself. Several days later Lamo was able to chat online with Danny. "For what it's worth, I'm not working with the guys out pounding on doors," he said, assuring Danny that he wasn't an informant. He added, "Let's just agree neither of us is going to share these logs." He subsequently provided the chat logs to investigators, though his intelligence-gathering activities never turned up a connection between Danny and WikiLeaks. Danny cut off contact with Lamo thereafter. At the end of that first Friday at HOPE, Danny got someone to jump his car battery and he drove through the middle of the night back to Boston. He would miss the drama that unfolded on Saturday and Sunday.

David House was sitting in the audience in the main lecture hall on Saturday afternoon when a middle-aged man wearing a backward-turned black baseball cap took the stage to introduce the keynote speaker. The man in the ball cap was Eric Corley, better known by his Orwellian alias, Emmanuel Goldstein, publisher of *2600*, radio show host, and prominent member of the hacker community.

Goldstein stood at the podium and smiled at the crowed. "Everyone having fun?" The crowd cheered. "There's a lot of feds here. I don't understand it," he said, cheekily. "There's all this interest in the conference this year for some reason." Goldstein laughed along with many in the audience. David sized up the stocky, bald guy sitting next to him in the audience, decided he was a federal agent, and saw more feds in figures standing at the back of the room. Goldstein thanked the audience for a successful conference thus far. Then he asked if anyone had seen the "Collateral Murder" video. More applause. "WikiLeaks is an organization that accepts leaks from people all over the planet," he said, "and, when appropriate, publishes them so that the world can see. I happen to think that's something that is extremely important, something the hacker world realizes is a valuable part of democratic society. And I think the person who leaked the video in the first place to WikiLeaks should be considered a national hero." For ten full seconds the audience roared in applause. Assange was not able to appear at the conference for fear he'd be arrested, Goldstein said. But there would be a WikiLeaks keynote address. "Without further ado I'd like to introduce—WikiLeaks."

A figure in a black hoodie bounded onto the stage pulling the hood off his head, revealing browline eyeglasses and a coy smile. "Hello to all my friends and fans in domestic and international surveillance," he said. The crowd chuckled. "I'm here today because I believe that we can make a better world."

The speaker was Jacob Appelbaum, another well-known character in the hacker world and now a public associate of WikiLeaks. Appelbaum had spoken before on different subjects at the Chaos Communication Congress in Berlin and was renowned for bold feats of bringing communications technology into dangerous areas, such as post-Katrina New Orleans and Kurdistan in the midst of the Iraq War. He was a chief spokesman for the Tor Project and now WikiLeaks' primary American representative.

"I want to make a little declaration for the federal agents that are standing at the back of the room and the ones that are standing at the front of the room." He said he had with him some money, the Bill of Rights, and a driver's license; no computer, telephone, keys, or anything else that should cause them to detain him. He was an American citizen, he said, who works with human rights activists, journalists, and others seeking "a positive change in this world."

"To quote from the movie *Tron*," he said, "'I fight for the user.'"

Appelbaum's "I fight for the user" lecture at HOPE would be pseudo-mythologized in hacker lore. Appearing publicly in lieu of Assange was a bold statement in defiance of the American investigation, for which he would pay a price in the coming months in the form of repeated detentions at American border crossings. The talk he gave was remarkably true to the WikiLeaks principles Assange had laid out years before. "Transparency is neutral," Appelbaum said, echoing Assange's earlier assertion that "in a world where leaking is easy, secretive or unjust systems are nonlinearly hit relative to open, just systems." Appelbaum rebuked the mainstream media for having a cozy relationship with the government and lauded WikiLeaks' commitment to disclosure at all costs—because the organization doesn't depend on access in the way other journalists do, it needn't fear losing the good will of press agents, he pointed out. The lecture was replete with anti-US abstractions and bold but vague condemnations of American foreign policy.

Appelbaum finally arrived at "Collateral Murder"—"The topic you all want to hear about," he said. He'd unzipped his sweatshirt to uncover a black t-shirt featuring the outline of a stop sign in neon green enclosing the words "STOP SNITCHING."

"Let's be clear about something. This is obviously in the air, and it's extremely important to state this," he said. "There is someone who has been alleged to be a source by a person who has no name in this community any more. Do I have agreement on that?"

The crowd gave him its most vigorous applause yet.

"I'm sorry, I didn't hear you. Can we try that again with a little sincerity?"

Even louder this time, with hooting and cheering. In Dante's *Inferno* the final circle of hell is reserved for traitors, and the target of this scolding was obvious. More than snooping federal agents, Barack Obama, George Bush, or the military industrial complex, the villain of the hour was the traitor among them: Adrian Lamo.

"This person prides themselves on being heard and thought about. Just forget them. They are irrelevant," Appelbaum said. "He doesn't exist, it isn't important, and he isn't important." He never said Lamo's name.

Appelbaum finished his talk with information about the Bradley Manning Support Network, encouraging those present to donate time or money to the cause. He called for the assembled crowd to get involved with WikiLeaks, run a Tor relay, and help expand the Tor network. "Think globally, hack locally," he said, and "together we will make a gigantic change in the world." He thanked the crowd for their support and received a standing ovation in return.

While the "Collateral Murder" video played on a screen behind the podium, Appelbaum donned his black hood and walked off the stage. He slipped out a back door while a decoy wearing an identical black hoodie left through the front, and hours later Appelbaum was on a flight to Berlin. Despite the endemic paranoia, on this particular visit to the United States Appelbaum was never approached by a federal agent.

When Adrian Lamo took the stage on Sunday to join a panel discussion titled "Informants: Villains or Heroes?" the vituperation began before he got to his chair. On the stage was Emmanuel Goldstein, the moderator, next to a lineup of convicted hackers, Kevin Mitnick, Ed "Bernie S." Cummings, and Mark "Phiber Optik" Abene. Audience members yelled unintelligibly at Lamo as he settled into his seat with a glass of water to one side and a bottle of the hacker-staple soft drink, Club-Mate, to the other.

"Good day, friends, neighbors, and opponents—although I would say from the get-go I don't feel that I'm the opponent of anyone in this crowd," Lamo said. "You may feel differently, and I respect your right to do so." Most of the audience did feel differently. David House walked out of the speech in disgust.

What followed was nearly a nearly hour-long inquisition, with a raucous audience shouting out of turn while Lamo defended his decision to turn in Brad Manning and deflecting cries of "Bullshit!" with an oddly irrepressible smile. Though a vocal minority of the audience applauded in support of Lamo several times, the tenor of the event revealed the presence of an angry, accusatory mob. During an extended Q&A session, people lined up to fold attacks into questions: "How long has it been since you've had an active restraining order against you for abusing your girlfriend?" Lamo responded calmly, "I have never been served with a restraining order, and there has never been one that is active against me." "Liar!" came the response.

There were brash denunciations: "From my perspective I see what you have done as treason." "I think you fucked it up hugely." "What you did is worse than treason! I think you belong in Guantánamo!"

Throughout the talk, Adrian Lamo remained remarkably poised for a man under verbal assault from thousands of allies turned enemies. He took time to respond to all questions posed to him and repeated that he'd acted on conscience after having been placed in an awful situation by a young man he'd never met. "I wish to hell that Bradley Manning had never said a word to me," he said. "Obviously it's been much worse for him, but it's certainly been no picnic for me, and I knew from the get-go that it was going to be a low point in my interactions with the community."

Near the end of the event he took a final question from the audience.

"Do you regret what you did?"

He thought a moment. "I regret not being a better friend to Manning," he said. "I wish that there was some way that it could have been done both ways. I wish so much that he had told me, 'I'm planning on doing this,' not 'I've already done this,' and that [the leaks] were out there and there might still be a possibility of interdicting them. I can't express in words how much I wish he had said that he was planning it and that I could have told him, 'Dude, you're gonna fuck your life up.'"

The conflict between Adrian and the audience of hackers ultimately reflected a clash of two divergent worldviews: Adrian Lamo's loyalty to the United States and to the nation-state system on the one hand, and an anti-nationalist creed, based on internationalism and anarchist principles, on the other. After the last question, one of the panel members, Phiber Optik, interjected a final comment and gave voice to the incongruity.

"I'd like to say something in closing—and I'm not here in any kind of capacity to pass judgment; I leave that up to our esteemed audience to do," he said, eliciting chuckles. "What I will say is that as long as the hacker underground has existed we've always held in very high regard our neutrality." Phiber Optik had been a prominent hacker since the 1990s and was something of an elder in the community. "We're internationalists and should remain so. As soon as you make up your mind to choose a side politically speaking, you cease to be a hacker."

Lamo took a long drink from his Club-Mate. "Why have you not renounced your citizenship?" he said.

"Why should I?"

"Because that's a side."

"I was born in this country. My citizenship is automatic."

"It's automatic," said Lamo, "but you're splitting that hair mighty thin there."

"I think you're changing the subject rather easily," said Phiber Optik. "My point I was trying to make was that you had a choice and you made the wrong choice. You could have simply walked away and none of this would have happened."

"I could've, but I wouldn't have been able to live with myself," Lamo said, followed by meager applause from his few supporters. The panel moderator, Emmanuel Goldstein, thanked the audience for a mostly civil dialogue on a controversial topic and adjourned the discussion.

The panel foretold Adrian's future as persona non grata in the hacker community. In the years that followed he was spurned by former friends and associates, including David House and Nadim Kobeissi. He put on weight and appeared heavily medicated at times, making numerous public appearances with droopy eyes and slurred speech. He received threats regularly, some more credible than others, and was the subject of a more or less constant current of invective online.

The leaks with which Adrian Lamo was confronted were of such a magnitude that turning Brad Manning in may have felt like as fraught an option as going on as though nothing had happened. Inside knowledge of such a consequential event can seem to demand action, impelling one to either tell someone or make a conscious decision to keep the secret. And the reasons a decision gets made in the proverbial heat of the moment often don't amount in retrospect to clear, well-considered logic.

But in looking back more than a year later on his decision to blow the whistle on the whistleblower, Lamo was confident, unrepentant, and clear about the fact that he felt he'd done the right thing. His decision to turn Manning in, he wrote in a Facebook note, "allowed the U.S. to adjust its readiness posture in relevant areas, warn collaborating native operatives (whom Julian Assange characterized as deserving of death) to run, not walk—to basically soften the brunt of a blow that would otherwise have been incredibly costly in lives, operations, and treasure."

The point Lamo makes in this justification is important. It is true that no significant harm has ever been demonstrated to have come from Manning's leaks, but it is too often forgotten that the government had several months to prepare for the bulk of them—months it would likely not have had were it not for Adrian Lamo.

Whatever his reasons for contacting the authorities, Adrian had to make a decision of profound consequence, he wrote, "out of sudden, unexpected urgency, with no significant time to second-guess." It was, he wrote, "just a decision devolved to someone who was never trained for it, which no one should have ever had to make in the first place had the machine worked right, but which was made with the best of intentions—appearances, peers, standing, and all that rubbish be damned."

"Does it bother you that people call you Snitch or Wanted, like in the poster you showed me?" an Al-Jazeera correspondent asked Lamo in a March 2011 interview.

"It's nice to be wanted," Lamo said, with a wry smile.

"Were the circumstances repeated," he went on to explain, "and if I had the same information then as I did then, and certainly with the information that I have now, I would take the actions necessary to interdict him from further leaks. I believe that he wanted to make the world a better place. He just didn't know how to do it."

■ ■ ■

On Sunday, August 15, after traveling nine hours from Boston to Quantico, Virginia, Danny drove onto Quantico Marine Base to visit Brad. He was admitted through the gate without a problem and drove freely around the base for over an hour in search of the brig before finally stopping to ask a group of marines on the street for directions. "Oh! Bradass!" the marines said, laughing, before they congenially pointed him in the right direction. He found the brig, came to a stop in the gravel parking lot, and then walked up a pathway and through a secure doorway into the building.

Danny told a guard he was there to see Brad Manning. The guards told him he was not on the visitors list. But he'd talked to Brad's JAG lawyer, he said, who assured him he was on the approved list. Nope, the marine guards responded, sorry. They told him he was free to leave certain approved items for Brad, like toilet paper, personal hygiene items, stationery, and money. *What? They don't give people toilet paper?*[1] Danny thought. Having traveled so many miles to see his friend, Danny was disheartened. He went back to the parking lot, grabbed a mostly unused roll of toilet paper he happened to have in his car, and handed it over to the guards along with the sixty dollars he had in his wallet. They gave him a receipt and sent him on his way.

Danny left frustrated. He tried contacting Brad's JAG lawyer but had trouble getting in touch with him. He wrote to Casey, Brad's sister, who wrote back: "We could get a really big box and put you in it and mail it to Brad. Of course we would need to put my name and address on the return label or a 3rd party vendor?" she joked—he couldn't even send a package without being on the approved list.

"Lol," he replied. "Thanks for the injection of humor, I really needed it."

On Saturday, August 21, Danny finally got in to see Brad. They hadn't seen each other since Brad's visit to Boston in January. Danny sat down on one side of a glass partition while his friend was escorted from his cell. The shuffling of jail slippers and the jingle of chains could be heard as Brad walked to the visitation center, his arms in handcuffs connected to shackles around his ankles by a chain that passed through a loop in a wide belt around his torso.

One of the first things Danny did was tell him about his earlier failed effort to see him. "Oh! You're the person the toilet paper and money were from!" Brad said, laughing.

"I guess what most surprised me was how upbeat he was," Danny said later. "It was almost sort of unnaturally upbeat. And one of the things that came out when I talked to him was that they did actually have him on antidepressants." Nonetheless, Danny was relieved. "He seemed OK, he seemed hopeful." They discussed the Bradley Manning Support Network, the fund-raising for his legal defense, and his new lawyer, David Coombs. Brad asked Danny to get in touch with

---

1. They do give people toilet paper.

a list of his friends from political circles in DC, especially people involved in fund-raising. Brad said he had faith in the military justice system and expected that soon his legal proceedings would begin. There was a flood of mail coming into the brig for Brad, which, he said, was slowing down the mail dissemination process for everyone, and he asked Danny to do something to get all the letters under control. In any case, he wasn't going to start randomly adding strangers to his approved mailing list. "It wastes stamps," he said.

During this period, Brad was getting visits from his lawyer, his father, his sister, his aunt Debbie, and now Danny Clark; his mother would eventually come to see him, but her health was too poor to make regular trips from Wales to the United States. It was a hectic time in the Manning family—in the short period of time while Brad was settling into life at Quantico, his grandmother passed away and he became an uncle. Danny was never able to convince any of the people Brad had asked him to get in touch with to visit Quantico.[2] From among Brad's group of friends before his arrest, only Danny Clark ever got involved in the movement to support him.

When he first arrived at Quantico on July 29, Brad had been placed on suicide watch, but his confinement status was relaxed to Prevention of Injury watch (POI) pursuant to an August 16 recommendation made by the brig psychiatrist. He spent twenty-three hours of every day alone in a jail cell equipped with a sink, a toilet, and a single bunk. Guards monitored Brad nonstop; they were not allowed to converse with him but were required to check on him verbally every five minutes. He was required to respond to verify he was still alive. Exercise inside the cell was strictly prohibited, and he generally spent his one daily hour of recreation walking figure eights in an empty gymnasium. He was allowed only brief access to a writing utensil and forbidden a pillow, sheets, or more than one piece of reading material at a time. Brad spent most of his time in his cell sitting

---

2. Though this writer has never seen evidence to support the notion and all research and reporting points to the contrary, it is certainly possible that one of Brad Manning's friends was placed on his visitors list and visited him in secret.

in quiet contemplation on his rack. Each evening, he had to remove his clothes, except his underwear, and surrender them to his guards. During their first visit, Brad told Danny the jail's policies were just a precaution for his own safety. Soon he'd be awaiting his court-martial in more hospitable circumstances, he assured him.

Danny continued visiting Brad throughout the fall of 2010, but carrying on a one-on-one conversation over several hours was not often easy for him, and doing so in the forced and intimidating context of a jail visit was simply untenable. Danny told Brad he had a friend who, like Brad, was interested in philosophy and who had an engaging, high-octane, conversational personality. His name was David House. They'd met once, Danny said, at BUILDS in Boston, but Brad didn't remember the name. On September 10, at Danny's recommendation, Brad added David to his list of approved visitors.

Danny joined David for his first visit with Brad. "David and Brad hit it off famously," Danny said. "They were just on the exact same intellectual wavelength. I had some part in the conversation, but it was basically the David and Brad show. They talked about philosophy, and they had had some similarities in their childhood experience. David had a very difficult time with his father, and Brad also had a fairly difficult time with his father." David became Brad's most regular visitor, making the trip from Boston to Quantico every other weekend to visit him. The Bradley Manning Support Network began covering the cost of his trips.

Brad and David spent their visits talking about a wide array of topics, but not about Brad's case—the purpose, as David saw it, was to provide company and intellectual stimulation, to provide a respite from life isolated in a cell. Often, they stuck to talking about their personal histories.

One story Brad recounted to David is apocryphal and likely the creation of Brad's imagination but entertaining nonetheless. Brad described an opportunity he had while working for Zoto in Oklahoma City to meet Senator Ted Stevens (R-Alaska), whose lack of technological savvy was long a running joke in American politics. Knowing that Stevens, being a longtime senator from Alaska, had a substantial knowledge of the oil economy, Brad tried to describe the functioning of the Internet to Stevens in terms he could understand. The Internet, he explained, was sort of like oil pipelines, only with information rather than hydrocarbons moving in a continuous flow into ever bigger pipes in the network—not a truck loaded up with information but more like a series of pipes. In the summer of 2006, days before Brad left Chicago for Debbie's place in Maryland, Senator Stevens spoke at a meeting of the Senate Commerce Committee explaining his opposition to net neutrality. In the course of his comments, he tried to explain the functioning of the Internet to his colleagues. "The Internet is not something you just dump something on. It's not a truck," he said, followed by the now-famous sentence: "It's a series of tubes." As he and David joked together, separated by a transparent partition at the Quantico brig, Brad Manning claimed credit for the meme.

Brad had access to a television for an hour each day—the guards would position a TV on a cart in front of his cell—but his channel choices were limited to local programming. During the hour he had allotted for TV time, typically 7:00 to 8:00 PM, no local news was showing. With visitor contact and limited access to media, Brad was aware that his name was in the news, but as WikiLeaks injected more classified material into the public sphere over the fall of 2010 he could not truly appreciate the degree to which he and his actions were rattling the status quo.

As the weeks dragged on, Brad became increasingly irritated with the conditions of his confinement. It was still unclear when the next step in his legal proceedings would come, but, with a mental health assessment yet to take place, his supporters assumed that by the following spring he would get an Article 32, followed not long thereafter by a court-martial. Brad expressed a deepening frustration to those visiting him that proceedings were moving so slowly. As a maximum security detainee under Prevention of Injury watch, Brad was awaiting trial in conditions that amounted to solitary confinement, or what in the American prison system is euphemistically called administrative segregation, often shortened to ad seg.

Ad seg is ostensibly designed to prevent the most dangerous prisoners from hurting themselves, guards, or others in the general prison population. But the extreme social isolation ad seg prisoners experience is not merely a result of their being necessarily segregated and closely monitored—it is expressly punitive. Bad behavior in ad seg, nonviolent or not, often results in a longer stint in ad seg. Innovative lines of communication between prisoners in an ad seg unit—passing notes through hidden pockets in library books, for example—are disrupted in an effort to keep those in ad seg cut off from even the most distant forms of human contact.

The United States is the only liberal democracy in the world that regularly uses solitary confinement in its corrections system—tens of thousands of Americans are living in solitary on any given day, some for ten or more years. The psychological results can be devastating, sending prisoners down a spiral of worsening antisocial behavior. Though ad seg as practiced in the United States is different in important ways from the solitary confinement inflicted upon people in squalid prisons in less developed countries—such as what Senator John McCain famously experienced at the hands of the Viet Cong—it is, crucially, not the squalor that drives the ad seg prisoner to madness. As Atul Gawande wrote in his 2009 opus on solitary confinement in the *New Yorker,* "Whether in Walpole or Beirut or Hanoi, all human beings experience isolation as torture."

David Coombs began calling for Brad's POI restriction to be lifted as soon as he became Brad's attorney. The effort started quietly; Coombs hoped to avoid antagonizing the government by making a public issue out of his client's pretrial living conditions. Instead he worked back channels. Ashden Fein, one of the JAG officers appointed to represent the government in the Manning case, had been Coombs's student at the JAG institute. The two had a healthy and amiable professional relationship, and Fein agreed that the POI restriction should be lifted. Coombs hoped to maintain good relations between the two camps by avoiding a public fight.

As Brad's birthday approached in December—he was soon to turn twenty-three behind bars—he remained in solitary confinement, though he did eventually get access to reading material. Coombs got him a subscription to his favorite magazine, *Scientific American*, starting with the November issue on dark matter. Brad also got to write a wish list of books, from which his family chose presents to buy him for his birthday and Christmas. His book list included *Decision Points* by George W. Bush, *The Selfish Gene* by Richard Dawkins, *A People's History of the United States* by Howard Zinn, as well as classics of military studies like *The Art of War* by Sun Tzu and *On War* by Gen. Carl von Clausewitz. He also received *The Good Soldiers*, in which the author David Finkel describes the Apache helicopter attack featured in the "Collateral Murder" video; *Propaganda* by Edward Bernays; and *Critique of Practical Reason* and, an old favorite of his, *Critique of Pure Reason* by Immanuel Kant.

The quiet campaign through the fall of 2010 to get Brad out from under the POI restriction wasn't yielding results. Some believed the government was deliberately holding him in inhospitable conditions to impel him to accept a plea deal and testify against Julian Assange. Certainly, the growing furor in Washington over the government secrets WikiLeaks was releasing established motive for the Pentagon to deliberately torment Brad Manning. And, as the State Department cables began appearing at the end of November, the furor was about to get worse.

■ ■ ■

Immediately following his arrest, Brad had been deeply emotionally distraught and unstable, but after arriving in Quantico, according to brig records, his conduct had "been excellent, so much so that is it apparent that he is extremely cautious about what he says or how he acts." Records show he was a compliant and respectful detainee, despite his ongoing frustration with living in solitary confinement. Repeatedly through the fall of 2010, two brig mental health experts recommended he be removed from POI watch. Only once did a brig psychiatrist recommend he remain on POI watch, and just three days later the recommendation was reversed.

On December 15, Glen Greenwald, writing for Salon, broke the story of Brad's unduly harsh pretrial confinement for the public. Two days later, Coombs spoke out publicly on the issue to a reporter for the Daily Beast. Coombs said the POI restrictions were patently unnecessary but remained cautious, insisting he felt the marines were simply acting out of an abundance of caution following the suicide of a marine captain in their custody earlier in the year. By the end of January 2011, the long campaign to get Brad Manning out of solitary confinement had reached a fever pitch.

The marines at Quantico were caught unprepared when, on January 17, 2011, a protest in support of Brad descended on the gates of the base. Chanting "Free Bradley Manning!" several handfuls of protesters defied repeated requests that they turn around and instead walked through the gates of the base, symbolically attempting to deliver blankets to their boy in the brig. There was minor physical contact between protesters and guards as the protesters were pushed back. The scene was largely nonviolent, at times chaotic, and certainly confrontational.

The next day, when four guards rather than the usual two or three came to take Brad out of his cell for recreation time, he sensed something was amiss. In a formal complaint issued weeks later, Brad described the scene in detail.

> When the guards came to my cell I noticed a change in their usual demeanor. Instead of being calm and respectful, they seemed agitated and confrontational. . . . The first guard told me to "turn left." When I complied, the second guard yelled "don't turn left." When I attempted to comply with the demands of the second guard, I was told by the first, "I said turn left." I responded "yes, Corporal" to the first guard. At this point, the third guard chimed in by telling me that "in the Marines we reply with "aye" and not "yes." He then asked me if I understood. I made the mistake of replying "yes, Sergeant." At this point the forth guard yelled, "you mean 'aye,' Sergeant."
>
> When I arrived at the recreation room, I was told to stand still so they could remove my leg restraints. As I stood still, one

of the guards yelled "I told you to stand still." I replied "yes Corporal, I am standing still." Another guard then said, "you mean 'aye' Corporal." Next, the same guard said "I thought we covered this, you say 'aye' and not 'yes,' do you understand?" I responded "aye Sergeant." Right after I replied, I was once again yelled at to "stand still." Due to being yelled at and the intensity of the guards, I mistakenly replied, "yes Corporal, I am standing still." As soon as I said this, I attempted to correct myself by saying "aye" instead of "yes," but it was too late. One of the guards starting yelling at me again, "what don't you understand" and "are we going to have a problem?"

Once the leg restraints were taken off of me, I took a step back from the guards. My heart was pounding in my chest, and I could feel myself getting dizzy. I sat down to avoid falling. When I did this, the guards took a step towards me. I instinctively backed away from them. As soon as I backed away, I could tell by their faces that they were getting ready to restrain me. I immediately put my hands up in the air, and said "I am not doing anything, I am just trying to follow your orders." The guards then told me to start walking. I complied with their order by saying "aye" instead of "yes."

According to his account of the incident, the guards let Brad walk undisturbed for an hour and returned him to his cell without further harassment. Brad started reading a book, but half an hour later the brig commander came to his cell and asked him what had happened during recreation time. "As I tried to explain to him what had occurred," Brad wrote, "CWO4 [Chief Warrant Officer] Averhart stopped me and said 'I am the commander' and that 'no one could tell him what to do.' He also said that he was, for all practical purposes, 'God.' I responded by saying 'You still have to follow Brig procedures.' I also said 'everyone has a boss that they have to answer to.'" Averhart, the head of the facility, ordered that Brad be placed again under suicide watch, the highly restrictive living regime he'd been under when he first arrived.

"Admittedly," Brad wrote, "once I heard that I would be placed under Suicide Risk, I became upset. Out of frustration, I placed my hands to my head and clenched my hair with my fingers. I did yell 'Why are you doing this to me?' I also yelled 'Why am I being punished?' and 'I have done nothing wrong.' I then asked CWO4 Averhart 'What have I done to deserve this type of treatment?'"

Thus began the peak of Brad's ordeal at Quantico. In suicide watch, he stayed under supervision in his cell twenty-four hours a day. His clothing and eyeglasses were taken away, and he was left to sit alone in a bare cell, in what he termed "essential blindness," except for limited periods during his television or reading time. He'd been placed on suicide watch against the recommendation of the brig psychiatrist and for reasons that were apparently punitive. A mere three days later, after a formal complaint was made by his attorney and swiftly processed through the chain of command, the suicide risk restrictions were lifted, and Brad returned to POI status. Chief Warrant Officer Averhart was relieved of his duties as brig commander, replaced by Chief Warrant Officer Denise Barnes.

Several days later, at a Pentagon press conference, Department of Defense spokesman Geoff Morrell responded to the growing outrage at Brad Manning's treatment with a display that must have embarrassed his coworkers. Morrell showed himself, in at least this instance, to be utterly inept and ill-prepared, as he admonished journalists to take care in how they reported the Manning story while he denied basic facts about the circumstances of Brad's incarceration. It became clear that Morrell quite literally did not know what he was talking about—he didn't understand the purpose of Prevention of Injury watch. "When one is confined in the brig it is not only for his protection that we are worried, we are also worried about our protection. He is charged with very serious crimes. That is why you isolate someone behind bars," Morrell said, growing more and more agitated as journalists pressed him on his inconsistencies.

In January, Brad had issued a formal Article 138 complaint—the recourse for a soldier who has been wronged by command—and he'd been waiting over a month for a response when, on March 2, he was informed that his request to be let out of solitary confinement was again denied. He asked a Quantico official what he could do to have the restriction lifted and was told there was nothing. He said sarcastically that the restriction was ludicrous—if he wanted to kill himself, he said, he could have done so long ago with the elastic in his boxers or the rubber in his sandals. In response to the quip, CWO Barnes, the brig commander, had him stripped naked at night. She was unable to have him placed under suicide watch again as the designation requires the approval of a brig psychiatrist, which Barnes did not receive.

The next morning Brad was awakened for morning inspection. By his account, he got up off his rack and walked, cold and naked, toward the front of his cell with his hands covering his genitals. He was ordered to stand at parade rest for inspection, his legs spread at shoulder width and his hands clasped behind his back. "The [Duty Brig Supervisor] looked at me, paused for a moment, and then continued to the next detainee's cell. I was incredibly embarrassed at having all these people stare at me naked," he wrote. After seven months in solitary confinement he'd been informed that a formal request for reprieve had been denied, and instead he was ordered day after day to stand naked for morning inspection. His lawyer called the new stripping procedures, absent any psychological necessity, to be plainly punitive. Brad had yet in his life to be convicted of a crime.

Brad Manning's public ordeal had become a nightmare circus. David House was speaking out publicly, insisting that Brad's mental state was decaying under the pressures of solitary confinement. Amnesty International called Brad Manning's living conditions "harsh and punitive," adding that they "undermine the principle of the presumption of innocence." Even Brian Manning, who had been visiting his son—but as late as January 2011 had never spoken to his son's lawyer—spoke out, granting a rare interview to *Frontline* to highlight Brad's jail conditions.

And the indignation wasn't limited to his supporters. The United Nations began a formal investigation, and the UN's special rapporteur for torture ultimately determined the United States was in violation of UN rules in denying him unmonitored access to the prisoner. Nearly three hundred scholars, including one who had been a professor to Barack Obama during his time at Harvard Law School, signed a letter in the *New York Review of Books* condemning the treatment of the accused soldier. Rep. Dennis Kucinich condemned Manning's treatment and was denied repeated requests to visit him. In a prepared statement in early March Kucinich asked, "Is this Quantico or Abu Ghraib?" State Department Spokesman P.J. Crowley, responding to a question in front of a small audience at MIT, said, "What is being done to Bradley Manning is ridiculous and counterproductive and stupid on the part of the Department of Defense." Days later Crowley resigned. He stood by his comments.

Behind the scenes, solitary confinement was changing Brad Manning, though not in the ways some feared. Rather than breaking, he had become hardened and stoic as he refocused on adapting to his new environment and controlling what aspects of his life he could. He spent long hours contemplating complex math, trying to apply cold reason and mathematical principles to his present conundrum. Unlike the period shortly after his arrest, he began shunning visitors—he would eventually remove both David House and his father from his visitors list.

When Danny visited Brad in April 2011, several months had passed since his last visit. He found his friend changed but still healthy. Brad described a recent trip he took off-base to receive a mental health assessment. The trip to the doctor's office in his three-car motorcade had taken him through Washington, DC. The cherry blossoms were in bloom and evoked pleasant memories of Brad's more carefree days years earlier, when he'd moved to Debbie's house outside of Washington and found a peaceful home life for the first time since he was a child.

To Danny, Brad appeared mentally fit but suddenly cold, lacking in empathy, and "snappy." He was preoccupied with his education and pressed Danny on what level of college Danny thought his knowledge in various fields would place him. "If he was in his current state back when I first met him. I don't think I would have been interested in being his friend," Danny said shortly after the visit.

Brad's arrest severely disrupted the lives of many who knew him. An association with Brad Manning had turned toxic for people in

DC political circles, as Brad's close friends and distant associates had to explain to bosses or investigators how they knew the world's most famous leaker. After he started traveling from Boston every two weeks to visit Brad, David House became the recipient of even more unwanted attention from federal agents. In November, while returning to the United States after a fishing trip to Mexico, he and his girlfriend were stopped at O'Hare Airport. David was detained and interrogated, and his laptop, thumb drive, and digital camera were confiscated. A full forty-nine days later his property was returned, nineteen days longer than border-search regulations allow and a day after the Americans for Civil Liberties Union sent a letter to the Department of Homeland Security demanding the items be returned. The government claimed they held on to David's computer for so long only because his combination Windows/Linux operating system, and his password, which he refused to divulge, confounded investigators. The ACLU filed a lawsuit against the government on David's behalf.

In the spring of the next year, both David House and Danny Clark were called to testify in a federal grand jury investigation into the WikiLeaks disclosures. Insisting they were prepared to go to jail, both refused to cooperate with what they felt had become a heavy-handed government investigation designed to harass Brad Manning's supporters as much as to investigate his alleged crimes. Neither of them was charged or incarcerated.

■ ■ ■

On April 19, without warning—David Coombs was as surprised by the news as the rest of the world—the Pentagon announced it was relocating Brad Manning to the new jail facility at Fort Leavenworth, in Kansas.

Brad described the Leavenworth jail as like summer camp—languid days spent reading, lounging, and eating with others in the dining facility, and hours of recreation time to play basketball and lift weights in the jail yard with views to the north of the rolling Kansas countryside beyond the fence. He lived with three other pretrial inmates in a pod that had four cells and a small common area with a television and a treadmill. Any day of the week he could receive visitors and meet them at a table in a large common area where they were free to embrace each other for the first time since his arrest. Brad got along fine, he told a visitor, with the other inmates in pretrial confinement. Another detainee, he said, had been arrested for smothering one of his children to death. The crimes Brad was accused of, as far as the other prisoners were concerned, were no comparison.

Brad Manning's move to Leavenworth was the final, irrefutable proof that the conditions under which he was held at Quantico were unjustifiably harsh and probably punitive. He awaited trial at Leavenworth without incident, neither a threat to himself or anyone else. In clear violation of the most basic principles of due process, the Pentagon had allowed the marines at Quantico to torment Brad Manning over the nine-month period that he was held under Prevention of Injury watch, in conditions tantamount to solitary confinement. The episode was an embarrassment for American jurisprudence. An internal Marine Corps investigation later found that brig officials had violated navy policy by keeping Brad on suicide watch against the recommendation of psychiatrists. In the fall of 2011, for reasons unrelated to Brad Manning, or so the Marine Corps said, the Pentagon announced it was permanently closing the Quantico brig.

The steady stream of controversy surrounding Brad Manning's confinement under various forms of suicide watch bolstered the image in the mainstream press of Brad as crazed and volatile. The image wasn't altogether false—he had indeed had volatile episodes throughout his rather difficult and chaotic life—but it was woefully incomplete. Still, the net result of the Quantico affair was not all bad for Brad.

In the first weeks after Courage to Resist began raising money for Brad's legal defense, about $40,000 came in donations. Then the flow receded to a steady lull. WikiLeaks' initial promise of a $50,000 contribution was eventually decreased to only $15,000, and it did not arrive for months after it was promised. The malfeasance perpetrated at the Quantico brig, however, turned the tide for Brad Manning. The outrage impressed his name in the popular consciousness more sympathetically, and more extensively, than ever before. As the uproar grew in early 2011, donations for his defense began pouring in again. His $120,000-plus legal bill was paid in full, with hundreds of thousands of dollars left over for the activities of his support network. In the final calculus, the ordeal at Quantico may have been a bit of disguised luck for the young soldier.

And luck he would need more of. Early that spring the military handed down twenty-two new charges, these much grimmer than the indictments they replaced. Manning was charged with five counts of violations under UCMJ Article 92, "Failure to obey (lawful) order or regulation," and sixteen counts under Article 134, for behavior detrimental to "good order and discipline . . . (and) of a nature to bring discredit upon the armed forces," eight of which were for violations of the Espionage Act. If convicted of these charges, he faced 150 years in prison. If Brad was found guilty of the most serious of his new charges, aiding the enemy, he could be sentenced to life in prison without the possibility of parole, or, if the military court felt the maximum punishment warranted, death.

11

Secrecy Is for Losers

"In some forty years of government work I have learned
one thing for certain. As I have put it, the central
conservative truth is that it is culture, not politics, that
determines the success of a society. The central liberal truth
is that politics can change a culture and save it from itself."

—Sen. Daniel Patrick Moynihan

By early 2012, the WikiLeaks moment looked like a flash in the pan. The financial blockade had left the organization nearly penniless and Assange's fight against extradition to Sweden had been lost. The original core group had all but disintegrated, leaving Assange to run WikiLeaks with a few former interns and a stable of remote working volunteers. In mid-2011 the group published the "Gitmo Files"—documents furnished by Brad Manning related to the Pentagon's jail at Guantánamo Bay, Cuba—to much less fanfare than their previous releases. After an impressive but heedless several-year ascent, Assange's experiment was collapsing under the burden of its own mercurial leader. What future there was for WikiLeaks looked pallid at best. The mainstream media, the political establishment, and the American public at large were deeply suspicious of Assange and the entire WikiLeaks enterprise.

WikiLeaks, and its brand of radical transparency, only truly came into maturity in 2010 with a series of major scoops, all of which came from a single source. The dearth of new groundbreaking leaks highlighted the reality that the truly revolutionary actor in the entire WikiLeaks drama had been Brad Manning; there was never a scarcity of people willing to accept and publish secrets. The odds were low that another person of Manning's inclinations would be similarly positioned, with access to gobs of tantalizing, poorly protected secrets, and the prospect of a comparable leak appeared, at least in the short term, very unlikely indeed.

But WikiLeaks had given rise to a whole new species of transparency activist. Groups like Domscheit-Berg's OpenLeaks were following in WikiLeaks' footsteps while working to avoid WikiLeaks' mistakes. Regional groups like BrusselsLeaks, IndoLeaks, and LocalLeaks cropped up, along with WikiLeaks copycat systems in mainstream media organizations like the *New York Times*. A new organization, Sannleik, run by a small coterie including former WikiLeaks volunteers, was founded to both accept leaks and to help would-be whistleblowers learn how to avoid the fate that befell Brad Manning. The group GlobaLeaks created an open source framework to make it easy for anyone—journalists, activists, corporations, governments, anyone—to set up their own WikiLeaks-style whistleblowing platform. The landscape of opportunities for a potential leaker had changed significantly since 2009.

But as Brad Manning's court martial neared there remained a fundamental unanswered question: if you build it, will they come?

■ ■ ■

On January 12, 2012, Lieutenant Colonel Paul Almanza, who had presided over Manning's Article 32 investigation, recommended that the private be court-martialed on all twenty-two charges brought against him. Significant revelations came out of the hearing, including a dramatic illustration of the harm Manning might have done through his extraordinary breach of state secrecy.

During the hearing the prosecutors repeatedly asked witnesses about what in the leaked documents might cause harm if made public. SIGACTS, like those Manning leaked, can include information on army TTPs (short for Techniques, Tactics and Procedures) for events like the kidnapping of an American soldier, responding to a bombing, indirect fire, assassination threats, and more. When, in its closing argument, the government showed a video of an al-Qaeda operative discussing Manning's leaks, it made for a poignant illustration of the otherwise obvious: that most of what Manning leaked had as a result become available to anyone with an Internet connection, including sworn enemies of the United States.

The defense attempted to address the same question of how much harm had been done. David Coombs requested a list of forty-eight witnesses to appear for the defense, including high-level officials like Secretary of State Hillary Clinton, Defense Secretary Robert Gates, and President Barack Obama, all of whom had commented publicly on the situation. Almanza allowed the ten defense witnesses who were requested by the prosecution, plus two of defense's unique thirty-eight, but he denied the people Coombs hoped to question regarding the harm done by the leak. Coombs was largely unable to make the case he emphasized in his closing argument, that Manning's leaks to WikiLeaks did little, if any, harm. Much of the case Coombs presented stressed the appalling information security that made such a leak possible, if not inevitable, and that expressed just how little the government valued those of its secrets Manning made public.

Brad Manning's leak might be best interpreted as a sort of gray-hat hack. It is true that little concrete evidence of *actual* harm was presented and that much good came of the leak. Tucked within the diplomatic cables, SIGACTS, and other reports Brad released were major revelations that contributed harmlessly to the public understanding of affairs of state. On the other hand, as the attorneys representing the government highlighted, soldiers and diplomats employ secrecy for important, sometimes life-and-death, reasons. Though, as Coombs said in his final statements of the hearing, "the sky has not fallen," the damage might have been significantly worse. The leak exposed not only the misdeeds and inconvenient secrets of world governments, but also the looming threat of secrecy abused in a digitized, interconnected world. Bradley Manning showed us just how bad secrecy is for secrets.

Studies on the dangers of too much secrecy in government are as old as government secrecy, at least in its modern form, which grew amid the expansion of the federal bureaucracy in the 1930s and 1940s. But the Commission on Government Secrecy chaired by Senator Daniel Patrick Moynihan was the first to see that the world had changed in crucial ways and that secrecy as it had been practiced was less tenable than ever. Moynihan, as they say, called it.

In 1997, the Moynihan commission clarified a discussion that tends by its nature to be murky when the commission's report pointed out that "secrecy is a form of government regulation." Over the long term, secrecy has the effect of impoverishing the well of public information, injecting an insidious inefficiency into the marketplace of ideas. It breeds skepticism among the citizenry, providing fodder for conspiracy theorists and the politics of the radical fringe. It oversimplifies complex challenges, and complicates simple ones. And it protects political elites from being held to account for their actions. Echoing Justice Potter Stewart's opinion in the Pentagon Papers case, the commission wrote that "when everything is secret, nothing is secret"—secrecy destroys itself.

In his 1998 book on the subject, *Secrecy*, Moynihan blamed secrecy for the key intelligence failure during his time in public service. While the State Department wanted to improve relations with the USSR and reverse the arms race that was driving the United States further into debt, a CIA submerged in the culture of secrecy warned against a powerful Soviet foe. Secretary of State George Schultz recounted: "In Washington, and especially from the CIA and its lead Soviet expert, [Robert] Gates, I heard that the Soviets wouldn't change and couldn't change. . . 'The Soviet Union is a despotism that works,' Gates said." Four years later, the Soviet system imploded.

Even more destructive intelligence failures caused by secrecy followed the release of Moynihan's book. The 9/11 attacks were attributed to the failure to share intelligence between agencies, a symptom of too much secrecy. Whatever its merits in retrospect, much of the Iraq War amounted to a series of intelligence failures, from preinvasion planning onward. The war in Afghanistan suffered from a similar misunderstanding of what military planners call "human terrain," the intricate web of tribal and clan politics that might have been better understood through an open, public dialogue. And American officials were, by all indications, caught completely by surprise when popular uprisings rippled across the Arab world in late 2010 and early 2011. We've paid for our secrecy at a very high price.

The last words of Moynihan's book are a prescient warning. "A case can be made," he wrote, "that secrecy is for losers. For people who don't know how important information really is. The Soviet Union realized this too late. Openness is now a singular, and singularly American, advantage. We put it in peril by poking along in the mode of an age now past. It is time to dismantle government secrecy, this most pervasive of Cold War–era regulations. It is time to begin building the supports for the era of openness that is already upon us." A little over a decade later Brad Manning brought openness to the government that left Moynihan's warning unheeded.

Hazardous though Manning's leak may have been, the principle he claimed as his inspiration—the notion at the core of the hacker ethic that "information should be free"—is not a radical idea but a conservative one. It is the foundation of an efficient marketplace and the principle at the heart of democracy. Manning's leak revealed some secrets that should never have been secret at all and illustrated the threat of secrecy gone out of control in a government out of touch with the times. But the leak also heralded a new epoch in which freely moving information has upended the traditions and customs with which society handled its secrets.

As a part of its grand jury investigation into WikiLeaks, the US Department of Justice issued a secret subpoena for records from Twitter accounts associated with WikiLeaks insiders such as Jonsdottir,

Appelbaum, and Assange. The government sought the IP addresses of locations from which the accounts had been accessed as well as "records of user activity for any connections made to and from" the accounts. Twitter challenged the secrecy of the order in court and won the right to inform its users that the government had demanded access to their account information. Three of the users appealed in federal court. Days before Alamanza's decision to send Brad Manning to a courtmartial, they lost their appeal. Notwithstanding the legal ins and outs of the issue, the episode put a spotlight on the logical difficulties that emanate from a philosophy of radical transparency.

Privacy for individuals and transparency for institutions is uncomplicated only as a slogan. WikiLeaks had been an agent in the biggest government information security failure in American history. The people who comprised WikiLeaks were hardly common, private individuals, and their internal communications were as central to the functioning of the WikiLeaks institution as the cables between diplomats were to that of the State Department. The notion that their institutional communications ought to be private secrets but the State Department's ought to be made public rests on dubious grounds at best.

The rippling effects of WikiLeaks put this conundrum into ever-starker relief. In response to Manning's arrest and as a general assault on the establishment, computer-savvy activists—hackers, as the media called them, operating under the name Anonymous—launched a series of attacks on various institutions, from which they purloined and published individuals' account information. Credit card data went online, along with the internal e-mails and text messages of law enforcement officials and others. Following his arrest, Manning's life story and private communications were of intense interest not only to the Department of Justice but to people all over the world fascinated by the then-unfolding events. Who was this young man who had ignited such passions? The press, including this writer, responded by investigating his private life and telling his secrets to the world. The records of his private communications with friends went online, as easily accessible as the State Department cables he leaked. In a dramatic illustration of the great privacy question of the digital age, a quiet and guarded young man with layers upon layers of secrets became a public story almost overnight. The life of Private Manning straddled the digital privacy divide, illustrating the final, irrefutable fact of the era proclaimed by his revolutionary leak: the world and its secrets have been forever changed.

Brad, the science lover and fervent atheist, has a favorite quotation he attributes to Charles Darwin. Its true origin is apocryphal—perhaps Clarence Darrow, the legendary jurist who defended John Scopes for exposing schoolchildren to evolutionary theory—but the adage has a special relevance for the world in the wake of WikiLeaks.

"It is not the strongest of the species that survives, nor the most intelligent, but rather the one most adaptable to change."

ACKNOWLEDGMENTS

First and above all, I am immensely grateful to the friends, relatives, and acquaintances of Bradley Manning who let me into their lives and trusted me with their stories. I hope this work reflects the duty I felt to act responsibly with that trust. A multitude of people, many of whom I am not at liberty to name, were generous with their thoughts and memories. I cannot list all of them here but I am particularly grateful to Danny Clark, David House, Jordan Davis, Bill Cooper, Rick McCombs, Diane Musil, Jason Edwards, and the folks at the Crescent Frontier Museum and Perry's Roadhouse. I also wish to thank the National Priorities Project, the Federation of American Scientists, the press relations offices at Fort Leonard Wood, Fort Leavenworth, and Fort Meade, and the team at Guardian Films.

This book would not exist but for my trusted mentor and friend, the editor in chief of This Land Press, Michael Mason, to whom I will be forever grateful and in whom I have tremendous faith. James Fitzgerald, my agent, is an unparalleled guide and a great friend. My editor Yuval Taylor has been an indispensable companion on this journey.

Numerous friends helped me at various points along the path, opening their homes to me and offering their counsel. I can't thank them all but I am particularly grateful to Makaira Casey, Gene and Sally Dennison, Leah Finnegan, Barry J. Whyte, Greg Hermann, Charlie Turpin, Unkle David, Lacy Post, Mitchell and Allison London, Keith Kobylka, Drew Baker, Daniel Jorgenson, Bernie Garland, Sean Barna, Spencer Livingston-Gainey, Sam Petulla, Laura Poitras, and Tyler Fields. Kat George is an excellent research assistant and an even better journalist in her own right.

This being my first book, I feel compelled to thank those who had a particular impact on my passage into journalism: Dale Maharidge, Jess Bruder, Sam Freedman, Paula Span, Howard French, Ziva Branstetter; Susan Ellerbach and Tina Brown for taking a chance on me; Tom Stone, John Clegg, John Waldron, and Rebecca Simcoe for teaching me what and how to read; Van Eden, Nancy Hermann, Jeannette Walls, Anne Weil, Judith Goldstein, Kathleen Hugley-Cook, and Dennis Cordell for inspiration and assistance.

Many names have been left out of these acknowledgments for sundry reasons, none of which was malicious. Dispensing with clichés about giants and their shoulders, I extend a heartfelt thank you to the many unnamed people who made this possible, without whom, indeed, the book would have been impossible. Last and above all I wish to thank my best friend and my hero, Dad, and my champion, Mom, for their unflagging, multifaceted support.

NOTES

Chapter 1: Crescent

Crescent, Oklahoma, appeared out of the wilderness in the fevered summer of 1899 . . . "The Eden of Oklahoma: Logan County," printed by the Oklahoma Development Company, 1903 (from the Crescent, Oklahoma, Frontier Museum).

Banks, a hardware store, and restaurants . . . Interview with Vickey Howard at Crescent Frontier Museum.

The young sailor was stationed at an Air Force Base . . . Brian Manning's LinkedIn profile, as of May 10, 2011, www.linkedin.com/pub/brian-manning/4/b46/132.

In 1976, on the day after Brian turned 21 . . . Ellen Nakashima, "Bradley Manning is at the center of the WikiLeaks controversy. But who is he?," *Washington Post*, May 4, 2010, www.washingtonpost.com/lifestyle/magazine/who-is-wikileaks-suspect-bradley-manning/2011/04/16/AFMwBmrF_print.html.

Unlike in Southern California . . . Ibid.

Brian and Sue had tried for years Ibid.

On some mornings, she squeezed . . . Interview with Diane Musil.

Bradley had acres of countryside to explore . . . Interview with Danielle Curtis; interview with Rhonda Curtis.

. . . would later describe him as a hummingbird . . . Nakashima op. cit.

He won the science fair three years in a row . . . Interview with Diane Musil.

. . . stuff, for that age, that was pretty deep . . . Interview with Shanée Watson.

. . . rode the Silver Bullet alone . . . Interview with Jacob Butts.

. . . pecking away at the keyboard . . . Nakashima op. cit.

Heavy flooding in the 1980s damaged the railroad . . . Interview with Vickey Howard; interview with Tom Copeland.

Sue didn't start drinking . . . Interview with Rhonda Curtis; interview with Bill Cooper; interview with Diane Musil; interview with anonymous source.

. . . once hiding in a tree . . .   Nakashima op. cit.

. . . skipping parent-teacher conferences . . .   Ibid.

. . . receive his trophy . . .   Ibid.

. . . hurling an iron . . .   Ibid.

. . . slinging insults . . .   Interview with Diane Musil.

. . . access the back end of programs . . .   Nakashima op. cit.

. . . I want to have my cake and eat it too . . .   Interview with Rhonda Curtis.

. . . Sue had to rely on attorneys . . .   Interview with Bill Cooper.

. . . gallon-bottles of vodka . . .   Interview with Diane Musil.

. . . Bradley seemed relieved by his father moving out . . .   Interview with Jordan Davis.

One evening, in the summer of his thirteenth year . . .   Ibid.

But try not to tell other people . . .   Nakashima op. cit.

I'm nobody now, Mum.   Ibid.

The three were in the backyard . . .   Interview with Shanée Watson.

Bradley, now the man of the house . . .   Nakashima op. cit.

They flew to Potomac . . .   Interview with Debra Van Alstyne.

Bradley never lost his entrepreneurial spirit . . .   Interview with James Kirkpatrick.

. . . a web interface to allow musicians . . .   Interview with Jordan Davis.

He missed his sister . . .   Ibid.

. . . drink herself to death . . .   Nakashima op. cit.

He's my son . . .   Steve Fishman, "Bradley Manning's Army of One," *New York Magazine*, July 3, 2011.

. . . started work at Zoto, a software start-up . . .   Nakashima op. cit.

When the police arrived at Brian Manning's house in Oklahoma City . . .   "The Private Life of Bradley Manning," *Frontline*, March 2011; interview with Jordan Davis; interview with anonymous source.

Chapter 2: Hack the World

He was always telling me about ideas . . .   Andrew Fowler, *The Most Dangerous Man in the World: The Explosive True Story of Julian Assange and the Lies, Cover-ups and Conspiracies He Exposed* (New York: Skyhorse Publishing, 2011), 41.

in a bikini, "going native" . . .   Stuard Rintoul and Sean Parnell, "Julian Assange, wild child of free speech," *The Australian*, December 11, 2010.

For eighteen months . . .   Fowler op. cit., 11.

. . . bestselling personal computer of all time . . . Adam Chowaniec et al, "Impact of the Commodore 64: A 25th Anniversary Celebration" (lecture, Computer History Museum), www.computerhistory.org/collections/accession/102695290.

It is like chess . . . Raffi Khatchadourian, "No Secrets: Julian Assange's mission for total transparency," *New Yorker,* June 7, 2010.

. . . living with his mother in Emerald . . . Suelette Dreyfus, *Underground* (Mandarin, 1997).

Piggybacking on the superior . . . Dreyfus op. cit.; Fowler op. cit., 18.

. . . seen e-mails saying as much . . . Fowler op. cit., 22.

. . . the evening of October 29, 1991 . . . Dreyfus op. cit.; Fowler op. cit., 22.

The so-called International Subversives were bound . . . Fowler op. cit., 19.

Using dials appropriated from telephones . . . Steven Levy, *Hackers: Heroes of the Computer Revolution* (Sebastopol, CA: O'Reilly, 2010), 9–10.

. . . the essence of the Hacker Ethic . . . Levy op. cit., 27–38.

The Jargon File, a regularly updated . . . The Jargon File, as of June 30, 2011, http://catb.org/jargon/html/index.html.

The Internet Engineering Task Force is the closest thing . . . Internet Engineering Task Force, Internet User's Glossary, as of June 30, 2011, www.ietf.org/rfc/rfc1392.txt.

The police ripped through Assange's house . . . Dreyfus op. cit.

Total damage claims from the hackers' activities . . . Dreyfus op. cit.

If there is a book whose feeling captures me . . . Julian Assange, "Jackboots," IQ.org, as of July 17, 2006, http://web.archive.org/web/20071020051936/http://iq.org.

It must have been more than a little gratifying . . . Robert Manne, "The Cypherpunk Revolutionary," *The Monthly,* March 2011.

Young scanned the report . . . Declan McCullagh, "He Digs 'Through' Gov't Muck," *Wired,* October 1, 1999.

. . . freedom of expression, privacy, cryptology . . . As of July 9, 2011, http://cryptome.org.

. . . an online archive of more than four thousand documents . . . Declan McCullagh, "FBI Pressuring Spy Archivist," *Wired,* July 21, 2000.

Julian Assange remained active on the Cypherpunks . . . Assange's Cypherpunk e-mails, hosted by Cryptome, as of July 9, 2011, http://cryptome.org/0001/assange-cpunks.htm.

Stallman had grown up in New York City . . . Sam Williams, *Free as in Freedom: Richard Stallman's Crusade for Free Software* (Sebastopol, CA: O'Reilly, 2002).

The two terms describe almost the same category of software . . .   Richard Stallman, "Why Open Source misses the point of Free Software," as of December 5, 2011, www.gnu.org/philosophy/open-source-misses-the-point.html.

They were easy to get . . .   Interview with Richard Stallman, July 26, 2011.

. . . started using his cryptography software . . .   Dreyfus op. cit.

. . . Assange reveled in the politically charged . . .   Fowler op. cit., 38.

Assange did wake often in the middle of the night . . .   Fowler op. cit., 39–40.

A leaky world, in Assange's estimation . . .   Julian Assange, "Conspiracy as Governance," IQ.org, December 3, 2006, as of December 5, 2011, http://cryptome.org/0002/ja-conspiracies.pdf.

Chapter 3: General Manning

. . . he was in surprisingly good spirits . . .   Interview with Jordan Davis, February 2011.

In mid-April, 2005, Brad and Jordan got jobs at Incredible Pizza . . .   Denver Nicks, "Manning in the Making," *This Land Press*, March 2011.

He was exhausted, mentally and physically . . .   E-mail exchange with Debbie Manning.

Montgomery County is near the top of the list . . .   Megan McNally, "Washington: Number One In College Degrees," The Brookings Institution, June 2003, as of December 5, 2011, www.brookings.edu/~/media/Files/rc/reports/2003/07washington_mcnally/education.pdf.

She tried to her best to feed him a proper diet . . .   E-mail exchange with Debbie Manning.

He later told a friend, "community college sucks" . . .   Chat logs of Zach Antolak (aka Zinnia Jones) and Bradley Manning.

He was used to everything coming easily . . .   Fishman op. cit.

Bradley, you're really not going anywhere . . .   Interview with Brian Manning, *Frontline*, February 28, 2011, as of December 5, 2011, www.pbs.org/wgbh/pages/frontline/wikileaks/bradley-manning/interviews/brian-manning.html.

The military was more diverse than ever before . . .   Ryan Kelty, Meredith Kleykamp, and David R. Segal, "The Military and the Transition to Adulthood," *The Future of Children* (Princeton University) 20, no. 1 (Spring 2010).

. . . an estimated 65,000 gays and lesbians . . .   "DADT Fact Sheet," Palm Center, as of December 5, 2011, www.palmcenter.org/files/active/0/DADT%20Fact%20Sheet.pdf.

A February 2005 Pew Research poll . . .   "Public Attitudes Toward the War in Iraq: 2003–2008," Pew Research Center, March 19, 2008.

. . . a Washington Post/ABC News poll . . . Dana Milbank and Claudia Deane, "Poll Finds Dimmer View of Iraq War," *Washington Post*, June 8, 2005.

. . . the deadliest year for American soldiers in Iraq . . . "Iraq Coalition Casualties: Fatalities By Year," iCasualties.org, as of December 5, 2011, http://icasualties.org/Iraq/ByYear.aspx.

Because the actual number of troops . . . E-mail exchange with Samantha Dana of the National Priorities Project.

In response to the dwindling supply . . . Lizette Alvarez, "Army Giving More Waivers in Recruiting," *New York Times*, February 14, 2007.

. . . the Marine Corps declined to discharge . . . Interview with Jeremy Johnson of the Palm Center.

Basically, when a drill sergeant . . . Interview with anonymous soldier.

It's traumatic walking into the discharge unit . . . Interview with anonymous soldier.

Copious amounts of masturbation . . . Interview with anonymous soldier.

Chapter 4: Dixie Charm

Swirling lights and thumping beats . . . Interview with anonymous friend.

Three weeks into his training Brad posted video messages . . . Kevin Poulsen and Kim Zetter, "WikiLeaks Suspect's YouTube Videos Raised 'Red Flag' in 2008," *Wired*, July 29, 2010.

. . . Cofer Black was in a conference room at the Hart Senate Building . . . Video on CSPAN.

Dana Priest, who'd spent years reporting on the military . . . Dana Priest and William M. Arkin, *Top Secret America: The Rise of the New American Security State* (New York: Little, Brown, 2011), 14.

Where everybody else was looking . . . "Top Secret America," *Frontline*, September 6, 2011.

With an initial down payment of a billion dollars . . . Priest op. cit., 6.

Between October 2006 and October 2009, federal . . . Petra Bartosiewicz, "To catch a terrorist: The FBI hunts for the enemy within," *Harper's Magazine*, August 2011.

In all, the government study found, more than 4.2 million people . . . "Annual Intelligence Authorization Act Report on Security Clearance Determinations For Fiscal Year 2010," Office of the Director of National Intelligence of the United States, as of December 8, 2011, www.fas.org/sgp/othergov/intel/clearance.pdf.

Diplomats designated cables for inclusion on SIPRnet . . .   Joby Warrick, "WikiLeaks cable dump reveals flaws of State Department's information-sharing tool," *Washington Post*, December 31, 2010.

Secrets cannot be totally secured by locks or code names . . .   Priest op. cit., 32.

In November, he made the hour-and-a-half drive . . .   Phim Her, "Teen hears peoples' stories at LGBTQ rally," Syracuse.com, November 17, 2008; Bradley Manning outed himself as her anonymous source on his Facebook wall.

Later in the year he started dating Tyler Watkins . . .   Interview with Danny Clark, April 2011.

Bradley was living the normal gay life . . .   Interview with anonymous source.

Gays have children less, socialize more . . .   Karen Schrock, "Monogamy Is All the Rage These Days," *Scientific American*, August 7, 2009.

. . . in the parlance of Dan Savage, monogamish . . .   Dan Savage, "Monogamish," *The Stranger*, July 20, 2011.

Pay to play politics, but open bars . . .   Chat logs of Bradley Manning and Danny Clark.

Such a change can be exhilarating . . .   Interview with Berin Szoka, July 2011.

He was kind of short, and a little small . . .   Interview with Jason Edwards, June 2011.

Sometimes there are these central and poignant events . . .   Interview with anonymous friend.

I hold on VERY close to my contacts . . .   Chat logs of Bradley Manning and Danny Clark.

"One day," he said, "we'll turn all the churches into lecture halls . . ."   Interview with Jason Edwards, June 2011.

There's always that sense with him . . .   Interview with Danny Clark.

It wasn't until I join[ed] the ranks . . .   Carly Carioli, "British newspapers out alleged WikiLeaks source, a soldier, as being gay; Queer-bashing has already begun," *Phoenix*, August 2, 2010, http://blog.thephoenix.com/BLOGS/phlog/archive/2010/08/02/british-newspapers-out-alleged-wikileaks-source-a-soldier-as-being-gay-queer-bashing-has-already-begun.aspx.

He put Tyler on the list of people to be alerted . . .   Text message logs of Bradley Manning and Danny Clark.

I answered with his name . . .   Chat logs of Bradley Manning and Zach Antolak.

On a Saturday evening in late February 2009, Brad was sitting at a computer . . .   Ibid.

He stayed at a hotel in Virginia and was busy during daylight hours . . .   Ibid.

He and Jason Edwards met up for dinner one night . . . Interview with Jason Edwards, June 2011.

On one early morning at Fort Drum in May 2009 . . . Jihrleah Showman testimony at Bradley Manning's UCMJ Article 32 investigation, December 20, 2011.

Tyler Watkins and his friend Danny Clark were preparing to carpool . . . Interview with Danny Clark.

In mid-June, Brad went to Boston for a long weekend with Tyler . . . Bradley Manning Facebook wall.

Hello, it's Brad Manning . . . Text message logs of Bradley Manning and Danny Clark.

Chapter 5: Building WikiLeaks

Notably, this first of WikiLeaks' disclosures appears . . . Internal WikiLeaks e-mails batch #1, Cryptome.org, as of December 9, 2011, http://cryptome.org/wikileaks/wikileaks-leak.htm.

One of the members of the WikiLeaks "advisory board" . . . Khatchadourian op. cit.; Guardian book.

We are going to fuck them all . . . Internal WikiLeaks e-mails batch #2, Cryptome.org, as of December 9, 2011, http://cryptome.org/wikileaks/wikileaks-leak2.htm.

. . . not favor automated or indiscriminate publication . . . Steven Aftergood, "Wikileaks and Untraceable Document Disclosure," *Secrecy News*, Federation of American Scientists' Project on Government Secrecy, January 3, 2007.

Public scrutiny of otherwise unaccountable and secretive institutions . . . Internal WikiLeaks e-mails batch #1 op. cit.

Among them was a German computer security specialist . . . Daniel Domscheit-Berg, *Inside WikiLeaks: My Time with Julian Assange at the World's Most Dangerous Website* (New York: Crown, 2011), 7–13.

Celebrating our first 10k followers! . . . WikiLeaks Twitter archive, October 2009, as of December 9, 2011, http://wlcentral.org/node/444.

Iceland had been hit particularly hard by the financial crisis of 2008 . . . ALDA, "Kaupthing's loan book exposed and an injunction ordered against RÚV," *The Iceland Weather Report*, August 1, 2009, as of December 9, 2011, http://icelandweatherreport.com/2009/08/kaupthings-loan-book-exposed-and-an-injunction-ordered-against-ruv.html.

I said it would be a bit of a prank to take him and see if they knew who he was . . . Andrew Gilligan, "Julian Assange wined and dined at US Embassy," *Telegraph*, December 13, 2010.

I crashed it under the guise of Birgitta's plus-one . . . Julian Assange, *Julian Assange: The Unauthorised Autobiography* (Edinburgh: Canongate, 2011), chap. 10.

First one member of the audience . . . Domscheit-Berg op. cit., 129.

Chapter 6: Carl Sagan

A conversation that started with their shared fondness . . . Interview with Danny Clark.

. . . Interlock Media, a film production company . . . As of December 9, 2011, www.interlockmedia.com/mission.html.

Briefly a chapter of the national Pi Kappa Alpha fraternity . . . As of December 9, 2011, http://pika.mit.edu/index.php?title=Home.

Do you come to Boston on work, or when on leave? . . . Chat logs of Bradley Manning and Danny Clark.

Back at Fort Drum, he was not getting along well in the army . . . Steve Fishman, "Bradley Manning's Army of One," *New York* magazine, July 3, 2011.

A turning point came when he clashed with a roommate . . . Interview with anonymous source.

Once back from "the swamps" . . . Bradley Manning Facebook wall.

I think I've just realized the outrageousness of the situation I am in . . . Chat logs of Bradley Manning and Danny Clark.

On one such weekend, they'd planned a kayaking trip . . . Interview with Danny Clark.

So what's rms [Richard M. Stallman] like? . . . Chat logs of Bradley Manning and Danny Clark.

Jason Edwards invited him to a quiet dinner at his friend Kevin's house . . . Interview with Jason Edwards; interview with Kevin Lees.

. . . in a rainbow sea of roughly 200,000 people . . . John Cloud, "The Gay March: A New Generation of Protesters," *Time*, October 12, 2009, as of December 13, 2011, www.time.com/time/magazine/article/0,9171,1930526,00.html.

He told me he was a little afraid . . . E-mail exchange with Debbie Manning.

On Sunday, October 11, Tyler Watkins was with friends . . . Interview with Keith Rose, conducted by *Guardian Films*.

Chapter 7: Shakoosh

Forward Operating Base (FOB, pronounced "fahb") Shakoosh appeared . . . David G. Fivecoat and Aaron T. Schwengler, "Revisiting Modern Warfare: Counterinsurgency in the Mada'in Qada," *Military Review*, November 2008; interview with anonymous soldier; interview with Dennis Carnelli.

At a staging area in Kuwait . . .   Chat logs of Bradley Manning and Danny Clark; interview with Dennis Carnelli.

Brad was surprised by how wet and cold the Mada'in Qada could get at night . . .   Bradley Manning Facebook wall.

Every so often a soldier at the FOB would commit suicide . . .   Interview with anonymous soldier.

. . . take slides from subordinate battalions, change wording . . .   Chat logs of Bradley Manning and Adrian Lamo.

His activities weren't restricted to FOB Hammer's Area of Operation . . .   Chat logs of Bradley Manning and Danny Clark.

In one instance, the Iraqi Federal Police had arrested fifteen Iraqis . . .   Chat logs of Bradley Manning and Adrian Lamo.

Not long after arriving in Iraq, he got in touch online . . .   Fishman op. cit.

He recognized immediately that the pager messages were . . .   Chat logs of Bradley Manning and Adrian Lamo.

. . . CIA detainee interrogation videos. While the CIA claims . . .   "WikiLeaks Most Wanted Leaks of 2009," as of January 6, 2010, http://web.archive .org/web/20110106024751/http://mirror.wikileaks.info/wiki/Draft_The _Most_Wanted_Leaks_of_2009/.

Later that evening Brad showed up to work forty-five minutes late.   U.S. Army Developmental Counseling Form (DA 4856, MAR 2006) for SPC/E-4 Bradley Manning, December 20, 2009.

Danny got to work preparing a care package for Brad . . .   Interview with Danny Clark.

Around New Year's Eve Brad was sitting at a laptop computer . . .   Chat logs of Bradley Manning and Adrian Lamo.

The SCIF was more secure in name than in reality . . .   Interview with anonymous soldier; Shane Shaneman and Cary Murphy, "Enhancing the Deployment and Security of SIPRNET and JWICS Networks using Intrinsic Fiber Monitoring" (Military Communications Conference 2007, Orlando, FL, October 2007).

. . . November 2009 seizure of assets in the United States, controversially including . . .   "Muslim-American group protests mosques' link to money laundering case," *CNN U.S.*, November 13, 2009, as of December 13, 2011, http:// articles.cnn.com/2009-11-13/us/mosque.seized.reaction_1_american -muslim-mosques-religious-freedom?_s=PM:US.

Chapter 8: Collateral Damage

Keith Rose walked into room 328, on the third floor . . .   Interview with Keith Rose, conducted by *Guardian Films*.

The first thing I learned was that chivalry isn't dead . . .   Chat logs of Bradley Manning and Adrian Lamo.

It was in this spirit that Brad called Danny on Wednesday afternoon . . .   Interview with Danny Clark.

David House arrived to a wintry Boston in January 2008 . . .   Interview with David House.

Brad schlepped with his large camouflage backpack . . .   Interview with Danny Clark; Amy Laskowski, "A Place to Hack or Just Hang: At BUILDS, computer science students find a playroom," *BU Today*, February 24, 2010, as of December 13, 2011, www.bu.edu/today/2010/a-place-to-hack-or-just-hang/.

. . . he moved around the room like a frenzied gentleman hacker . . .   Interview with David House.

After the event, Brad piled into Danny's car . . .   Interview with Danny Clark; interview with anonymous lockpicker.

To make it easier for them to communicate securely about DADT-sensitive issues . . .   Ibid.

Shortly after Brad got back to Washington, the first inches . . .   Bradley Manning Facebook wall.

After their speaking engagement at the Chaos Computer Conference . . .   Domscheit-Berg op. cit., 142.

. . . WikiLeaks announced it had met its minimum . . .   WikiLeaks Twitter archive, February 2010, as of December 13, 2011, http://wlcentral.org/node/448.

Before I completely lost my shit, I booked a flight home . . .   Domscheit-Berg op. cit., 145.

He described how he took a writeable CD labeled Lady Gaga into the SCIF . . .   Chat logs of Bradley Manning and Adrian Lamo.

Brad would later describe aspects of the relationship . . .   Ibid.

As New Yorker writer Raffi Katchadourian noted in blog post . . .   Raffi Khatchadourian, "Manning, Assange, and the Espionage Act," NewYorker.com, May 20, 2011, as of December 13, 2011, http://www.newyorker.com/online/blogs/newsdesk/2011/05/manning-assange-and-the-espionage-act.html.

I remember my primary emotions . . .   Interview with Danny Clark.

What I kept hearing over and over and over . . .   Interview with Jason Edwards.

Assange told the reporters that the leak of the video . . .   Khatchadourian op. cit.

. . . as seen through a soda straw . . .   Julian E. Barnes, "Gates says video of U.S. helicopter attack in Iraq out of context," *Los Angeles Times*, April 14, 2010, as of December 13, 2011, http://articles.latimes.com/2010/apr/14/world/la-fg-gates-video14-2010apr14.

They're in a combat situation. The video doesn't show . . .   Evan Harris, "Gates on Wikileaks Video: 'Not Helpful' but 'Should not Have Lasting Consequences,'"

ABC News, April 11, 2010, as of December 13, 2011, http://abcnews.go
.com/blogs/politics/2010/04/gates-on-wikileaks-video-not-helpful-but
-should-not-have-lasting-consequences/.

Back in Iraq, Brad was exhilarated by the airing of "Collateral Murder" . . . Kim
Zetter and Kevin Poulsen, "Army Intelligence Analyst Charged With Leaking
Classified Information," Wired.com, July 6, 2010.

According to an army investigation, portions of which . . . Nakashima op. cit.

Brad broke down an e-mail to Sergeant Adkins trying to explain . . . Notes taken
during Bradley Manning's UCMJ Article 32 investigation, December 22,
2011.

He'd sent a Facebook friend request in mid-March to Jonathan Odell . . ." E-mail
exchange with Jonathan Odell; Nakashima op. cit.

Near the end of his senior year of high school, in Florence, Alabama . . . Interview
with David House.

Adrian Lamo grew up in Boston, San Francisco . . . Jennifer Kahn, "The Homeless Hacker v. The New York Times," *Wired,* April 2004; Matt Palmquist, "A
Duty to Hack," *SF Weekly,* April 16, 2003.

In the end, Adrian was sentenced to six months . . ." Kevin Poulsen, "Feds say
Lamo inspired other hackers," *SecurityFocus,* September 15, 2004.

Geek syndrome. Engineer's disorder . . . Steve Silberman, "The Geek Syndrome,"
Wired, December 2001.

Adrian Lamo's longtime contact in journalism, Kevin Poulsen . . . Kevin Poulsen,
"Ex-Hacker Adrian Lamo Institutionalized, Diagnosed with Asperger's,"
Wired.com, May 20, 2010.

But the Asperger's article wasn't the only press Adrian Lamo received . . . Kevin
Poulsen, "Lost Hacking Documentary Surfaces on Pirate Bay," Wired.com,
May 20, 2010.

I'm an army intelligence analyst . . . Chat logs of Bradley Manning and Adrian
Lamo.

The two had exchanged several e-mails back and forth . . . Adrian Lamo's testimony
at Bradley Manning's UCMJ Article 32 investigation, December 21, 2011.

In any case, Adrian would later state . . . Adrian Lamo, "Informants: Villains or
Heroes," panel discussion (The Next HOPE Conference, New York City, July
2010).

I felt a responsibility as a witness to a crime . . . Monica Villamizar, "I'm sorry that
I could not be a friend to Manning," AlJazeera.com, March 13, 2011.

What followed was one of the more bizarre episodes . . . Clint Hendler, "WikiLeaks
Alleges Collusion: Wired's happy to set the timeline straight," CJR.org, June
18, 2010, as of December 13, 2011, www.cjr.org/campaign_desk/wikileaks
_alleges_collusion.php.

Did I, in the end, keep him talking . . .   Adrian Lamo's Facebook profile.

Look again at that dot . . .   Carl Sagan, *Pale Blue Dot: A Vision of the Human Future in Space* (New York: Ballantine Books, 1997).

In 1984, in response to the publication of Steven Levy's book . . .   Levy op. cit., 465.

On May 26, Adrian called Kevin Poulsen to tell him . . .   Kim Zetter and Kevin Poulsen, "Update: Ex-Hacker Denies Alleged WikiLeaker Gave Him Classified Documents," Wired.com, August 1, 2010; Hendler op. cit.; e-mail exchange with Kevin Poulsen.

Chapter 9: WikiLeaked

Julian Assange was scheduled to appear beside Daniel Ellsberg . . .   Micah L. Sifry, *WikiLeaks and the Age of Transparency* (Berkeley, CA: Counterpoint, 2011), 31.

Later that evening Assange was riding in a car . . .   Fowler op. cit., 141.

The Pentagon didn't publicly acknowledge . . .   E-mail exchange with Kevin Poulsen.

I only contacted Kevin as a sort of insurance policy . . .   Interview with Adrian Lamo, conducted by Steve Fishman.

. . . it wasn't until his colleague Nick Davies read . . .   David Leigh and Luke Harding, *WikiLeaks: Inside Julian Assange's War on Secrecy* (New York: Public Affairs, 2011), 92–99.

One of the oldest newspapers in the world . . .   Sarah Ellison, "The Man Who Spilled the Secrets," *Vanity Fair*, February 2011.

These war logs—written in the heat of engagement . . .   "Afghanistan war logs: the unvarnished picture," *Guardian*, July 25, 2010.

The behind-the-scenes frustrations of soldiers on the ground . . .   Mark Mazzetti, Jane Perlez, Eric Schmitt, and Andrew W. Lehren, "Pakistan Aids Insurgency in Afghanistan, Reports Assert," *New York Times*, July 25, 2010.

US authorities were prepared with a raging response . . .   "Statement of National Security Advisor General James Jones on Wikileaks," The White House, Office of the Press Secretary, July 25, 2010.

Mr. Assange can say whatever he likes . . .   Robert Winnett, "Wikileaks Afghanistan: Taliban 'hunting down informants,'" *Telegraph*, July 30, 2010.

. . . to borrow from Blake Hounshell . . .   Blake Hounshell, "The logs of war: Do the Wikileaks documents really tell us anything new?" ForeignPolicy.com, July 25, 2010, as of December 14, 2011, http://blog.foreignpolicy.com/posts/2010/07/25/the_logs_of_war.

The disclosure of what are mostly battlefield updates . . .   Greg Jaffe and Peter Finn, "WikiLeaks disclosures unlikely to change course of Afghanistan war," *Washington Post*, July 27, 2010.

If they won't charge him with treason . . . David Gura, "Congressman: If Brad-ley Manning Gave Reports, Video to WikiLeaks, Execute Him," NPR.org, August 3, 2010, as of December 14, 2011, www.npr.org/blogs/thetwo-way/2010/08/03/128957337/congressman-if-bradley-manning-gave-reports-video-to-wikileaks-execute-him.

On August 8, Ginger Thompson, writing for the New York Times . . . Ginger Thompson, "Early Struggles of Soldier Charged in Leak Case," *New York Times*, August 8, 2010.

But Danny did not wonder if desperation for acceptance . . . Interview with Danny Clark.

Look at the disaster one gay created under our punishing . . . Ann Coulter, "Bradley Manning: Poster Boy for 'Don't Ask, Don't Tell'," Townhall.com, December 1, 2010.

The record shows that Manning allegedly betrayed the United States . . . Cliff Kincaid, "MSNBC Weeps for Accused Traitor Bradley Manning," *Accuracy in Media* December 17, 2010, as of December 14, 2011, www.aim.org/aim-column/msnbc-weeps-for-accused-traitor-bradley-manning/.

Once PVT Manning embraced the gay lifestyle . . . Richard Swier, "Wikileaks, Bradley Manning and the Gay Agenda," *Red County*, November 29, 2010.

. . . removed all higher-level political motivations from him . . . Michael Calderone and Ryan Grim, "WikiLeaks Editor Julian Assange Calls Media Coverage of Bradley Manning 'Apalling'," *Huffington Post*, May 25, 2011, as of December 14, 2011, www.huffingtonpost.com/2011/05/25/wikileaks-julian-assange-bradley-manning_n_866980.html.

On Wednesday, August 11, Assange flew from London to Stockholm . . . Fowler op. cit., 169–170.

. . . she didn't want to go any further but that it was too late to stop . . . Leigh and Harding op. cit., 148.

Illuminated by the spotlight of global publicity . . . As of December 14, 2011, http://cryptome.org/0001/wikileaks-audit.htm.

Ultimately, of course, it was Julian who made the decisions . . . Domscheit-Berg op. cit., 219.

If you do not answer the question, you will be removed . . . Ibid., 223.

Assange had expanded the group of media partners . . . Leigh and Harding op. cit., 138.

Iraq Body Count *found* . . . David Leigh, "Iraq war logs reveal 15,000 previously unlisted civilian deaths," *Guardian*, October 22, 2010.

The logs documented copious instances . . . James Glanz and Andrew Lehren, "Use of Contractors Added to War's Chaos in Iraq," *New York Times*, October 23, 2010.

Also on evidence were hundreds of reports . . .   Nick Davies, Jonathan Steele, and David Leigh, "Iraq war logs: secret files show how US ignored torture," *Guardian*, October 22, 2010.

. . . dump of documents on Afghanistan in the summer . . .   "Wikileaks's leaks mostly confirm earlier Iraq reporting," *Washington Post*, October 26, 2010.

. . . recall ever having been the subject of such absolutely, relentless vituperation . . .   Michael Calderone, "NY Times reporter defends profile of WikiLeaks' Assange," *The Upshot*, October 26, 2010.

. . . an unprecedented look at back-room bargaining . . .   Scott Shane and Andrew Lehren, "Leaked Cables Offer Raw Look at U.S. Diplomacy," *New York Times*, November 28, 2010.

. . . irresponsible, reckless, and frankly dangerous . . .   Matthew Lee, "U.S.: WikiLeaks Is 'Irresponsible, Reckless, Dangerous', Won't Cooperate With Anti-Secrecy Group," *Associated Press*, September 1, 2011.

But a review by the Associated Press . . .   Bradley Klapper, "AP review finds no threatened WikiLeaks sources," *Associated Press*, September 10, 2011.

Now, I've heard the impact of these releases on our foreign policy . . .   As of December 14, 2011, www.defense.gov/transcripts/transcript.aspx?transcriptid=4728.

If we have an American citizen that is willing . . .   As of December 14, 2011, http://m.theatlanticwire.com/politics/2010/12/ron-paul-vigorously-defends -wikileaks/18230/.

The most dramatic—and disputed—illustration of how . . .   Tom Malinowski, "Whispering at Autocrats," ForeignPolicy.com, January 25, 2011; Sofiane Ben Haj M'Hamed, "How WikiLeaks Rocked Tunisia," IWPR.net, July 6, 2011.

When WikiLeaks released a fund raising commercial . . .   Robert Mackey, "Assange Claims Credit for Egypt's Revolution," *New York Times*, July 6, 2011, as of December 14, 2011, http://thelede.blogs.nytimes.com/2011/07/06/assange -claims-credit-for-egypts-revolution/; Dan Murphy, "Julian Assange: The man who came to dinner, the man who saved Egypt," *Christian Science Monitor*, July 5, 2011, www.csmonitor.com/World/Backchannels/2011/0705/Julian -Assange-The-man-who-came-to-dinner-the-man-who-saved-Egypt.

Chapter 10: Saving Private Manning

The Acetarium 2.0, according to its website . . .   As of December 15, 2011, http:// acetarium.com/.

It had been over a week since Danny had heard from Brad . . .   Interview with Danny Clark; Bradley Manning Facebook wall.

. . . Danny had received a call from Adrian Lamo . . .   Interview with Danny Clark.

Immediately after the call, Danny e-mailed Brad's Aunt Debbie.   Danny Clark e-mail archive.

Poulsen was still trying to verify that Brad Manning . . .   E-mail exchange with Kevin Poulsen.

The next day, Tyler Watkins sent a message online to Danny.   Chat logs of Danny Clark and Tyler Watkins.

Mike Gogulski grew up in Orlando, Florida . . .   Interview with Mike Gogulski.

. . . meteoric career path, going from hobbyist hacker . . .   As of December 15, 2011, www.nostate.com/284/why-slovakia/.

Back in Cambridge, Danny Clark was mobilizing too . . .   Interview with Danny Clark; Danny Clark e-mail archive.

Brad's Aunt Debbie became the family's point person for his case . . .   E-mail exchange with Debbie Manning.

A native of Boise, Idaho, a golfer and a fisherman . . .   As of December 15, 2011, www.linkedin.com/pub/david-coombs/19/744/944; as of December 15, 2011, www.armycourtmartialdefense.com/attorney-CV.pdf.

. . . because of the potential for lengthy continued pretrial confinement . . .   Pentagon press release #20100729-001, July 29, 2010.

The July 2010 HOPE Conference (Hackers on Planet Earth) . . .   Quinn Norton, "HOPE: the lost article," *Quinn Said*, October 3, 2010, as of December 15, 2011, http://quinnnorton.com/said/?p=397.

There are other conferences that relate on certain themes . . .   Ibid.

The caravan of Boston hackers was thus abuzz . . .   Interview with David House; interview with Danny Clark.

Several days later Lamo was able to chat online with Danny . . .   Adrian Lamo's testimony during Bradley Manning's UCMJ Article 32 investigation, December 21, 2011.

Goldstein stood at the podium . . .   The Next HOPE keynote address, as of December 15, 2011, www.youtube.com/watch?v=5U7dAujk5E4&feature=related.

When Adrian Lamo took the stage on Sunday . . .   The Next HOPE "Informants" panel, as of December 15, 2011, www.youtube.com/watch?v=jMz3p_2yOeo.

On Sunday, August 15, after traveling nine hours from Boston to Quantico . . .   Interview with Danny Clark.

We could get a really big box . . .   Danny Clark e-mail archive.

When he first arrived at Quantico on July 29 . . .   Memorandum from PFC Bradley E. Manning to Col. Daniel J. Choike, March 10, 2011; David Coombs, "PFC Bradley Manning Is Not Being Treated Like Every Other Detainee," January 26, 2011, as of December 15, 2011, www.armycourtmartialdefense. info/2011/01/pfc-bradley-manning-is-not-being.html.

One story Brad recounted to David is apocryphal . . .   Interview with David House.

As Atul Gawande wrote in his 2009 opus . . .   Atul Gawande, "Hell Hole," *New Yorker*, March 30, 2009.

As Brad's birthday approached in December . . .   Denver Nicks, "Bradley Manning's Life Behind Bars," *Daily Beast*, December 17, 2010.

On December 15, Glen Greenwald . . .   Glenn Greenwald, "The inhumane conditions of Bradley Manning's detention," *Salon*, December 15, 2010.

When the guards came to my cell . . .   Memorandum from PFC Bradley E. Manning to Col. Daniel J. Choike, March 10, 2011.

Behind the scenes, solitary confinement was changing Brad Manning . . .   Interview with Danny Clark.

After he started traveling from Boston every two weeks to visit Brad . . .   Interview with David House.

Brad described the Leavenworth jail as like summer camp . . .   Interview with anonymous visitor.